PLATE 18
E ware Vessel 4. The carbonized deposits running over the broken edges of the vessel are clearly visible.
(*Reproduced courtesy of Glasgow Museums: Kelvingrove Art Gallery and Museum*)

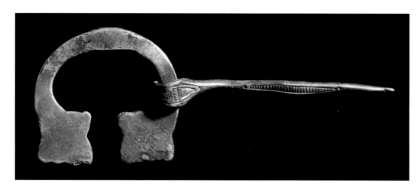

PLATE 19
a) Front view of the brooch with pin in position; b) back view of brooch.

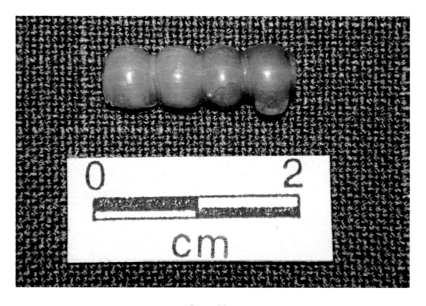

PLATE 23
The silver-in-glass bead.

PLATE 29

Cadmug Gospels, 8th century. (Fulda, Landesbibliothek MS Bonifatianus 3 folio 51v). The evangelist John with a possible book satchel in his left hand.
(*Reproduced courtesy of Hessische Landesbibliothek Fulda*)

PLATE 31
Quern LGQ3 showing the concentric circles of iron staining around the central hole on the upper surface.
(*Reproduced courtesy of Glasgow Museums: Kelvingrove Art Gallery and Museum*)

A Crannog of the First Millennium AD

# A Crannog of the First Millennium AD

*Excavations by Jack Scott*
*at Loch Glashan, Argyll, 1960*

ANNE CRONE and EWAN CAMPBELL

with contributions by
Colleen Batey, Ann Clarke, Jon Henderson, Rob Lewis, Bernard Meehan,
Effie Photos-Jones, Anita Quye, Clare Thomas, Penelope Walton Rogers

Edinburgh 2005
SOCIETY OF ANTIQUARIES OF SCOTLAND

Published in 2005 by the Society of Antiquaries of Scotland
Authors: Anne Crone and Ewan Campbell

Society of Antiquaries of Scotland
Royal Museum of Scotland
Chambers Street
Edinburgh EH1 1JF
Tel: 0131 247 4115
Fax: 0131 247 4163
Email: administration@socantscot.org
Website: www.socantscot.org

*British Library Cataloguing-in-Publication Data*
A catalogue record for this book is available from the British Library

ISBN 10-digit: 0 903903 36 9
ISBN 13-digit: 978 0 903903 36 3

The Society gratefully acknowledges grant-aid towards the publication of this volume from Historic Scotland.

Typeset in Bembo by Waverley Typesetters, Galashiels
Design and production by Lawrie Law and Alison Rae
Manufactured in Great Britain by The Bath Press, Bath

*This volume is dedicated to the memory of*
# JACK SCOTT

# Contents

# Jack G Scott: an appreciation

Jack Gillespie Scott was born in Northumberland in 1913 and in the 1930s he worked in the Leicester Museum. On the outbreak of war he enlisted in the army, was commissioned, and rose to the rank of captain. He did not talk much about his wartime experiences, but liked to tell of the time, during service in the Western Desert, when the truck he was driving ran over a land mine. Jack escaped unscathed as the main force of the explosion was on the unoccupied passenger side where the wheel was blown off, leaving him uninjured.

For a short time after the end of the war, he returned to Leicester Museum and also undertook some lecturing, eventually coming to Glasgow to work in the Glasgow Museum and Art Gallery at Kelvingrove in 1948. In those days the staff was limited, so that Jack and other colleagues returning from war service had to cover an extensive range of museum work. His remit was wide and he gradually acquired an expertise in a number of fields, including history and archaeology, in time becoming Keeper of Archaeology, Ethnography and History.

He married his wife, Margaret, about the time he came to Glasgow, and they were a true team, working together on many projects, including numerous archaeological excavations in the west of Scotland. Margaret was also involved in making museum models and replicas of archaeological structures and sites. They undertook the re-arrangement and updating of collections in some of the smaller museums in the region, including Bute, Campbeltown and the Stewartry Museum in Kirkcudbright.

Jack was elected a Fellow of the Society of Antiquaries of Scotland in 1949 and later served on the Society's council and as its representative to the Scottish Field School of Archaeology. He submitted a thesis on the Neolithic period in Kintyre for his MA degree from Liverpool University in 1960. He became early on an Associate Member of the Museums Association and was later elected a Fellow of the Association – a tribute to his professionalism in museum work. He joined the Glasgow Archaeological Society shortly after coming to Glasgow, and served on the council and as treasurer. He edited the final volume of the old *Transactions* of the Society and, in the late 1960s, he and other members of the Society's council decided to modernize and rename the *Transactions*, which had been appearing since the middle of the 19th century. He then edited the first two volumes of the new *Glasgow Archaeological Journal* in 1969 and 1971, and volume 4 in 1976. In 1972 he was elected President of the Glasgow Archaeological Society for a term of three years.

During his long service in the museum at Kelvingrove, Jack was constantly involved in writing and research, and produced many papers and articles in various scientific and learned journals. His major field of study was the origin and development of the Neolithic chambered tombs of the 'Clyde Group' in Kintyre, mid-Argyll, Arran, Bute and Ayrshire. He carried out many excavations on these and other archaeological monuments and the results were published in the *Proceedings of the Society of Antiquaries of Scotland*, in the journal *Antiquity* and in the *Glasgow Archaeological Journal*. There was never any lack of volunteers to take part in his fieldwork, and he was an inspiring excavation director, always ready to explain or discuss the work in hand, to the team or to visitors to his sites.

An interesting, truly local, project was his excavation of the earthwork at Camphill, Queens Park, Glasgow, in 1951. The excavation was sponsored by the Corporation of Glasgow, the first time in Scotland that an archaeological excavation had been supported by a civic authority. He produced the first regional study of archaeology in Scotland with his book *South-West Scotland*, in the Heinemann Regional Archaeologies series, in 1966.

Jack's interests and research ranged well beyond the Neolithic period and he often wrote notes and appendices on material from excavations other than his own, such as an appendix on the pottery from a Food Vessel cist burial at Doonfoot in Ayrshire, where he coined the phrase 'Machrie Vase' to describe a type of Food Vessel, neither Irish Bowl nor Yorkshire Vase, found at Doonfoot and on Machrie Moor, Arran. He undertook the investigation of the stone circles and cist burials at Temple Wood, Kilmartin, Argyllshire, between 1974 and 1980. He also studied the Roman occupation of south-west Scotland and was involved in research into the petrography and distribution of prehistoric stone implements in Scotland. His work in later periods included the excavation of the crannog in Loch Glashan in Argyllshire in 1960, the subject of the present report, and the analysis of medieval finds including a romanesque crucifix from Dorothy Marshall's excavations at Macewen's Castle, Loch Fyne, Argyllshire.

If museum exhibits were labelled with the names of the staff who were responsible for their presentation, we would be able to say that Jack Scott was best known to the great majority of the general public who visited the Art Gallery and Museum at Kelvingrove for the wonderful Arms and Armour display. This much-acclaimed exhibition was based on the material from various bequests to the museum, the largest of which was presented in 1939 by R L Scott of the shipbuilding family. The collection has been visited and praised by specialists from all over the world, and Jack Scott also wrote the accompanying booklet *European Arms and Armour at Kelvingrove* in 1980.

Jack retired from his position in the Kelvingrove Museum in 1978 and, sadly, his wife Margaret died shortly afterwards. Since retirement he had been living at Creebridge, Newton Stewart, and had continued his writing and research right up to his death, latterly concentrating more on the later, historical period in the Dumfries and Galloway region as work in the field became more difficult for him.

A serious-minded man with a quiet sense of humour, Jack was greatly respected in Scotland and beyond. He was a scholarly and prolific writer who did much to advance our knowledge of the archaeology and history of the west of Scotland. He shared that knowledge and insight generously with friends and colleagues over the years and his great breadth of interest will be greatly missed in this era of growing specialization.

This Bibliography is far from complete, but will serve to demonstrate Jack's wide range of experience and knowledge.

## BIBLIOGRAPHY

1951   With H Fairhurst 'The earthwork at Camphill in Glasgow', *Proc Soc Antiq Scot*, 85 (1950–1), 146–57.

1954   'Walton Farm, Cardross' [chambered cairn excavation]. *Scottish Regional Group, Council for British Archaeology, 9th Annual Report*, 9.

1956   'The excavation of the chambered cairn at Brackley, Kintyre, Argyll', *Proc Soc Antiq Scot*, 89 (1955–6), 22–54.

1961a  'The excavation of the chambered cairn at Crarae, Lochfyneside, Mid Argyll', *Proc Soc Antiq Scot*, 94 (1960–1), 1–27.

1961b  With Campbell, M & Piggott, S 'The Badden cist slab', *Proc Soc Antiq Scot*, 94 (1960–1), 46–61.

1961c  'The excavation of the crannog at Loch Glashan, Mid Argyll', *Archaeological News Letter*, 7, 1 (July, 1961), 20–1.

1962   'Clyde, Carlingford and Connaught cairns – a review', *Antiquity*, 36, 97–101.

1964   'The chambered cairn at Beacharra, Kintyre, Argyll, Scotland', *Proc Prehist Soc*, 30, 134–58.

1966   *South-West Scotland* (Regional Archaeologies), London.

1967   'Report on the pottery', in J M Davidson, 'A Bronze Age cemetery at Doonfoot, Ayr', *Trans Glas Archaeol Soc*, 15, pt. 4, 159–70.

1968   'A radiocarbon date for a west Scottish Neolithic settlement', *Antiquity*, 42, 296–7.

1969a  'A romanesque censer from Bearsden, Glasgow', *Glasg Archaeol J*, 1, 43–6.

1969b  Chapter 6 – The *Clyde* cairns of Scotland, Chapter 7, The Neolithic period in Kintyre, Argyll, in T G E Powell *et al*, *Megalithic Enquiries in the West of Britain*. Liverpool, 175–222.

1971   'A food vessel burial from Cour, Kintyre, Argyll', *Glasg Archaeol J*, 2, 27–30

1973a  'The Clyde cairns of Scotland', in G Daniel & P Kjaerum (eds), *Megalithic Graves and Ritual* (papers presented at the 3rd Atlantic Colloquium, Møsegard, 1969), Copenhagen, 117–28.

1973b  'Axeheads of Group IX from Kintyre, Argyll', *Proc Prehist Soc*, 39, 469–71.

1976a  'The Roman occupation of South-west Scotland from the recall of Agricola to the withdrawal under Trajan', *Glasg Archaeol J*, 4, 29–44.

1976b  'A note on Beacharra Pottery', *Antiquity*, 51, 240–3.

1980   *European Arms and Armour at Kelvingrove* (Glasgow Museums and Art Galleries).

1981   With P R Ritchie. *Petrography of Scottish Stone Implements* (unpublished research report).

1982   'An early sheriff of Dumfries?' *Trans Dumfries Galloway Natur Hist Antiq Soc*, 57, 90.

1983   'A note on Viking settlement in Galloway', *Trans Dumfries Galloway Natur Hist Antiq Soc*, 58, 52–5.

1985   'Finds', in H McFadzean, 'A prehistoric chipping-floor of agates on the hills of south Bute', *Trans Buteshire Natur Hist Soc*, 22, 35–38.

1988   'The origins of Dundrennan and Soulseat Abbeys', *Trans Dumfries Galloway Natur Hist Antiq Soc*, 63, 35–44.

1989a  'The stone circles at Temple Wood, Kilmartin, Argyll', *Glasg Archaeol J*, 15, 53–124.

1989b  'The hall and motte at Courthill, Dalry, Ayrshire', *Proc Soc Antiq Scot*, 119, 271–8.

1990 'A romanesque crucifix from Macewen's Castle, Loch Fyne, Mid Argyll', *Glasg Archaeol J*, 16,

1991 'Bishop John of Galloway and the Status of Hoddom', *Trans Dumfries Galloway Natur Hist Antiq Soc,* 66, 37–45.

1993 'Galloway in the 1100s: notes, footnotes and some comments', *Trans Dumfries Galloway Natur Hist Antiq Soc*, 68, 131–3.

ALEX MORRISON
2004

# The Jack Scott archive

Aware of the importance of his archaeological excavation records, Jack Scott made provision in his will for the safe keeping of his papers in the archive of the Royal Commission on the Ancient and Historical Monuments of Scotland (RCAHMS). In August 1999, staff from RCAHMS worked with a representative from Jack's solicitors, Faulds, Gibson & Kennedy, to identify and remove all archaeological material from his house in Newton Stewart.

The J G Scott collection of material is now housed in the RCAHMS premises at John Sinclair House, 16 Bernard Terrace, Edinburgh EH8 9NX, and comprises a wealth of material relating to a lifetime of archaeological research and excavation, including photographs, negatives, slides, drawings, notes, correspondence and a quantity of artefacts. Numerous sites are represented in the collection and include: Templewood, Argyll; Loch Glashan, Argyll; Camphill, Queen's Park, Glasgow; Shiels, Govan, Glasgow; Barmore Wood, Argyll; and Monybachach, Argyll. There are some 5,000 items in the collection which is currently awaiting detailed research and cataloguing to make it fully accessible.

LESLEY FERGUSON
2005

# List of contributors

COLLEEN BATEY
Department of Archaeology, Gregory Building, University of Glasgow, Lilybank Gardens, Glasgow G12 8QQ

EWAN CAMPBELL
Department of Archaeology, Gregory Building, University of Glasgow, Lilybank Gardens, Glasgow G12 8QQ

ANN CLARKE
Rockville Lodge, by Kingston, North Berwick, East Lothian

ANNE CRONE
AOC Archaeology, Edgefield Industrial Estate, Loanhead, Midlothian EH20 9SY

JON HENDERSON
Department of Archaeology, University of Nottingham, University Park, Nottingham NG7 2RD

ROB LEWIS
The Burrell Collection, 2060 Pollokshaws Road, Glasgow G43 1AT

BERNARD MEEHAN
Keeper of Manuscripts, Trinity College, Dublin, Ireland

EFFIE PHOTOS-JONES
Scottish Analytical Services for Art and Archaeology, Unit J, 47 Purdon Street, Glasgow G11 6AF

ANITA QUYE
National Museums of Scotland, Chambers Street, Edinburgh EH1 1JF

CLARE THOMAS
Stillness, Weem, Aberfeldy, Perthshire PH15 2LD

PENELOPE WALTON ROGERS
The Anglo-Saxon Company, Marketing House, 8 Bootham Terrace, York YO30 7DH

# List of figures

# List of plates

# Acknowledgements

The finds assemblage from Loch Glashan has been curated by the Kelvingrove Art Gallery and Museum since the excavation. We are indebted to Colleen Batey and Jenny Rose for their assistance in providing information and access to the collection. The bulk of the paper record from the excavation is now curated by the National Monuments Record for Scotland and we would like to thank Miriam McDonald for her assistance in providing frequent access to the record.

Many colleagues have provided advice and support during the project. These include John Barber, Damian Goodburn, Rupert Housley, Heather James and Adam Welfare.

All the artefacts were drawn by Sylvia Stevenson except for figures 35, 54f and 56 which were drawn by Jill Sievewright and figure 55a-c which were drawn by Tom Borthwick. Alan Hunter Blair prepared all the other illustrations in this report, except figures 44 and 45 which were drawn by Graeme Carruthers.

Historic Scotland commissioned many of the specialist reports and funded the publication project.

*Bernard Meehan* wishes to thank the following for their generous assistance in the preparation of his paper: David Clarke, Andy Halpin, Peter Harbison, Isabel Henderson, Colum Hourihane, Ruth Johnson, Eamonn P Kelly, Paul Mullarkey, Dáibhí Ó Cróinín, Raghnall Ó Floinn, Felicity O'Mahony, Stuart Ó Seanoir, Tony Roche, Grellan Rourke, Michael Ryan and Alison Sheridan. He is grateful to Paul Mullarkey for permission to cite his unpublished work.

*Effie Photos-Jones* wishes to thank Ms Ruiz-Nieto of SASAA and R MacDonald of Glasgow University for IT and technical support respectively.

# Chapter 1

# History of the Project

The crannog was discovered in 1960 as a result of dam construction in Loch Glashan. The loch had been selected by the former North of Scotland Hydro-Electrical Board as a reservoir to operate a hydro-electric power station at nearby Loch Gair. In order to increase the capacity of the loch the Board decided to build a dam across the outlet into Loch Gair, but before the foundations of the dam could be laid it was necessary to lower the existing water level by approximately 3.6m, thus exposing former beach deposits and lacustrine silts (plate 1). By coincidence, the extraction of the gravel for the dam from a terrace

PLATE 1
Aerial photograph showing Loch Glashan after the lowering of the water level. The dam is under construction. The dun lies to the left of the dam; the medieval island settlement and crannog are visible projecting from the shoreline just to the right of the dam. (© *Meridian*)

1

at Bruach an Druimein, Poltalloch, led to the rescue excavation of a contemporary site (Cregeen 1960; Abernethy forthcoming).

In the spring of 1960 a forestry worker found a logboat partially buried in the silts at the edge of the lowered water level and the then Ministry of Works Inspectorate of Ancient Monuments and Historic Buildings was contacted. An Assistant Inspector, Mr P R Ritchie was despatched to investigate the logboat and in the course of his visit noticed what looked like a pile of stones sitting partially submerged in the water at the very edge of the exposed silts. Closer inspection brought the startling discovery of what he recognized as a virtually complete E ware pot (vessel 5) standing upright on the surface of the stony mound. This was not all – he recorded that 'one almost complete pot, fragments of three others, four whetstones, eight querns, iron slag and what may be a wooden yoke were recovered during the surface examination' (letter 7 June 1960) – and surmised that the crannog had been untouched since its abandonment. A further 13 possible quern fragments were eventually removed from the surface of the crannog before excavation began.

Recognizing the significance of his discovery a rescue operation was mounted and Ritchie approached the Kelvingrove Art Gallery and Museum for help in staffing a small excavation. He asked specifically for Jack Scott (referred to hereafter as JGS), then Keeper of Archaeology at Kelvingrove, because he was one of the very few with first-hand experience of crannog excavation, having worked on the excavation of the Milton Loch I crannog.

The excavation lasted for 3½ weeks, from 25 July to 16 August 1960. JGS was assisted throughout by his wife Margaret and Miss Anne Ward, then Trainee Assistant at the Kelvingrove, who was present for the third week. The Hydro-Electric Board also paid for the services of two men to work on site for the duration of the excavation. Indeed, the excavation was very much a collaborative effort; the Ministry of Works provided funds and equipment, the Forestry Commission provided access to the site, various facilities and the services of a keeper for one day, while the Kelvingrove Museum provided the often urgent transport to Glasgow of finds in need of immediate conservation, as well as seconding JGS to the excavation.

JGS was assiduous in publishing interim accounts immediately after the excavation (Scott 1960; 1961a; 1961b). The rich assemblage of wood and leather artefacts recovered during the excavation was conserved promptly at Kelvingrove using techniques which were

novel for their time. In 1963 Kelvingrove mounted an exhibition about the discoveries from the crannog and over the next few years JGS also lectured frequently on the subject.

Over the course of the following decades elements of the artefact assemblage formed the subject of various individual studies. A scientific examination of the brooch was undertaken by the British Museum (Werner 1963). The querns were catalogued as part of an undergraduate dissertation by Stuart Dobbin, of Glasgow University (Dobbin 1977). Caroline Earwood examined a selection of the wooden artefacts as part of her PhD thesis (Earwood 1990). The E ware and crucibles were examined by Ewan Campbell in the course of his PhD (Campbell 1991). The evidence from the crannog was summarized in the Royal Commission volume on Argyll (RCAHMS 1988, 205–8). The leather items were included in a study of leather artefacts as part of an undergraduate dissertation by Mhairi Matson, again of Glasgow University (Matson 1998). As part of a project to construct an Early Historic tree-ring chronology for Scotland two timbers recovered from the excavation were the subjects of dendrochronological investigation (Crone 1998).

It was not until his retirement, and the completion of other, equally pressing projects, that JGS was able to take up the task of drawing together all the evidence from Loch Glashan for full publication. Historic Scotland undertook to fund the outstanding post-excavation tasks, and reports on the assemblages of leather, wood and metallurgical waste were commissioned. JGS had already prepared plans and sections for publication and had just begun the task of writing the introductory text when he was tragically killed in 1999. He had willed his entire archaeological archive to the National Monuments Record at the RCAHMS and this was examined by one of the authors (AC) to assess what remained to be done.

As well as the completion of the remaining post-excavation tasks some additional work was proposed that would complement the existing record and enhance the final report. The evidence for the dating of the crannog resided entirely in some of the artefacts (Chapter 4) but, given our reservations about the nature of their deposition (Chapter 3.5) it was considered essential to gather more dating evidence relating to the actual structure of the crannog. Consequently, a diving exercise, undertaken by a team from Nottingham University, was mounted to sample *in situ* oak timbers for dendrochronological analysis (Chapter 3.4). Radiocarbon dates were obtained for some of the artefacts and previously curated structural timbers (Chapters 5.2 and 5.3). A sidescan sonar survey of the crannog was also undertaken to ascertain its full extent (Chapter 3.4).

The following sections (2 and 3) are based on text that JGS had begun to prepare, together with evidence gleaned from the archive, primarily the original finds record, the site daybook and the photographic archive. Unfortunately, the original site plans and sections have never been located and so the text relies on those illustrations which JGS had already begun to prepare for publication, which already incorporate an element of interpretation. It hardly needs stating that much has changed since 1960, particularly our understanding of site formation and post-depositional processes at work on archaeological sites (for example, Schiffer 1996; Simpson 1997). The more recent excavations at Buiston crannog (Crone 2000) have also forced us to re-examine some of the assumptions which underpinned the observations of the earlier 19th-century crannog excavations and which also informed JGS' interpretations of what he was excavating. Consequently, some of his observations and interpretations are disputed by the authors. In Chapter 3.3 the evidence is described as impartially as is possible and then, in Chapter 3.5 JGS' interpretations are presented, followed by our own re-interpretations. Any phrases in quotation marks are direct quotations from the daybook.

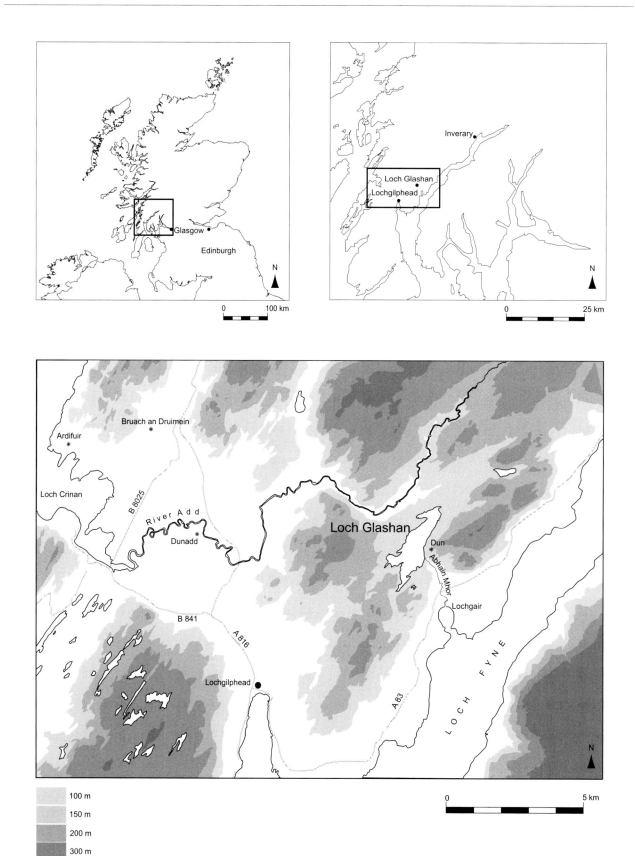

FIGURE 1
Map showing location of Loch Glashan and some of the other nearby archaeological sites mentioned in the text

# Chapter 2

# Site and Setting

## 2.1 THE PHYSICAL SETTING

Loch Glashan is a small inland loch lying to the west of Loch Gair, on Loch Fyneside, in mid-Argyll (figure 1). It lies some 1.7km from the sea at Loch Gair into which the main outlet from the loch, *Abhainn Mhor*, originally drained. Before the construction of the dam the loch was originally about 1.9 × 0.8km in size, its surface lying at 96m above OD. To the south, east and north-east it is hemmed in by hills rising steeply to between 200m and 300m in height (plate 1). To the north the ground rises more gradually to a height of nearly 300m. To the west the ground undulates much more gently for 2 miles, then rises to a height of about 210m, overlooking the valley of the River Add near Kilmichael Glassary. Fairhurst (1969, 47) points out that a relatively easy route across this part of mid-Argyll starts from Loch Gair, rounds the north shore of Loch Glashan, then crosses to the Add valley. Thence there is a route to the north to Loch Awe, and another running south, past the Early Historic stronghold of Dunadd, to the sea at Loch Crinan. The loch is now completely enclosed by coniferous plantations but prior to this it lay in open moorland, with deciduous woodland only to be found on the lower banks of the *Abhainn Mhor* and along the shore of Loch Fyne (OS 1925).

A small island had always been visible lying approximately 10m off the original shoreline; the medieval settlement on the island was also excavated once the island became accessible when the water levels were reduced (Fairhurst 1969; and see below). The crannog lay approximately 50m off the south-western corner of the island (plate 2) and also approximately 50m from the original shoreline.

## 2.2 GEOMORPHOLOGY AND WATER LEVELS IN THE LOCH

The top of the crannog lay at 93.8m OD meaning that the crannog had lain some 2.2m under the pre-1960 water surface (figure 2). In order to better understand the original position of the crannog and its relationship to the shoreline and water level JGS asked Dr W W Bishop of the Department of Geology, University of Glasgow, to examine the geomorphology of the loch basin – the following is based on the report he wrote in 1960 (also see Fairhurst 1969, 47–8).

The sequence around the loch consists of boulder clay overlain by laminated still-water silts interbedded with fine sands which were thixotrophic when saturated (figure 2 and plate 3). Above this was a detrital peat horizon between 0.3–0.6m in thickness which was in turn overlain by beach gravels up to 0.6m in depth. The surface exposed between the crannog and the shore as a result of the lowered water level, was that of the peaty horizon which made for a treacherous approach to the crannog (plate 3). Towards the shore the peat was humified and contained many drifted birch logs and hazelnuts but towards the crannog it became a peaty silt some 0.15m in thickness which contained rhizomes indicative of the *in situ* growth of reeds and other plants. Dr Bishop thought that this peaty horizon probably underlay the crannog. What is not clearly explained in his account is the difference in level of approximately 2m between the surface of the peat at the shore (95.1m) and near the crannog (approximately 93m). Bishop only observed the sequence at the shoreline and so the relationship between the peats, silt and crannog is not fully understood.

Dr Bishop considered that the water level in the loch had stayed at c 96m OD for most of its existence – this is indicated by a negative break in slope at this level just behind the beach gravels. He also argued that at one point the loch levels must have dropped to c 94.9–95.1m OD to allow the peat to become interbedded with still water sediments near the loch margins. Dr Bishop observed evidence of slumping at the southern end of the loch, and surmised that it was the drying-out and subsequent contraction of the newly exposed deposits that had caused the lowering of all the exposed strata. However, he did not think that the slumping accounted for the level of the crannog, presumably because the deposits around and under the crannog were never fully exposed and therefore had not been able to dry out. He concluded that what change in level there may have been would have been as a result of the crannog mass settling over a period of time into the thixotrophic silts.

PLATE 2

View of the crannog from the island, looking south. The crannog emerges as a low stone mound lying on the very edge of the shallow, peat-covered
lacustrine silts exposed when the loch levels were lowered. (© *Crown copyright: RCAHMS Jack Scott collection*)

## 2.3 THE ARCHAEOLOGICAL BACKGROUND

The development of the Loch Glashan crannog can be
seen in relation to the later Iron Age and Early Historic
period occupation of mid-Argyll. This discussion
will concentrate on this area of mainland Argyll, as
the offshore islands of the Inner Hebrides have their
own set of controversies, particularly relating to the
date of brochs (MacKie 1974; Lane 1990; MacKie
1997), but no broch has been certainly identified on
mainland Argyll. While this period is relatively well
known in terms of archaeological survey of settlement

types (RCAHMS 1988; 1992), significant problems
remain in outlining a coherent settlement sequence and
chronology (summarized in Harding 1997). Specifically,
there is controversy over the date and classification of
Iron Age settlements, and a lack of evidence for the
timing of the shift from hilltop fortified settlement to the
dispersed settlement pattern of the medieval and post-
medieval periods. While a few important sites, such as
Dunadd, have been excavated and published to modern
standards (Lane & Campbell 2000), for most others we
have only antiquarian accounts or the morphological

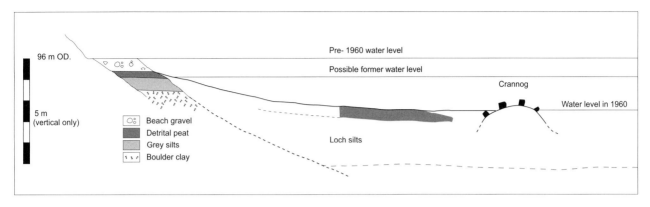

FIGURE 2
Geomorphological profile of deposits on shoreline near the crannog (after W W Bishop) and water levels in loch

forms of surviving monuments to assist in interpretation. For the Early Historic period, the traditional picture of Scots migrating from north-eastern Ireland to Argyll in the 6th century AD and founding the kingdom of *Dál Riata* has been challenged on archaeological, historical and linguistic grounds (Campbell 2001).

The characteristic settlement form of Argyll in this period is the hilltop dun, which differentiates this region from other areas of Scotland where brochs, wheelhouses and forts dominate (Henderson 2000, fig 1). Duns are stone-walled, sub-circular enclosures, which by some definitions are small enough to have been roofed. Other types of settlement include a variety of hillforts, crannogs, some cave occupation, and unenclosed settlement. There are over 300 recorded duns in Argyll, mainly coastal in distribution, and located on defensible crags near to areas of low-lying agricultural land. Most debate has centred on their dating. Traditionally they have been seen as belonging to the earlier Iron Age, and a few excavations have provided evidence of construction and occupation at this period. However, many others have produced clear evidence of occupation, and sometimes construction, in the Early Historic period (Alcock & Alcock 1987; Nieke 1990). Recent debate on the issue (Harding 1997; Henderson 2000; Gilmour 2000) has suggested that the issue is complex, with the simple term 'dun' encompassing a number of morphologically distinct forms; dun-houses (which could be roofed) and dun-enclosures, which potentially have different dates. In this view, sites such as Ardifuir, which have produced Early Historic material, were re-occupied at that time, but originally constructed as complex Atlantic roundhouses in the first millennium BC. Without the excavation of larger numbers of sites it will be difficult to resolve this debate.

The other major site type in the region is the hillfort. The Royal Commission adopted a definition of hillforts as being differentiated from duns by enclosing more than 375sqm (corresponding to an approximate internal diameter of 11m). As with the duns, there are a variety of morphological forms in Argyll. It has been suggested that sites with angular, rather than contour-following, ramparts are late in the sequence and fall into the second half of the 1st millenniun AD (Gilmour 2000). This is certainly the case at Dunadd, where an angular outer rampart replaces a curved one in the 8/9th centuries AD (Lane & Campbell 2000, 92–5, illus 3.6, 3.7; Campbell 2003, illus 22). It has also been proposed that hillforts lie at higher altitudes than duns, but a study of mid-Argyll and Lorn shows little variation (Breslin 1999, 34–42). The chronological sequence at Dunadd, which shows development from a summit dun to successively larger hierarchically arranged enclosures of the 'nuclear fort' (Lane & Campbell 2000, 87–97) illustrates the problem of defining sites on a morphological basis alone. It also demonstrates clearly that nuclear forts are an introduction of the Early Historic period, rather than an adaptation of earlier Iron Age fortifications as Feachem proposed (1966). However, there is no doubt that other types of fort were built in the early Iron Age (Nieke 1990).

Some 50 possible crannogs have been identified in Argyll, 20 of which are located in Loch Awe alone (Morrison 1985, 31–3), the remainder occurring mainly as single instances in small lochs (RCAHMS Vols 1–7). Although Loch Glashan is the only crannog in Argyll to have been excavated in modern times, two others have antiquarian accounts. The first of these recorded the ground-breaking use of divers by the Rev Mapleton in Loch Coille-Bharr in 1870, though few other details were recorded (Butter 1999, 77; Morrison 1985, 6).

PLATE 3

View of the crannog siting, looking north. In the foreground the sequence of peat overlying the yellow lacustrine silts can be seen. The stoniness of its surface is clearly visible. (© *Crown copyright: RCAHMS Jack Scott collection*)

The other records the excavation of a crannog in Lochan Dughaill, Clachan, Kintyre, which produced little of chronologically diagnostic value (Munro 1893). However, the similarity between the timber structure exposed at Lochan Dughaill, with its mortised radial timbers pinned around the perimeter by stakes and surfaces of tangentially-set timbers, and that recorded at Buiston (Crone 2000, figs 11 and 16) is so close as to hint at an Early Historic date.

Most of the crannogs in Loch Awe were located for the first time during an underwater survey (Morrison 1985) but only one was sampled for radiocarbon-dating. A structural timber from the crannog at Ederline produced a radiocarbon date of $2320 \pm 45$ BP (Morrison 1981) indicating that a tradition of crannog-building existed in Argyll as early as the early Iron Age. This has been confirmed by radiocarbon dates obtained during a recent underwater survey in which timbers from five crannogs were sampled: three producing Iron Age dates, one an Early Historic date and one a medieval date (Cavers forthcoming). More recently, excavations at Ederline in 2004 have produced E ware, confirming it was occupied in both the Iron Age and Early Historic periods (Henderson *pers comm*). Finally there is the problem of the massive settlement shift which took place to form the basis of the modern dispersed settlement pattern. Current ongoing work on the deserted settlements of mid-Argyll has identified both the longevity of some settlements, and possible medieval building forms (James 2003). The medieval settlement on the island in Loch Glashan can be dated at least as far back as the 14th century on archaeological grounds (Fairhurst 1969). The latest dates, both scientific and typological, from forts and duns cluster around the 8th/9th centuries (Nieke 1990), apart from a possible 10th/11th century re-use of the summit dun of Dunadd for feasting purposes (Lane & Campbell 2000, 96). There is, therefore, a gap, possibly of almost half a millennium, in the settlement sequence. Only excavation of a number of medieval settlements will establish when exactly they were founded. However, the cluster of settlement sites at Loch Glashan, with a dun, crannog, medieval and post-medieval sites in close proximity (figure 3), have the potential to suggest some models of settlement sequence.

These neighbouring sites require a short introduction because they may have a bearing on our understanding of the nature of occupation on the crannog. A circular dun (NR99SW 8) is located on a knoll above the steep slopes bordering the eastern shore of the loch. The location of the dun would have given it clear views to the south and west over the loch but restricted views to the east and north, perhaps suggesting that the focus of its interest was the loch. It would certainly have been visible from the crannog. Excavations in 2003 produced evidence of middle Iron Age occupation in the form of a bead and radiocarbon dates of the 1st to 4th centuries BC (Gilmour & Henderson *pers comm*).

Excavation of the settlement on the natural island which lies only 50m to the north-east of the crannog was undertaken in 1961, also in advance of the dam construction (Fairhurst 1969). An artificial terrace contained behind a stone revetment had been built on the landward side of the island using materials very reminiscent of crannog construction: large logs, brushwood and organic-rich soils (*ibid*, 51). A range of three small buildings lay along the artificial terrace. Coins and green-glazed pottery indicated a 14th-century date for the construction of the terrace and these buildings. One building was of superior construction and had the size and alignment

consistent with a small chapel, an interpretation enhanced by the quantities of wrought stones found on the island. Fairhurst suggested that the settlement represented the beginnings of an ecclesiastical settlement which, for whatever reason, had failed. However, more recent surveys of late medieval island dwellings in Argyll provide an adequate secular context for these

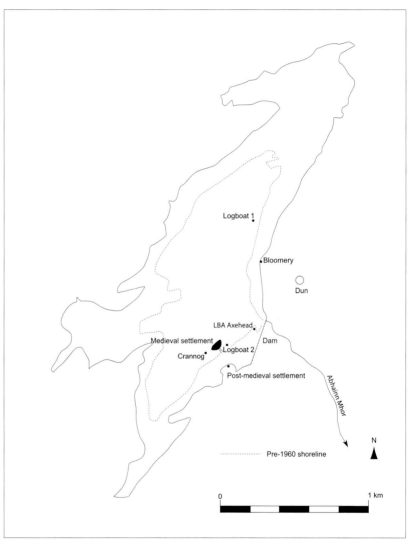

FIGURE 3
Loch Glashan showing location of archaeological sites in and around the loch

buildings (RCAHMS 1992, 306). Most pertinent to the excavations on the crannog, Fairhurst found no evidence of earlier activity on the island, although few of the trenches were fully excavated down to the natural subsoil.

A rough causeway of stones connected the island to the shore and at the northern end of the strait between island and shore the remnants of a logboat were found

(Fairhurst 1969, 47; Logboat 2 on figure 3). Nothing more than its location was noted and it was left *in situ*. As described earlier, it was another logboat that initially drew archaeological interest to the loch, resulting in the discovery of the crannog. Logboat 1 was found at the northern end of the loch (figure 3; NR99SW 11) and fared rather better than Logboat 2. It was retrieved by JGS with the help of a team of 20 men from the Territorial Unit of the Royal Engineers and was subsequently conserved. It has been fully reported by Mowat (1996, 58). The logboat is not dated and could therefore be associated with any one of the settlements in and around the loch.

A post-medieval settlement, consisting of at least two sub-rectangular buildings, lies on the present shore of the loch on what was presumably once a small platform of slightly higher land (James 2003, 107–8). One other site has been noted in the vicinity of the loch. During low water levels in 1987 a bloomery site was exposed on what is now the eastern shoreline of the loch (Gladwin 1987; and see figure 3). The hearth area was clearly visible surrounded by a wide scatter of slag. Again, no dating evidence was retrieved but elsewhere in Scotland these sites tend to be late medieval in date (Photos-Jones *et al* 1998; and see Chapter 4.6). Finally, one stray find which may be of significance is an unusual decorated Late Bronze Age axehead (RCAHMS 1988, illus 26B). This was recovered from the loch shore, near the outlet of the *Abhainn Mhor* in 1960, when the water level was lowered, and may indicate that this area of the loch was used for votive deposition in the later prehistoric period.

# Chapter 3

# The Excavation

## 3.1 THE SITE BEFORE EXCAVATION

The crannog first appeared as a low, stone-covered mound some 0.9m in height, approximately 17m long north to south, and 10.75m from west to east (plates 2 and 3). It lay on the peat-covered shelf at the very edge of the water. It was clear that part of the structure had already slumped into the deeper water beyond, the effect of which had been to loosen and open up the structure of the rest of the crannog (plate 4).

The surface of the crannog was covered by stones (figure 4 and plate 5), amongst which were the querns and other inorganic artefacts collected by Ritchie (see Chapter 1). The stones were large, angular stones, as much as 0.5–0.60m along their long axis, very similar

PLATE 4
Horizontal timbers at the water's edge, showing the degree of slumping into the deeper water just off the shelf. The island is visible in the background.
(© *Crown copyright: RCAHMS Jack Scott collection*)

11

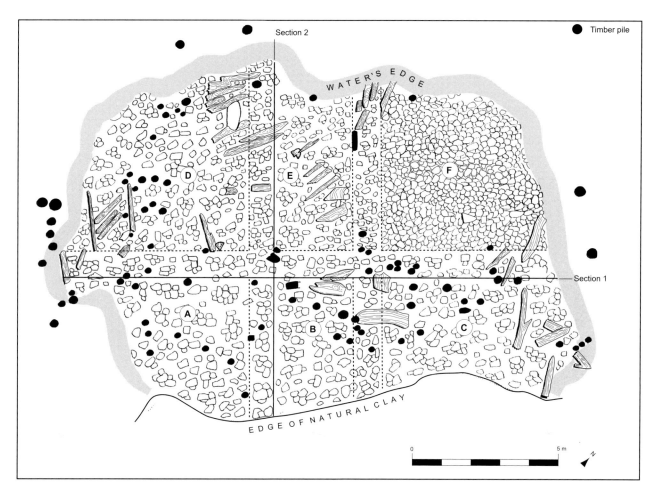

FIGURE 4
Plan of the crannog before excavation (after J G Scott)

to those found along the old beach. Waterlogged horizontal and vertical timbers protruded through the stones in places.

## 3.2 METHODOLOGY

The exposed crannog surface was divided into six sectors, separated by 0.91m baulks, with a long baulk running approximately north and south, separating three landward sectors (A, B and C) from three lochside sectors (D, E and F) (figure 4). The three landward sectors were excavated to a point at which infiltration of water brought the work to a halt. The baulks between them were then removed. Of the three lochside sectors only the central one (E) was excavated to water level in the time available (plate 6). A complete cross section and a complete longitudinal section of the crannog, down to water level, were drawn (figure 6). Backfilling was not considered necessary, since the site was shortly to be inundated.

Parts of the crannog remained water-covered throughout the excavation and could not be excavated. Consequently, the original dimensions of the structure could not be ascertained. Timbers were visible below the water, but the foundations in the lochside sectors could not be established.

## 3.3 THE CRANNOG STRUCTURE

SUBSTRUCTURE

It was possible to insert a 6ft ranging rod to its full extent into the silts under the horizontal timbers. It is therefore clear that there were no stone foundations underpinning the crannog infrastructure. It was also noted that the surface of the crannog tilted, or quaked when walking upon it, again implying that there was no solid foundation to the structure. The core of the crannog above the water level consisted of a compact mass of 'brushwood' at least 0.8m at its maximum visible height. Bark, twigs and leaves were well-preserved throughout this layer and mosses and rushes were also observed in places, but it is not clear whether there were substantial quantities of brushwood in the form of bundles as was the case at other crannogs. In photographs this layer appears as highly comminuted organic debris (ie plates 14 and 15). It is recorded as a homogenous deposit throughout the crannog. Horizontal timbers, some up to 0.34m in diameter were also contained within it, some of which were identified as birch. It is clear from section 2 (figure 6 and plate 7) that the horizontal timbers were more densely concentrated in the western half, on the loch side. In section 1, which skirts the edge of the crannog, the horizontal timbers are much more scattered throughout this layer (figure 6). Occasional stones were scattered throughout the brushwood mound.

PLATE 5
The surface of the crannog before excavation. The sand and gravel layer is visible between the stones and piles can be seen projecting up through the layer.
(© Crown copyright: RCAHMS Jack Scott collection)

PILING

The crannog appears to have been encircled by a halo of wooden piles driven into the brushwood layer (figure 5 and plate 6). They lie in a thick swathe along the eastern, landward side of the crannog, curving around the southern, unexcavated portion of the site. Although not clearly represented on section 2 this halo of piles marks the transition from scattered to more densely packed horizontal timbers and demarcates the extent of the sand and gravel layer (figure 6), something which is more clearly seen in plan (figure 5). Very few piles are visible in the interior of the crannog, ie within the halo of piling (figure 5). As the piling appears to act as a boundary defining the crannog proper one might have expected to observe a difference between the brushwood layer within the piling and that outside it, particularly as all the organic artefacts were found in the latter (see below), but no such distinction was recorded by JGS.

The piles range in diameter from 0.15–0.25m and are mainly undressed roundwood, probably birch

(see below). Scattered throughout the piling were a number of squared oak timbers (plate 8) all of which are described as being charred. JGS also identified other piles as charred and commented in the daybook that 'timbers in [Sector C] appear badly burnt'. Three forked timbers were also observed in Sector A, one of which was apparently *in situ* (Timber 2: figure 5 and plate 9). This appears to have originally been an upright and also lies within the band of piling. The tips of the fork (also recorded as charred) would have stood approximately 1.8m above the point at which the stem snapped off. There was no evidence for any horizontal timber component to prevent sideways movement of the piling, such as the radial mortised framework recorded at Buiston (Crone 2000, 90).

Some of the piles cluster around a massive oak log, prompting the suggestion that the log may have been deliberately pinned in position by the piles (Timber 1: figure 5). A large, gnarled lump of oak also lies alongside the log (Timber 3: figure 5). JGS suggested

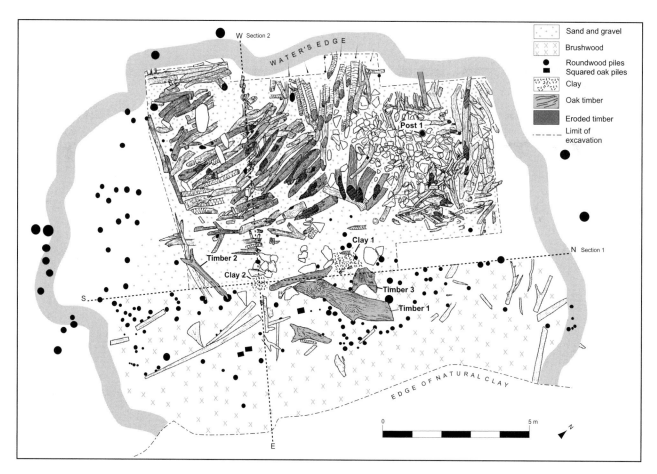

FIGURE 5
Plan of the crannog showing all features discussed in text (after J G Scott)

PLATE 6
View of the crannog from shore showing the band of piling around the landward side of the structure. Section 1 runs north–south across the crannog.
The three landward sectors, A, B and C have been removed. Behind Section 1, Sector D has been excavated down to the surface of the peat.
(© *Crown copyright: RCAHMS Jack Scott collection*)

that these large pieces of oak had been laid down to form an approach to the shore (plate 10).

### HORIZONTAL TIMBER HORIZON

A horizon of large, horizontal logs lay directly over, and in some places appeared embedded in, the brushwood layer (figure 6). In the southern half of the crannog these timbers formed a distinct rectangular area, or 'platform', 4.4m wide and at least 5.5m long, the long axis lying

west/east (figure 5 and plate 11). The western end of the 'platform' could not be excavated as it lay below the water level. The logs in the 'platform' were a mixture of oak and other species (see below), and some were as much as 0.35m in diameter and up to 2.3m long. The logs had been laid down in two abutting rows in such a way that the ends interdigitated with each other. It was noted that the upper surfaces of some of the logs appeared flattened but there was no clear evidence for

15

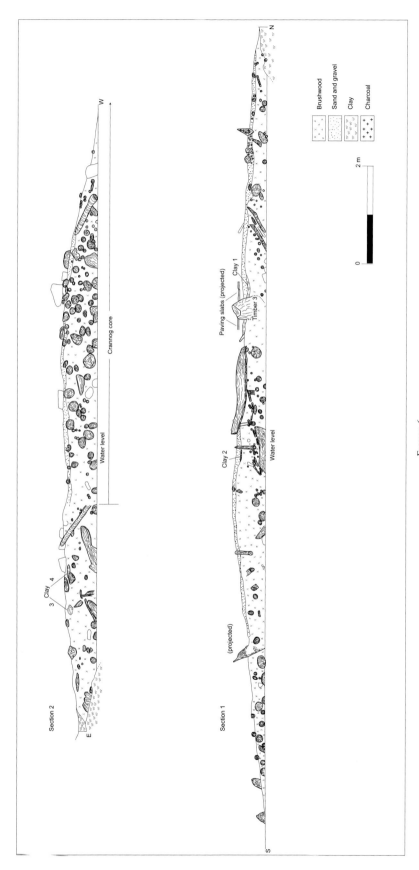

FIGURE 6
Sections 1 and 2 (after J G Scott)

PLATE 7
Section 2 running west–east across the crannog. The concentration of horizontal logs in the 'core' of the crannog is visible in this section.
(© Crown copyright: RCAHMS Jack Scott collection)

any deliberate shaping. Holes, interpreted as sockets for posts, were recorded in one or two of the timbers.

Another group of horizontal timbers lay immediately adjacent to the northern edge of this rectangular 'platform' (figure 5). These timbers were aligned west/east, ie at right angles to those in the 'platform', and were only partially exposed above the water line. They

had apparently slumped into deeper water so that their exposed ends jutted up into the air (plate 4).

It is not clear what happens to this horizon in the northernmost section of the site because it was not fully excavated down to the lacustrine silts. JGS records that under the pile of stones in Sector F (see below) large timbers were encountered, 'more or less radially set',

17

and lying at odd angles 'as though the whole structure had sunk'.

CLAY DEPOSITS

Several discrete patches of clay were found lying directly on top of the brushwood layer, immediately within the halo of piling. Clay 1 is recorded in both section (figure 6) and plan (figure 5), although it does not appear to have been fully exposed when planned. Large flat stones and sand appear to lie over its northern end (plate 12) but JGS commented in the daybook that there was no apparent relationship between them. When fully exposed it was 1.6m wide and some 0.07m thick. Clay 2 was only recorded in plan where it appears as a patch, approximately 0.6m in diameter. A further two lenses of clay are recorded in section 2 (Clay 3 and 4: fig 6) where they appear to lie within the brushwood mound outwith the halo of piling. JGS also mentioned patches of clay in Sector F in the daybook but they are not recorded in section or plan.

SAND AND GRAVEL HORIZON

The entire surface of the brushwood mound within the interior of the piling was covered by a layer of sand and gravel up to 0.12m thick in places (plates 5 and 11). It was found in the interstices between the horizontally-laid logs and, on occasion overlay the logs (figure 6). It also overlay the clay patch, Clay 1 (figure 6).

STONE HORIZON

When first discovered the crannog was covered in a layer of large angular stones (figure 4 and plate 5), from which all but one of the querns were retrieved. The stones were thinly scattered across the site except in the Sector F (figure 5), where excavation revealed that they had been deposited to a depth of at least 1m, which had the effect of levelling the surface of the crannog. In the centre of this deposit of stones was a large upright post (Post 1: figure 5).

It should be noted here that, in the plans that JGS had begun to prepare for publication and on which

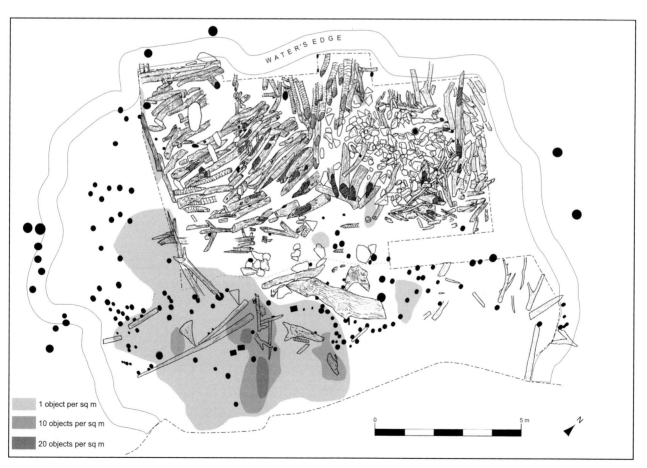

1 object per sq m

10 objects per sq m

20 objects per sq m

0        5 m

FIGURE 7
Plan of the crannog showing the distribution of the artefacts

figures 4 and 5 are based, the stones have been drawn schematically and do not approximate to the size and distribution of stones that are visible in the photographs. In the daybook he records that all the visible timbers were planned but not the stones because they did not display any patterning.

FINDS DISTRIBUTION

The bulk of the artefacts recovered during the excavation were found on the landward side of the crannog, in a remarkably discrete area amongst and outwith the halo of piling (figure 7). All of the organic artefacts recovered were found within the brushwood layer in this area. This deposit also yielded the brooch, the axe, and potsherds from Vessels 1, 3 and 4, as well as numerous coarse stone implements, a single quernstone (SF39; plate 13), and four animal teeth, the surviving one of which has been identified as cattle (*Bos* sp; Murray Cook *pers comm*). JGS recorded all the finds three-dimensionally, measuring their position as offsets from the baulks and recording their depth within the brushwood layer.

No artefacts were retrieved from the brushwood deposits lying within the piling. In this area, only inorganic artefacts were found in the sand and gravel horizon on top of the crannog. These included the two crucibles, potsherds from Vessels 1 and 2, quantities of slag and coarse stone implements. It will also be remembered that Ritchie found one almost complete E ware pot (vessel 5), three E ware sherds (from Vessel 1), four whetstones, 21 possible querns and slag lying on the exposed surface of the crannog when he first visited it (see Chapter 1). The concentration of stones in the north-western section of the crannog was devoid of finds, although minute fragments of burnt bone were observed.

NOTE ON WOOD SPECIES

Six samples of wood from the crannog were sent by JGS to Professor Preston of the Department of Botany, University of Leeds who carried out an experiment in dating the timbers on the basis of their water content.

PLATE 8
The piling under excavation. A squared pile can be seen collapsed between two undressed roundwood piles. The stump of another squared post is visible at the righthand edge of the photograph. (© *Crown copyright: RCAHMS Jack Scott collection*)

As a preliminary he identified the species of the samples: five were birch and one was disconcertingly identified as sycamore, a species which was not introduced to the British Isles until the 15th/16th century (Jones 1945). JGS identified oak (*Quercus* sp) timbers on his plans (figure 4); the two timbers that he retrieved, Timbers 1 and 2, were recently confirmed as oak so there is no reason to doubt the veracity of his other identifications.

NOTE ON EVIDENCE FOR CONFLAGRATION

Many of the structural timbers and wooden artefacts were described as charred. The level at which the charring occurred is not recorded but the piles did not protrude much above the level of the brushwood mound, ie *c* 93.8m. To become charred the piles would have had to be exposed to the air at this level and yet there is no evidence that the water levels were ever this low in the past (Chapter 2.2). Furthermore, such an extensive burning episode as is implied would surely

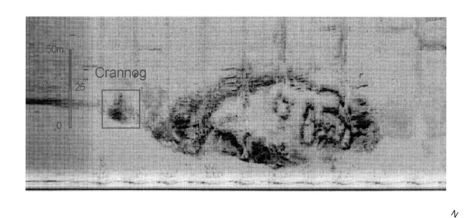

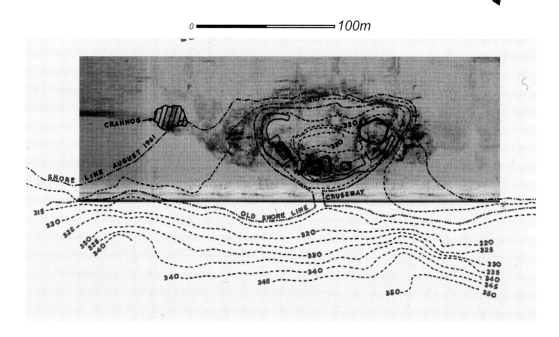

FIGURE 8
a) Sonograph of the crannog lying to the south-west of the submerged natural island; b) Sonograph overlain with plan of
island settlement and crannog (from Fairhurst 1969, fig 2)

have left a thick deposit of charcoal on the surface of the brushwood mound, whereas the only charcoal recorded is a scatter at the northern end of section 1 (figure 6). Timber 2, the prongs of which had been recorded as charred, has since been examined and displays no evidence of burning. Examination of the wooden artefacts revealed evidence of burning on only one object (Chapter 4.1). Similarly, the brooch had been described in the daybook as 'largely destroyed by burning' but the condition of the amber studs showed that the brooch had not been exposed to fire (Werner 1963). Overall, there is no evidence to support the thesis of a conflagration on the crannog. It seems most

likely that, in the case of the wood, the discoloration caused by submersion in the peaty loch compounded by drying-out during a year of exposure above the water, causing the surface to craze, was mistakenly identified as charring.

## 3.4   THE UNDERWATER SURVEY

### *Jon C Henderson*

AIMS

Although the arc of the piling appears to continue around the crannog, the full extent of the crannog on the loch side could not be recorded during the excavations

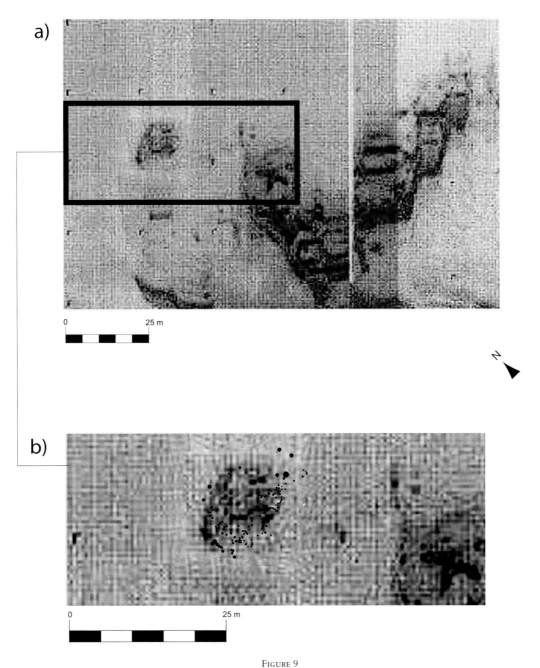

FIGURE 9
a) Higher resolution sonograph of the crannog. The frequency of the sidescan has been adjusted to penetrate the covering silts to produce a more accurate representation of the size and extent of the site; b) Sonograph overlain with plan of piling (the piles have been doubled in size to show more clearly against the sonograph)

in 1960 (figure 5). Consequently, a side-scan survey and underwater examination of the area around the crannog and the submerged island was carried out in June 2003. The aims of the work were twofold;

- to survey the full extent of the crannog and locate the piling around the perimeter

- to sample those oak timbers which were clearly identifiable as structural elements of the crannog for dendrochronological analysis.

METHODOLOGY
Sidescan sonar was the principle method of prospection used to locate and plan the extent of the

PLATE 9
a) Timber 2 *in situ*; b) Timber 2 held upright. (© *Crown copyright: RCAHMS Jack Scott collection*)

crannog. Sidescan sonar is a specialized surveying technique in which short pulses of acoustic energy are transmitted along the sea or loch bed in fan-shaped beams (narrow in the horizontal plane and wide in the vertical plane) from a submerged transducer unit (towfish) towed by a moving vessel. The return echoes from any objects in the path of these beams are electronically processed and continuously recorded side-by-side on a graphic display to create an image called a sonograph. Different loch bed environments have different acoustic properties (textures) and the images recorded on the sonographs reflect this. The acoustic impedance between rock, gravel and wood is stronger than that of silt, sand or mud. The former materials will therefore appear darker on a mixed lakebed sonograph (figures 8 and 9). Areas of positive and negative relief (loch bed topography and anthropogenic objects such as crannogs) can also be detected as topography determines the reflected energy strength from the sonar beam. For example, inclined slopes facing the towfish are better reflectors than declined slopes. The latter will appear darker on the record, because of the lower angle of incidence of the sonar pulse as it encounters the loch floor.

At Loch Glashan, an *EdgeTech* Model 260-TH recorder with a dual-frequency *EdgeTech* 272-TD towfish was used, operating at frequencies of 400–500 kHz. A scanning range of either 150m (ie 150m to either side of the towfish transducer) or 75m per channel was employed. The towfish was towed by a hard bottomed RIB vessel at surveying speeds of 2–3 knots to produce sonographs which most closely approximate true scale images (Duck & McManus 1987, 224). The sidescan traverses were accurately fixed geographically by GPS readings (linked to the recorder and taken constantly throughout the process). An area 250m by 200m was covered by the sidescan sonar. Areas of interest indicated by the sidescan sonar were marked with buoys and visually inspected by members of the dive team. Underwater photography and videoing was attempted but was rendered impossible due to the dark, silty conditions of the loch.

RESULTS

The site of the crannog was located at NR 9168 9252 lying some 47m west of the submerged medieval island settlement (figure 8). Underwater inspection revealed that the site lay underneath at least 2m of very soft silts in some 16m of water. The very soft nature of the silts, coupled with the relatively deep nature of the site, created very poor visibility (less than 1m) and meant that diving conditions were treacherous. The depth of silt made the location and recovery of structural timbers

impossible without excavation, which would have involved the use of a water dredge.

Soft fluidized silts and muds are commonly found in reservoirs and are sometimes referred to as 'ooze layers'. Due to the damming of the loch the sediment input to the loch is not naturally flushed away but instead builds up behind the dam. The close location of the site to the dam itself (figure 2) may account for the very soft silts obscuring the crannog. Sonograph traces of the sites were only obtained by changing the resolution of the sidescan to penetrate silts. Consequently, only a general outline of the crannog could be obtained and the position of piling around the crannog could not be determined (figure 8a). The sonograph trace accords well with the 1961 plan of the crannog and medieval island settlement (figure 8b).

By adjusting the frequency of the sidescan a more detailed image of the crannog was obtained (figure 9a). In figure 9b the sonograph trace of the crannog

PLATE 10
View of the crannog from the shore. Timber 1 is just visible lying behind two large piles. JGS thought this group of timbers might form an approach from the crannog to the shore. (© *Crown copyright: RCAHMS Jack Scott collection*)

PLATE 11
Horizontal timbers forming a rectangular 'platform'. Note that the surfaces of these timbers appear eroded rather than deliberately flattened. To the left of the photograph the sequence of stones over sand-and-gravel over timbers is clearly visible. (© *Crown copyright: RCAHMS Jack Scott collection*)

has been overlain with a plan of the piling recorded in 1960. The close correlation in size and shape between the sonograph and the arc of piling suggests that the crannog was not much larger than the area exposed in 1960 and that it probably was oval in plan. If a line is drawn through the surviving arc of piles and projected out into the water it appears to describe an oval approximately 18m by 13m. This is a very rough-and-ready estimate and its final shape and size may well have been determined by post-depositional slumping.

## 3.5  STRUCTURAL INTERPRETATION

The stratigraphy of the site as recorded during the excavation is very simple (figure 6). A mound of organic debris consisting primarily of brushwood, with some larger timbers and occasional stones lies on top of lacustrine silts. This mound is covered by a layer of large horizontal timbers, over and between which is a layer of sand and gravel. Finally, a layer of stones covers the site. The brushwood mound is reminiscent

of the *Packwerk* construction revealed at Buiston (Crone 2000, 14) and intimated on other crannogs (Munro 1882, 262). This type of construction was first defined by Davies (1942) and consisted of materials such as brushwood, stones, peat, turves, bracken, branches and midden debris dumped onto the lochbed to form a mound which was probably contained and pinned down by encircling piles. The piling is driven through the periphery of the brushwood layer, either to contain the mass of the crannog infrastructure or to provide a defensive perimeter, a palisade. A midden has built up in the brushwood deposits outwith the piling.

THE BRUSHWOOD LAYER

A conflict is immediately apparent with the recorded stratigraphy in that the midden, which must have formed *after* occupation, is embedded in a layer, the 'brushwood' layer, which was supposedly laid down as part of the crannog substructure *before* occupation began. There are two ways of resolving this conflict. One is to assume that the brushwood layer inside and outside the piling is homogenous and represents the

24

primary layer of the packwerk mound. The corollary of this assumption is that all the artefacts found in the brushwood layer must have been incorporated in the mound during its construction and therefore *pre-date* the crannog occupation. The fact that all the artefacts were found in a discrete area mainly outside the piling and are not dispersed throughout the brushwood layer within the piling strongly militates against this interpretation. The alternative is to assume that there must have been a distinction, which was not observed, between the brushwood layer within the piling and that outside. The only distinction that is apparent in the recorded stratigraphy is that the horizontal timbers within the brushwood mound are more densely concentrated within the halo of piling, suggesting that this was indeed the core of the crannog (plate 7). In this interpretation the brushwood layer within the piling represents the primary deposit of the packwerk mound while the 'brushwood' layer outside the piling developed during and/or after the crannog occupation.

### INTERPRETATION OF THE FEATURES ON THE SURFACE OF THE CRANNOG

JGS interpreted the layers overlying the brushwood mound as remnants of the original occupation surface (Scott 1960). He saw the timber 'platform' as the sub-floor of a rectangular building, the upper surfaces of the timbers having been deliberately flattened for this purpose. He proposed that the forked timber, Timber 2, might have formed a corner post. The timber sub-floor was then covered by a floor of sand and gravel, the eastern end of which was roughly paved. The patches of clay, Clay 1 and 2, which also lay at the eastern end, were interpreted as the remains of domestic hearths (plate 12). The artefact-rich brushwood deposits in and around the piling were interpreted as midden and JGS concluded that the artefacts therein must therefore pre-date the pottery found on the surface of the crannog. Finally, he suggested that the concentration of stones in the northwestern section of the crannog represented the foundations of a circular hut some 3.7m in diameter built around a central post. As the spread of stones had partially buried some of the horizontal logs adjacent to the rectangular building JGS concluded that the round hut post-dated it.

### AN ALTERNATIVE INTERPRETATION: CONFLATION

A glimpse at figure 5 shows that this interpretation is, indeed very plausible. However, there are a number

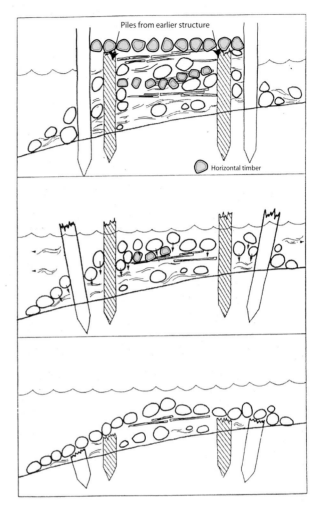

FIGURE 10
Schematic section through crannog showing the process of deflation

of observed features which cannot be accommodated within this interpretation and which therefore cast doubt on its integrity. Principal amongst these is the capping of stones over the crannog and the concentration of so many inorganic artefacts within this capping. How did an almost complete pot come to be sitting on the surface of the crannog after at least a millennium of submersion under the loch waters? One possible explanation is that the stone capping and the inorganic artefacts represent a conflation deposit, ie all that is left after the organic matrix in which they were originally embedded has decayed and eroded away.

Many crannogs in Highland lochs often appear as small stony islands, prompting the description of 'crannog-cairn' (Davies 1942), but excavation has demonstrated that at least in the excavated cases, these crannogs have a large wood component at the core and that the stones are merely a capping (ie Dixon 1984). It has been suggested that the stone capping represents a later phase of refurbishment, taking place after the piles had rotted to the level of the protective organic deposits (Dixon *ibid*). However, why so many crannogs would be treated to such refurbishment is unclear (but see below). It seems more likely that such a ubiquitous feature as the stone capping is the result of a natural, post-depositional process in which degradation of the organic component causes the structure to collapse

PLATE 12
The putative hearth and flagstones. The ranging rod lies across Clay 1, with the flagstones behind it. (© *Crown copyright: RCAHMS Jack Scott collection*)

inwardly. This process continues until the stones, which may have been distributed throughout the mound as weighting material (as at Buiston) or formed some element of the structure/s on top of the crannog, come to settle as a continuous layer, thus providing a protective layer over the remaining organic deposits below (Crone 1988, 47 and see figure 10). In this model the inorganic artefacts found in the capping are the residue of a much larger artefact assemblage, the organic component of which has decayed away.

If we accept that the conflation model provides a feasible explanation for the layer of stones and inorganic artefacts this also implies that there was a greater depth of mound material than has survived, something that is also intimated by the evidence of the water levels. At the pre-1960 level of 96m (Chapter 2.2; figure 2), over 2.2m of material would have been needed to bring the surviving surface of the crannog to a habitable level above the water. The geomorphological evidence indicates that there was a period when the water levels in the loch were c1m lower; if the crannog was built during this period then at least 1.2m of deposits would still have been needed. The stone capping and its contents would therefore represent the conflation deposit from between 1.2–2.2m depth of material.

This means that the excavated features would originally have lain beneath up to 2.2m of deposits, thus casting doubt on their interpretation as the occupation surface. There are a number of observations that also militate against this interpretation. JGS thought that the flattened upper surfaces of the horizontal timbers were deliberate but examination of the photographic record (plate 11) indicates that these timbers were quite degraded at the time of excavation. They had been exposed for a year prior to excavation and had never been fully protected by the capping of stones during their long submersion. The flattened surfaces are thus more likely to represent an erosion surface. The 'sockets' were only recorded on plan and so their interpretation cannot be corroborated. The sand and gravel deposits interpreted as a floor surface over the timber sub-floor are also susceptible to alternative interpretation. This horizon is not limited to the boundaries of the rectangular timber 'platform' but covers the entire surface of the crannog within the halo of piling (figure 5). This horizon could represent the accumulation of the smaller mineral component of the packwerk mound, possibly brought on to the mound either as deliberate dumps of beach deposits or as turves. Finally, the clay patches are not convincing as hearths. They are located too close to the piling palisade to have

PLATE 13
The quern, SF39, *in situ*. (© *Crown copyright: RCAHMS Jack Scott collection*)

functioned as such (figure 5), and have no edging or signs of burning. Furthermore, the recording of clay lenses within the brushwood mound just outside the palisade (figure 6) and in Sector F suggests that these lenses were simply another inorganic component of the packwerk mound.

An alternative explanation for the observed features is that the 'platform' of horizontal timbers was just one element in a patchwork of log layers which were laid down to build up the core of the mound. The horizontal timbers, which can be seen dipping into the water adjacent to the northern edge of the rectangular 'platform', appear to be a similar area of parallel-laid logs (figure 5 and plate 5). This interpretation is proposed here as that which best fits the available evidence but it is unfortunately untestable, at Loch Glashan at least. If we accept JGS' interpretation that the surviving surface of the crannog was the original occupation surface then we must find an explanation as to why it ended up some 2.2m below the surface of the loch. Bishop (Chapter 2.2) proposed one possible explanation, that the weight of the crannog

mass may have caused it to gradually settle into the lacustrine silts until it sank below the surface of the loch. If this happened during the occupation of the crannog the subsidence would surely have been compensated for by the addition of more deposits to build up the surface, thus burying earlier occupation surfaces, as happened at Buiston (Crone 2000, 65–6). If subsidence continued after final abandonment then there was still a long period when the deposits on the exposed surface of the crannog had time to decay and erode away before sinking below the water. It is possible that the conflation of the deposits ceased at the level of a buried floor surface leaving us with the recorded features but the observations presented above cast doubt on that interpretation.

MULTI-PERIOD OCCUPATION?

We have no stratigraphic evidence as to whether the original crannog mound consisted entirely of packwerk deposits on top of which there was a single phase of occupation, or whether there were several phases of occupation, each of which would have left evidence within the mound. The conflation deposits may therefore represent more than one phase of occupation. There were a number of observed features which indicate that there may have been some chronological depth to occupation on the crannog. SF15, a small, tub-shaped wooden vessel was found in a very fragmented state (Chapter 4.1) around the base of a pair of birch stakes in the palisade (plate 14). JGS suggested that the vessel had been rammed down around the stakes but the logic for such an action is hard to fathom. It seems more likely that the vessel had been pierced by the insertion of the stakes, implying that the vessel had already been deposited by the time the piling was inserted. The palisade consists of both untrimmed roundwood birch stakes and squared oak stakes (figure 5 and plate 8), JGS describing the latter as 'firmly fixed', presumably in contrast to the less firmly embedded birch stakes. This mixture could simply reflect use of whatever was to hand, the squared oak stakes possibly being re-used within the palisade, but it may also reflect refurbishment of the palisade, an event which occurred frequently on Buiston crannog (Crone 2000, 66).

POST–OCCUPATION ACTIVITY?

Although we have argued that the spread of stones over much of the crannog mound was the result of decay of the organic matrix the concentration of stones in the north-western sector does appear to be a deliberate deposit. Unfortunately, the findspots of the artefacts found on the surface of the crannog before excavation were not recorded so we do not know if they were also found scattered over the north-western section. If this were the case then it could be argued that the concentration of stones in this area was a pre-conflation event. In his daybook JGS observed that the feature was 'almost certainly later than the subsidence of the crannog on the lochside' and it does seem most likely that it was formed some considerable time after abandonment of the crannog, at a time when deflation of the organic mound was well-advanced. If the crannog lay just below the surface of the water it will have formed a hazard to boats on the loch and it is possible that a cairn of stones, with a projecting post, was built up on the crannog to signal the hazard.

# Chapter 4

# The Artefact Assemblage

The artefacts were originally numbered in a site catalogue in a sequence running from SF1 to SF219, though often several items were listed under one number. These numbers have been retained where possible in this report for ease of reference to the original archive, but in a number of instances this has proved impossible. The surviving leather, for example, has been designated L1 to L74 due to difficulties in matching fragments to the original catalogue. The querns were never numbered, and have been designated LGQ1 to LGQ21. The pottery was separately listed, from 1 to 21, and this numbering has been retained. A number of additional items, primarily a few wooden objects which did not have surviving finds numbers and the whetstones found prior to excavation, have been designated X1, etc. The finds are all deposited in Kelvingrove Museum, Glasgow Museums and Art Galleries, Glasgow, and the archives, including detailed finds catalogues, in the RCAHMS premises at John Sinclair House, 16 Bernard Terrace, Edinburgh.

## 4.1 THE CONSERVED WOOD ASSEMBLAGE
*Anne Crone*

### INTRODUCTION

All the wooden objects were conserved in Carbowax™ (chemical name: polyethylene glycol, molecular weight unknown) soon after excavation but no analysis of the assemblage was undertaken until Caroline Earwood reported on a selection of the more interesting items as part of a larger study into wooden domestic artefacts (Earwood 1990; 1993a). Although the original finds list recorded 128 wooden objects some could not be located and in all 106 objects were examined during this study.

This report attempts to present a comprehensive overview of the assemblage but it is always more difficult to analyse a wood assemblage *after* conservation because certain categories of information can no longer be obtained. In the case of the Loch Glashan assemblage the carbowax deposits on the surface of the objects have tended to obscure evidence of toolmarks and wear patterns and occasionally identification of the conversion method is impossible. In most cases it has also been impossible to identify the wood species used (see below).

A complete catalogue of all the surviving wooden artefacts is lodged with the site archive. Catalogue entries are presented only for those objects which have been illustrated. While the function of some of the artefacts is clear, that of the majority is more ambiguous; the question marks after many of the sub-headings in the catalogue reflect this. Where possible, the artefacts are grouped and discussed below according to the activity or product they represent. Individual artefacts are only discussed where additional comment can supplement the catalogue entry.

### CONTAINERS

Seven containers were recovered from the crannog. The majority are carved one-piece containers but a single fragment of a turned bowl was found and there is also indirect evidence for the use of stave-built vessels. The handle of a container lid was also found. This mixture of container types is characteristic of wooden artefact assemblages from other crannogs, ie Buiston (Crone 2000), Ballinderry 1 (Hencken 1936), Ballinderry 2 (Hencken 1942), and Lagore (Hencken 1950), although at the latter two sites the commonest type of container by far was the stave-built tub or bucket. The evidence from Loch Glashan is discussed below by category.

### *Carved containers*

All but one of this group are shallow trough-shaped containers. The exception, SF15 (figure 11 and plate 14), is a small tub-shaped container, between 180–190mm in diameter. It was carved out of a log of ash by hollowing out the interior of the trunk, perhaps the simplest and easiest means of creating a wooden container but not one which displays an understanding of the properties of wood. This method of conversion would have rendered the container weak because the grain ran down the length of the body, making it vulnerable to vertical splitting. It may have been made rapidly for immediate use and disposal with no long-term function in mind; it has been roughly finished and fragments of bark are still in place. It is possible that it

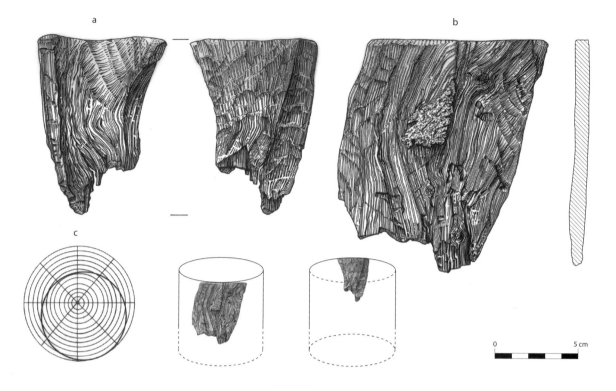

FIGURE 11

Fragments of SF15, the tub-shaped container, showing the flat rim and the tub-like profile: a) from left to right, interior and exterior of one fragment:
b) exterior of the largest fragment; c) position in which the container was carved out of the log; d) reconstruction of container.

was bound by small hoops to prevent vertical splitting but there were no signs of hoop marks on the walls although, admittedly, the longest surviving fragment was only 146mm. An oak tub of similar dimensions and construction, from a 10th-century AD context in Southampton, was bound with two hazel hoops some 70mm above its base (Holdsworth 1976, 43–4). There is no evidence to indicate whether the base was a separate element or carved in one with the walls.

This type of container has a long history. The earliest example found in the British Isles, a tub from Allt Garadh Ealabais, Islay, dates to the Bronze Age (Earwood 1998) while the 10th-century AD example from Southampton has already been mentioned. A one-piece tub of willow of similar dimensions but with a band of carved decoration below the rim was found at Ballinderry 1 (Hencken 1936, 137); carved tubs from the later prehistoric Glastonbury Lake Village were also decorated (Earwood 1993a, 58–9). Containers of similar construction but much larger in size to the examples mentioned have been found in both Scotland and Ireland, several of which contained bog butter (Earwood 1993b).

The other carved containers have been more sensibly converted from the log. SF82 (figure 14), 83 (figure 14), 120 (figure 13) and 121 (figure 13; see also plate 31) have all been converted from half-logs while SF55 (figure 12; see also plate 31) has been converted from a whole log. In all cases the grain runs across the vessel, thus minimizing the risk of vertical splitting. Only two of the vessels, SF82 and 83, could be confidently identified as alder but this species would have been ideal for the production of all the containers, being easy to carve and not susceptible to splitting. Furthermore, it apparently imparts no flavour to foodstuffs contained within (Taylor 1981, 45). It is the species most commonly used in the past for the manufacture of carved containers (ie Crone 1993; 2000; Earwood 1993a).

Two of the containers, SF55 and 120, are very similar in that they are rectangular and relatively straight-sided, and at each end the rim extends out horizontally to form ledge handles. They belong to a class of container commonly known as troughs, examples of which have been found elsewhere in Scotland, Ireland and the Continent, mainly in Early Historic and later contexts

(Earwood 1993b). A ledge-handled trough from Durness, Sutherland has been radiocarbon-dated to 940 ± 80 BP (OxA-3010: *ibid*, 361).

There is a considerable difference in size between SF55 and 120, the former being over twice as long as the latter and half as high again. SF120, at 430mm long, is the smallest known to date. Other ledge-handled troughs display similar variety in size; an example found near the late medieval crannog at Eaderloch is 1.65m long, prompting the excavator to suggest that it was a small cargo boat (Ritchie 1942, 58), while the trough found at Lochlee, a crannog of probable Early Historic date (Munro 1882, 93 and see Crone 2000, 106), was only 570mm long. Mowat (1996, 96) has calculated the capacity of the Loch Glashan examples at 18 litres for

SF55 and 4.4 litres for SF120, a difference which must surely relate to function. Earwood (1993b, 357) suggests a number of possible uses, from food preparation and storage, to the dyeing of textiles. Food storage seems unlikely, particularly in the case of SF55, given that there is a large surface area to keep covered, but two of the Scottish troughs, from Durness, Sutherland and Midton, Ross-shire, did contain bog butter when found (*ibid*). SF120 is certainly small enough for use as tableware or for food storage within the house. SF55 is of a size to have had a semi-industrial function, such as leather tanning or flax retting. The ledge handles are clearly designed for ease of carrying and it is possible that the larger examples were simply designed for the transporting of goods by two persons.

PLATE 14
The wooden container, SF15, pierced by two stakes. (© *Crown copyright: RCAHMS Jack Scott collection*)

31

FIGURE 12
Trough SF55

SF120 and SF121 (figure 13) were found together, in such a way as to suggest that one had been stacked inside the other (plate 15), and are therefore assumed to be contemporary. SF121 is also a large, low trough-like container, measuring 620mm in length, but it is more bowl-shaped in profile, with rounded corners and curving walls. More importantly in terms of function, it has a very small handle at each end, neither of which

PLATE 15
Wooden containers, SF120 and SF121, as found. The nature of the 'brushwood' layer in which the containers are lying, is clearly visible in this photograph. (© *Crown copyright: RCAHMS Jack Scott collection*)

can be easily gripped and which would have made the carrying of the container very difficult. The handles are also positioned differently, a feature which may simply be a mistake made during manufacture. However, several other wooden vessels have similarly assymetric handles, ie the prehistoric dish from Stornaway, Lewis (Earwood 1993b, 357) and the bowl from Bracadale, Skye (Crone 1993) so it may well be a deliberate feature relating to function. It seems most likely that this container, given its large size and non-operational handles, was intended for a stationary purpose. The trough from Stornaway has been radiocarbon-dated to $2370 \pm 90$ BP (OxA-3012: Earwood 1993b, 361) while the Bracadale bowl was radiocarbon-dated to $1930 \pm 50$ BP (UT-1698: Crone 1993).

SF82 and 83 (figure 14) are very similar in size and, with the exception of the tub, are substantially smaller that the other carved containers. This alone would suggest a very different function, possibly as dishes for use on the table or in the kitchen. Despite their small size they both have thick end walls which substantially reduce the internal volume so carrying capacity may not have been a consideration. They may have been used for pounding herbs, spices or nuts, etc. Both vessels are boat-shaped but SF82 is markedly so. The single handle on SF82, which projects only 22mm from the end wall, cannot have been designed to function as such and it is possible that it was a design feature carved out to emphasize the prow-like shape of that end.

SF82 is the only one of the carved containers to retain evidence for the method of its manufacture. Crescentic marks at each end indicate that the half-log was placed flat side down and a small axe, working in a downwards motion, was used to shape the rounded ends. A knife was then used to pare the profile of the dish foot, cutting in from the sides towards the handle in the centre of the end wall. A few insubstantial cut-marks are also visible in the angle between the interior wall and base on SF120 and 121 but conservation has obscured any more detail.

### Turned containers

SF149 is the only example of a turned bowl found on the crannog. It has been made from ash, a wood prized by turners for the decorative pattern of its grain, and used in many early examples of turned vessels (ie Buiston-Crone 2000, 111–12; Glastonbury-Earwood 1988; Morris 1984, 231). All that survives is a fragment with a finely made everted rim and a smooth, apparently globular profile (figure 15). However, we cannot be absolutely certain about the original profile of the bowl

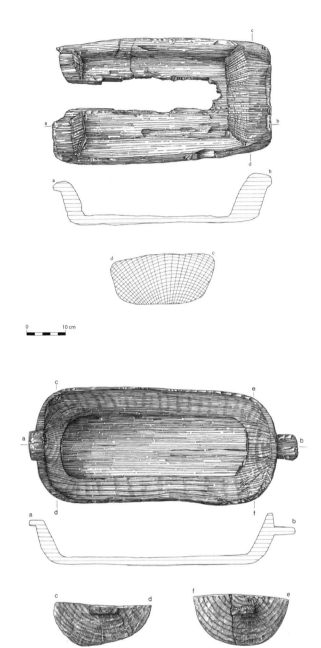

FIGURE 13

Top – trough SF120. Cutmarks are visible in the angle between base and wall at the left-hand end of the trough; bottom – carved container SF121

because the surviving fragment is only 55mm in height and will have suffered some distortion during burial.

Large numbers of lathe-turned bowls have been found on some of the Irish crannog sites, ranging from shallow, open bowls to more sophisticated profiles with everted rims and decorative grooves (ie Ballinderry 1; Hencken 1936, 148 and 172). Hencken suggested that

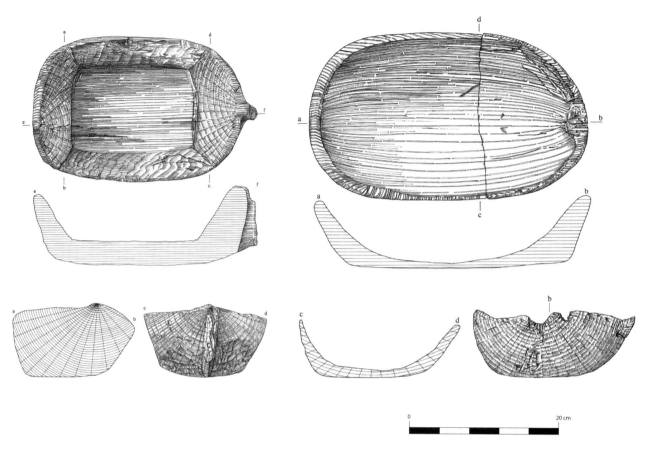

FIGURE 14
Carved containers; left – SF82; right – SF83

those vessels with everted rims imitated pottery forms, although he could not specify what type of pottery (Hencken 1950, 156). Earwood (1990, 85) has gone further and suggested that SF149 is a copy of one of the E ware vessels found on the crannog, Vessel 5 (figure 32), but given the uncertainty about the original profile of the wooden bowl, this comparison may not be valid (see Chapter 4.2).

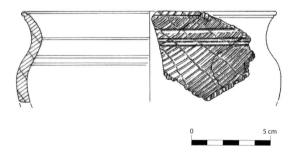

FIGURE 15
Turned bowl, SF149. The grooves on the interior and exterior are the results of turning rather than deliberate decorative elements

*Stave-built containers*

Although there are no staves in the assemblage there are three finds which indicate that stave-built vessels were also being used on the crannog. SF111, 140 and X6 are all chords cleft off lengths of withies (figure 16), provisionally identified as hazel. Despite being incomplete (at least one end is broken off on all three items) their surviving lengths are substantial, 825mm, 660mm and 910mm respectively. They are between 35–38mm wide and the bark has been stripped off so that the smooth sub-bark surface is revealed. Two of the chords have been manufactured so that they thin out towards one end. SF140 has been cleft in such a way that its thickness reduces from 17mm to 6mm while on SF X6 the sub-bark surface has been cut away for part of its length, reducing its thickness from 11mm to 6mm. These chords were intended for use as hoops and the deliberate tapering in thickness along their length was designed to allow a neat overlap of the hoop ends as they encircle the vessel. The overlapping tapered ends would then be secured by small pegs or were

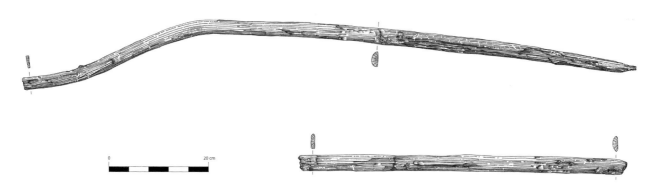

FIGURE 16
Barrel hoops X6 (upper) and SF140 (lower). Note the deliberately tapered ends to the left

bound together (for examples see Earwood 1993a, 178–80).

Although it is impossible to estimate the diameter of the vessel for which they were intended the stoutness of these hoops suggests that they were intended for a relatively large vessel. For comparison, the two hoops from the Early Historic rath at Seacash, Co Antrim were only 25mm wide and encircled a tub 1m in diameter at the rim (Lynn 1978, 69). A complete hoop from Ballinderry 1 was 35mm thick and encircled a diameter of 0.65m (Hencken 1936, 151). We can also only guess at the shape of the stave-built vessel. Although the craft of barrel-making, with fitted base and head, was introduced to the British Isles by the Romans (Earwood 1993a, 181) there is very little evidence for the manufacture and/or use of barrels by the native populations. Straight-sided and splay-sided stave-built vessels are found throughout the British Isles from the later prehistoric period (Earwood 1993, 76–80) and are commonly found on almost every Early Historic site in Scotland and Ireland on which waterlogged deposits have survived. However, only two sites from that period have produced unambiguous evidence of barrels; two bellied staves were found at Lagore (Hencken 1950, 153) and a chord of a coopered barrel lid was found at Buiston (Crone 2000, 114).

There is no curvature along their length and no fixture marks on the tapered ends so these hoops had not yet been used. Their presence on the crannog therefore indicates that stave-built vessels were either being manufactured, or at least repaired there.

*Container lid*
The stave-built vessels described above or the one-piece tub such as SF15 could have been either open-topped or closed with a separate lid. The lids were often of an integral design, ie lid and handle were carved as one piece out of the half-log. SF157 (figure 22a) is probably the fragment of a C-shaped handle from such a lid. The upper part of the handle has been flattened while the underside, where the fingers would clasp, has been rounded for comfort. It becomes much stouter at the point at which the handle curves downwards to join the lid and the surfaces have all been carefully smoothed. A complete lid from Ballinderry 1 displays a similar shaped handle (Hencken 1936, 171; and see figure 22b). A fragment of a similar C-shaped handle was also found at Lagore (Hencken 1950, fig 80, W119).

TOOLS

Included in this category are objects which have clearly been deliberately shaped for a specific purpose and appear to have a 'working' end and 'handle' end.

*Spoon-shaped spatulae*
This is a small group of very distinctive objects, variable in dimensions but unified by their method of manufacture (figure 17a-c). SF44, 56 and 94 have all been cut out of thin chords cleft off a branch, the sub-bark surface forming one face. The bark has not been stripped off SF94 suggesting that it is unfinished, although a small patch of bark still adheres to the back of SF56 which in all other respects appears to be complete. No other shaping has been undertaken other than to trim the edges so that they are vertical. The blades of the spatulae vary in length from 46–70mm and in width from 37–61mm and they are also variable in shape. SF94 is almost exactly circular while SF44 and 56 are more classically spoon-shaped. SF56 is the most complete and appears to have a tang rather than an integral handle. They do not display any deliberate

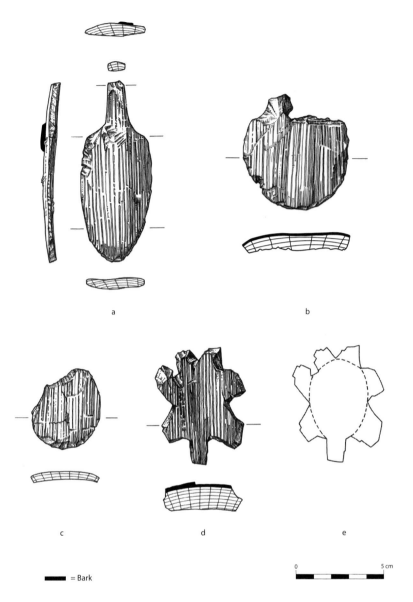

= Bark

FIGURE 17
Spoon-shaped spatulae: a) SF56; b) SF 94; c) SF44; d) SF 16; e) illustrates how a spatula might
have been cut out of SF16

converted in the same fashion, but they appear to have integral handles (444/22 and 185; Barber 1981, 345). A circular spatula with very narrow handle was found at Lagore but its curvature suggests that it was carved (Hencken 1950, 170).

A curious cog-shaped object, SF16 (figure 17d) may belong with this group. It has also been cut out of a chord and the bark is still in place on one face. The seven irregular 'spokes' have been created by cutting in towards the centre from two directions with a knife and then breaking off the intervening piece, thus leaving the internal angle rough. This would have been an easy method of reducing the chord to the required size. The 'spokes' are now small enough to be easily cut off with a knife, leaving a roughly oval shape, approximately $40 \times 30$mm, which can be more finely dressed to create the spatula (figure 17e). The longer 'spoke' at one end may have been intended as a tang.

*Leaf-shaped spatulae*
There are only two items in this category and they are very dissimilar in size and manufacture to the group described above. SF57 is a complete example of this type, with a leaf-shaped blade extending symmetrically from a small rounded handle (figure 18a). SF181 (figure 18b) appears to be a fragment of the same type although the blade is slightly smaller than that of SF57. They have both been carved from a radially-split lath of wood and pared to a lenticular cross-section although SF181 does not display the pronounced ridge seen on the 'back' of SF57. The handle of SF57, with its slightly bulbous end, fits comfortably in the palm of the hand and could have been used for spreading or smoothing. A very similar spatula was found at Ballinderry II (Hencken 1942, fig 26, W500). Mowat (1996, 95) has suggested that SF57 may be a model of a boat paddle, presumably because of the similarity between the blade and that of SF8, a fully-sized boat paddle (see below).

curvature across their width or down their length other than that which would occur naturally in a thin piece of wood so they were clearly not designed to function as spoons. Carved bowl-shaped spoons and ladles were certainly being manufactured during this period (for examples see Earwood 1993a, 116–17) so the distinctiveness of these objects suggests that they were manufactured for a specific function. It is difficult to find comparable objects in other assemblages, partly because analysis of conversion methods has not been undertaken until recently. Two spoon-shaped objects were found at Iona, one of which may have been

## Spatulate knives

This is a group of objects which differ from the group of spatulae described above in that they do not display any differentiation between blade and handle. SF138 and 205 (figures 19a and b) are virtually identical. They have both been fashioned from radially-split laths and are lenticular in cross-section, creating a blade with one long edge thinner than the other. Both are slightly bulbous at one end while the other end appears to taper to a rounded point, although in both cases, this end is damaged. They are both small (78mm long and 63mm long respectively) and can only be gripped between thumb and fingers. This suggests that they were used for some delicate work, the blade being used for scraping, perhaps. Other objects in the assemblage are similar in size and morphology, ie SF131 (figure 19c) and 204, and may have been used for the same type of function. A group of very similar spatulate tools were found on Iona, all made of pine (444/19–21, 26; Barber 1981, 345). The blades are all 25mm wide but they vary between 60–90mm in length, very thin in cross-section and pointed at the tip.

SF148, a complete tool made of oak (figure 19d), also falls into this group although it is substantially larger and the handle and blade are more clearly differentiated. It is 218mm long, with an oval handle which narrows to a spatulate blade 5mm thick. The design and size suggests that it was for a very different function than those spatulae described above; it is very similar in size and shape to a modern table knife but has no sharp edge for cutting. The slender blade would have lent itself to spreading and smoothing.

## Miscellaneous tools

SF119, a complete tool made of ash (figure 20a; see also plate 31), has a large flat blade which has been deliberately set assymetrically on the handle. It has been described as a beater or scutch, a tool used in the preparation of flax (Earwood 1990, 92). After retting, the flax stems are broken with a flat blade to remove the fine linen fibres. However, the assymetric design of SF119 means that the heavier side swings downwards when held. Furthermore, the curved edge on the heavier side does not have the crisp profile of the straight edge and is quite battered, suggesting that this was the working edge. A large wooden knife was often used to break up the flax stems after retting and SF119 could have been used for this purpose. SF119 is perhaps a hybrid of a flax knife and scutch, intended to do both jobs. Similar implements have been found at Ballinderry 1 (Hencken 1936, 131), Lagore (Hencken 1950, 164), Viking sites in

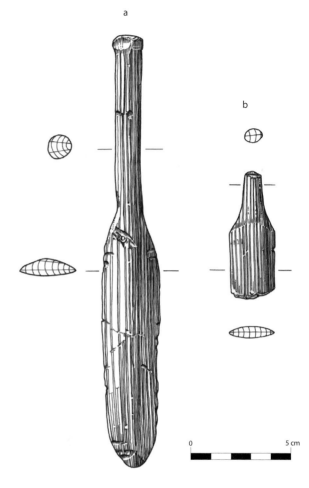

FIGURE 18
Leaf-shaped spatulae: a) SF57; b) SF181

Dublin (Earwood 1993, 130) and at Coppergate, York (Walton Rogers 1997, 1724) but these all have blades which sit symmetrically to the handle.

SF27 (figure 20b) is a complete, carefully made implement with a 'handle' which sits very comfortably in the hand with the thumb resting along the top and a tapered 'blade' ending in a blunt rounded tip. The hole, together with the shape of the 'blade', suggests that it may have been used for threading something like rope, wool or leather. A weaving shuttle usually has two pointed ends and a central point of attachment for the weft so it would be unsuitable for that purpose (Thea Gabra-Sanders *pers comm*). One other possible function which was explored was that of a 'needle' in the fabrication of fishing nets but, again it does not have the facility for 'loading' twine around the shaft that more recent net needles display (Linda Fitzpatrick *pers comm*). A very similar object was found at Buiston

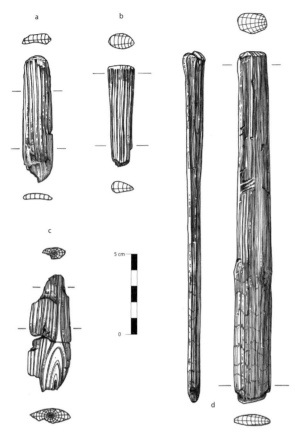

FIGURE 19
Spatulate knives: a) SF138; b) SF 205; c) SF131; d) SF148

(Crone 2000, 125). It was similar in shape and profile but did not have a hole.

*Tool handles*

There are only two objects in the assemblage which can be unambiguously described as handles yet neither is of a length which is comfortable to grip. SF23 and 195 (figure 21) are both stubby, round handles, simply fashioned from a length of roundwood, with a short tang socket at one end. SF23 has not been shaped beyond trimming the ends and inserting the socket but SF195 has been pared down its length so that it tapers towards the socketed end. They are 65mm and 66.5mm long, respectively, which is too short to grip comfortably in the fist. This type of handle may have been intended for attachment to a tool, the tip of which could be hammered down, such as a gouge or chisel, rather than a tool which needed to be gripped. Numerous examples of this simply-made handle exist, all of which are very similar in size and appearance. An

example from Iona (444/18; Barber 1981, 345) is only 65mm long while an identical type of handle from the Norse site of Tuquoy, Westray was only 55mm (Crone unpubl). The 7th-8th century carved wooden box from Evie, Orkney contained nine wooden handles, as well as handles of bone, antler and horn, all with tang holes; the wooden examples ranged from 94mm to 60mm in length (Stevenson 1952). This assemblage of tool handles was initially thought to represent a wood-carvers toolkit although latterly it has been described as that of a leather-worker (Foster 1996, 69).

There are a number of possible handle roughouts in the assemblage. SF85 is very similar in cross-section to SF195 and has been pared to reduce the diameter from one end to the other, although, at 83mm, it is longer. However, it does not have the definitive socket and, like many objects in the assemblage, could equally well be a stopper or even a trenail (see below). SF X1 also belongs in the same category.

SF29 may be the fragment of a scoop handle (figure 22c). With its neatly rounded, projecting end, SF29 is almost identical to the upper section of a scoop handle from Lagore (Hencken 1950, 159 and see figure 22d). It is slightly smaller than the Lagore example but would still have been large enough to be comfortably gripped. The ring-pattern visible at the end of SF29 indicates that the original scoop was probably carved out of a half-log with the grain running the length of the scoop. Scoops such as these were a frequent find on the Irish crannogs; a scoop of willow with a similarly designed handle is illustrated in the Ballinderry 1 report (Hencken 1936, fig 19). The scoop would have been ideally suited for handling goods such as flour and butter.

PINS, PEGS AND TRENAILS

As on many waterlogged occupation sites the bulk of the wood assemblage is made up of objects which fall into this category. It encompasses a miscellany of objects of differing sizes, shapes and therefore, presumably, different functions. This very general category has been divided up, for ease of discussion, into different groups on the basis of size and/or differentiation between head and shaft but there was almost certainly plenty of overlap between the different groups.

*Trenails*

Trenails were used to secure joints in structural frameworks and in furniture and, as they were intended for permanent insertion, there was no need for a distinct head. Typically a trenail would have one slightly expanded end, the edges of which were bevelled, and this would serve as the head which would stand just proud of the surface into which it was hammered. All the examples from Loch Glashan have been carved out of pieces of roundwood, mostly between 60–100mm long and 15–25mm in diameter, and the shafts are either round, square or hexagonal. SF22, 37, 99b, 103, 158, 160, 169, 175, 190 and 206 fall into this category.

*Pegs*
The objects in this category are generally larger than the trenails. Their heads are no more differentiated from the shaft; rather the shaft imperceptibly expands to form a head which can be slightly rounded, flat or faceted to a blunt crown. Such pegs would also have been used for securing joints, amongst other things, but they would have projected from the surface into which they were hammered and were probably used in more rough-and-ready situations. SF48, 134, 203, 176, 184 and 189b fall into this category.

*Loom pegs*
This group of pegs have strongly differentiated heads which suggests that they were designed to be moved in and out frequently. The heads vary from the carefully carved globular heads of SF112 and 187 (figure 23a and b), the more prosaic drum-like head of SF76 (figure 23c), to the roughly carved square head of SF118 (figure 23d). Pegs very similar to SF74 and 76 have been found at Buiston (Crone 2000, 121), Deer Park Farms (Earwood unpubl), Lochlee (Munro 1882, 120, figs 113–115), Ballinderry 1 and 2 (Hencken 1936; 1942) and Odell, Bedfordshire (Morris 1984, fig 28). Morris (*ibid*, 71) has suggested that they may have been the type used to support the rod-heddle on an upright warp-weighted loom (for example, Forbes 1987, fig 32). Such pegs would have had to be easy to grip so that they could be removed and inserted easily. The design of the head on SF112, with its collar and smooth globular profile, is more elaborate than would have been necessary, and must have been designed to be ornamental.

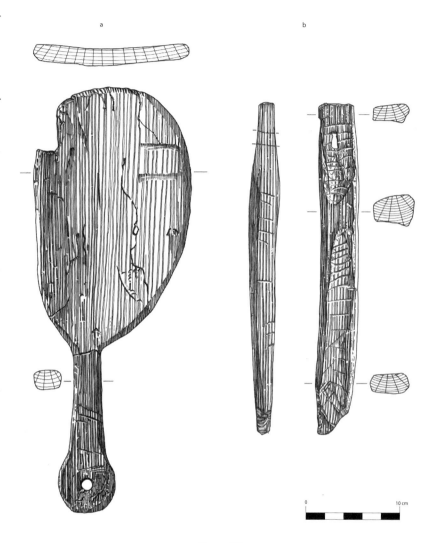

FIGURE 20
Miscellaneous tools: a) SF119; b) SF27

*Furniture/instrument pegs?*
Four pegs, SF84, 95b, 107 and 152a, have a very distinctive design which sets them apart from all others in this category (figure 24). They consist of a head with a flat top and a 'blade' which is the same width as the head in one plane but in the other, has been reduced to a thin lenticular cross-section which lies axially to the handle. These objects have been carefully made, with bevelled edges at either end of the head. SF107 and 152a are complete and are 91mm and 94mm long, respectively. They could be tools but they are uncomfortable to grip. They may be furniture pegs, or keys, used to secure the horizontal elements of rustic furniture against movement between the uprights (Chinnery 1986), or possibly pegs of the kind used on musical instruments.

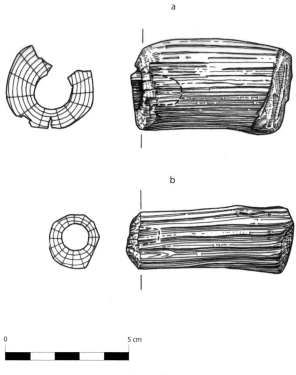

a

b

0          5 cm

FIGURE 21
Socketed tool handles: a) SF23; b) SF195

*Pins/spindles?*

None of the five pin-shaped objects in the assemblage (SF43, 114, 152b, 196 and 207) is more than 10mm in diameter at the top and 86mm in length, although all are missing either heads or tips except for SF152b (figure 25c). The tips of SF114 (figure 25b), 152b and 196 are quite large and blunt and would not have been fine enough for piercing cloth. Only 152b and 196 have intact heads and these are plain and flat. It is possible that some of the broken pins are actually the ends of spindles.

Spindles can be such simple objects, requiring no more than a piece of roundwood with tapered ends and a bulge midway along its length to support the whorl (ie Buiston – Crone 2000, fig 101a; Ballinderry 2 – Hencken 1942, fig 26, W158). One object fits the description better than most. SF150/151a (figure 25a), a splinter of conifer wood, would have been at least 223mm long and has been deliberately carved so that it expands from a smooth, rounded cross-section, 9mm in diameter, to a rough hexagon, 18×12mm across, before tapering away to a blunt, faceted tip. The two stone whorls found at Loch Glashan, SF5 and SF77, had central holes, 12mm and 9mm in diameter respectively

(Chapter 4.12); the former would have sat comfortably above the bulge on SF150/151a.

AGRICULTURAL EQUIPMENT?

SF45 (figure 26) is a large, crude implement, over 1.24m long, and displays a number of features which were clearly deliberate elements of its design and use. A log with a projecting side branch has been deliberately selected in order to utilize the natural angle in the side branch. The parent log has been cleft in half and a rough notch cut into the upper, cleft surface. The side branch has been chopped off to form a short 'foot', the 'toe' of which is very rounded, possibly from wear. The end of the parent log has been neatly rounded off, while the junction between log and branch has been emphasized by chopmarks which have created a distinct right angle.

It is possible that this object was an ard-like implement for cultivating the soil. If the parent log were the 'beam' of an ard the side branch with its 'foot' would move through the soil at right angles to the direction of pull. The notch cut into the upper surface of the 'beam' may have been used to attach something to the 'foot' using a strap, possibly of cloth or leather. The notch is reminiscent of the notches on the two crook ards from Buiston which were probably used to attach the stilt to the beam (Crone 2000, figs 98 and 99) but, otherwise, this implement is unlike any of the other ards found in this country (Rees 1979). The angled set of the side branch in relation to the parent log is reminiscent of the construction of hay scythes; what survives may be the handle end, the 'working' of which has broken off.

BOAT EQUIPMENT

SF40 (figure 27) is very like a modern rowlock and compares well in size with modern examples. It would have acted as a swivelling fulcrum for the oar and would have sat within a socket in the top strake of the boat (for example, McGrail 1987, 212). The seat of the socket for the oar is well-worn. Rowlocks themselves are an unusual find although logboats with slots for rowlocks have been found at both Ballinderry 2 (Hencken 1942, 60) and Lagore (Hencken 1950, 152). Damian Goodburn (*pers comm*) has pointed out its similarity to rowlocks used in boats which are propelled by a standing oarsman.

SF28 (figure 27) is almost identical to SF40 in terms of shape and size except that the stem is much stouter and the area where the socket might have been has eroded away. It is possible that it is a paddle rather than

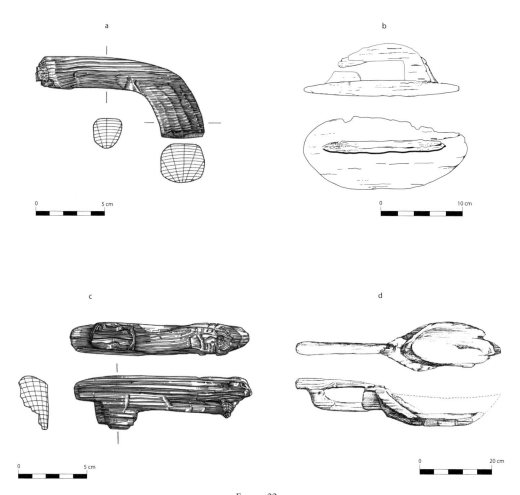

FIGURE 22
Handles: a) SF157; b) lid with similar handle from Ballinderry 1 (after Hencken 1943, 171, fig 35D); c) SF29; d) scoop
with similar handle from Lagore (after Hencken 1953, 159, fig 79, W22)

a rowlock. Certainly, Mowat (1996, 93) identifies it as such and it was made of ash, a species commonly used in the manufacture of paddles or oars (Damian Goodburn *pers comm*). SF8 (figure 27) is clearly a boat paddle. The blade is rather short, suggesting that it was used for paddling rather than skulling within rowlocks.

### STRUCTURAL?

SF155 contains three lengths of oak which are identical in morphology and cross-section although they cannot now be fitted together. SF153, 168a and 168b are similar in size and morphology, although these seem to be more fragmentary pieces chopped of the original timber, presumably after it had fallen into disuse. They were all found close together (figure 31) and may represent a single object; their combined length is

1.89m. The key feature of these objects is a protruding lip which runs along one edge of the squared log and is pierced by a series of small sub-rectangular holes at regularly spaced intervals (figure 29). The holes are clearly intended to attach something to the timber but their small size (they are all roughly $9 \times 6$mm) precludes the use of wooden fixtures which would be too weak. Thin leather straps, however, would fit easily through the holes, suggesting that it is part of some sort of sewn, or lashed construction. The rounded profile of the lip suggests a hinge but it, too, is small and could easily break if anything heavy was hinged off it. Meehan (1994a, 140) describes how, to make parchment for manuscripts, skins were tensioned on a frame to which they were attached by cords. It may have been part of such a frame, although it seems over-elaborate for such a function.

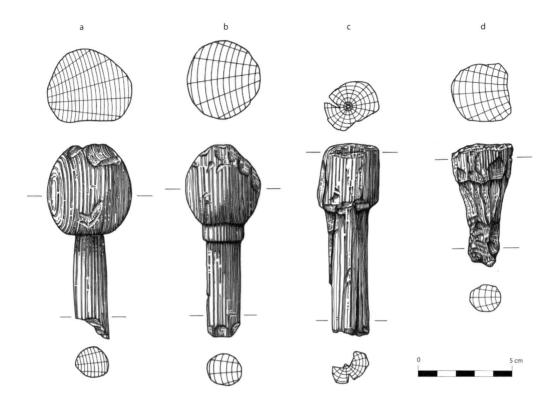

FIGURE 23
Pegs: a) SF112; b) SF187; c) SF76; d) SF118

GAMING COUNTERS

The likely function of the objects, SF151b and SF123, was as gaming counters (figure 30). Both have been fashioned from burrs of wood deliberately selected for the decorative pattern of the grain and the surfaces have all been highly polished. SF151b is finished; it has a flattish base 21mm in diameter and a domed profile 22mm high. SF123 is unfinished but knifemarks are visible around the belly signifying that the maker intended to cut the egg-shaped object in half, making two counters. Dome-shaped gaming counters, more often made of glass, amber, bone or ivory and with metal pegs inserted into the base, are a relatively common find in Viking contexts (Owen 1999). A set of whalebone counters from the 9th/10th-century Viking boat burial at Scar, on Sanday are very similar in both profile and dimensions to the Loch Glashan finds; they range from 18–27mm in height and 21–34mm in base diameter (*ibid*, 128). The Loch Glashan counters do not have the metal pegs which were used to secure them to the game board (*ibid*) but the unfinished example SF123 indicates that this set of counters were in the midst of production. Earwood has pointed out that the swirling pattern of

the grain on the Loch Glashan counters echoes that of white glass counters found in Viking Dublin (Earwood 1993, 123).

MISCELLANEOUS

SF211 (figure 28) is a complete object consisting of a half-log with a large oval hole at either end and a projecting branch almost exactly midway along its length which has been pared to a stake-like point. No comparanda for this object have been found and it is difficult to suggest a function, although it was clearly deliberately designed.

SPECIES COMPOSITION

No analysis of the artefacts was undertaken before conservation so there is no information about the species composition of the assemblage. As it was impossible to remove thin-sections for species identification from the conserved objects an attempt was made to identify the wood species using macroscopic characteristics. In the case of the ring-porous species, oak, ash and elm, this is straightforward because their pore-patterns are so distinct. Occasionally it is possible to attribute a species identification on the basis of attributes such as colour and ring-pattern but, in such cases, these can only be provisional identifications. Of the 104 objects examined 39 have been firmly identified, 22 objects as oak (*Quercus* sp) and 17 as ash (*Fraxinus excelsior*). A further eight have been provisionally identified as specific diffuse-porous species such as hazel (*Corylus avellana*) or alder (*Alnus glutinosa*). A single example of a conifer, possibly Scots pine (*Pinus sylvestris*) was identified. The remainder of the assemblage consists of diffuse-porous species but it is not possible to be any more specific.

Ash is usually specially selected for objects such as handles and turned and carved bowls, for which it is admirably suited (Taylor 1981). The ubiquitous use of ash throughout the assemblage, to make pegs, pins and spatulae, as well as handles and vessels, presumably reflects its easy availability in the surrounding landscape (MacKintosh 1988). Oak was used to make trenails and pegs, and was selected for the agricultural implement, SF45, where strength was presumably required.

All of the species identified would have been available in the surrounding landscape but there is evidence that the inhabitants also gathered driftwood for building work from the shores of Loch Fyne. One object, SF31

(plate 16), which is either a stake or structural offcut, is penetrated by the galleries of a marine bivalve and must, therefore, have been in the sea for some time.

EVIDENCE FOR THE TOOLKIT

As discussed in the introduction the method of conservation has almost always obscured the evidence of toolmarks and wear patterns. A few objects still retain toolmarks and provide some information about the types of tools used. SF15, the small carved tub (figure 11) has small axemarks, >25mm across, on the external and internal faces. The most complete axemarks are visible on the end walls of the carved dish, SF82 (figure 14) and indicate that a small axe, 30mm wide, was used to shape the vessel.

A blade, probably a knife, was used for the final shaping and dressing of many of the objects. Knifemarks are visible in between the 'spokes' of SF16 (figure 17d), on the external surface of SF15, around the handle of SF82 and on the surfaces of SF27 (figure 20b). On the latter the knife kept jerking against the grain creating 'chatter' marks, which suggests that it was not sharp enough.

Small vertical toolmarks on the internal surface of SF15 suggest the use of a small chisel, 11mm wide. The toolmarks display the striae, or signatures, caused by a

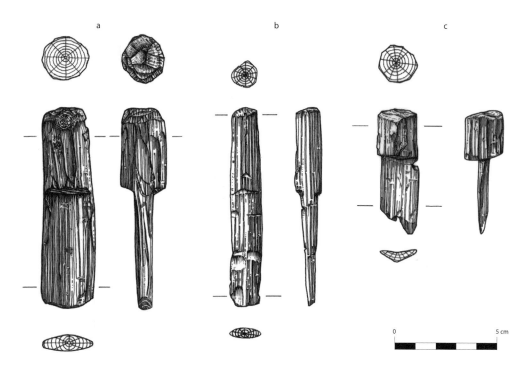

FIGURE 24
Pegs/tools?: a) SF152a; b) SF107; c) SF95

nicked blade. On one of the lengths of timber in SF155 there are shallow grooves cut into the surface just in front of two of the holes. These may have been created by a small chisel or gouge used to cut out the small, rectangular holes. If so, the tool would have been only 9mm wide.

There is some evidence for the use of a spoon augur. The only complete example is the hole in the handle of the flax scutch, SF119 (figure 20a), which is neatly

PLATE 16
Possible stake, SF31, showing bivalve tracks.
(*Reproduced courtesy of Glasgow Museums: Kelvingrove Art Gallery and Museum*)

drilled and indicates the use of a tool with a 12mm bit. The tang sockets in the handles, SF23 and 195 (figure 21), are 16mm and 12mm in diameter respectively, and could have been drilled out. There are also chords of holes on the offcuts, SF61 (7mm diameter) and 199 (at least 16mm diameter).

DATING EVIDENCE

As with most archaeological wood assemblages there are few artefacts which are chronologically diagnostic on the basis of association and/or typology.

The radiocarbon-dating of organic artefacts has demonstrated that carved containers like the tub and troughs from Loch Glashan were in use from the 1st millennium BC through to the medieval period (Earwood 1993b, 361). Similarly, while the bulk of known stave-built containers are generally later prehistoric the earliest examples were found at the Wilsford Shaft, a late Bronze Age site (Earwood 1993a, 69). Scoops and spoon-like spatulae are also known from late Bronze Age contexts

in the British Isles (*ibid*, 29). Hencken (1936, 222) pointed out that the design of the Ballinderry scoop (see above) was no different to that of 20th-century Welsh butter scoops and examples found in the Norse boat burials at Oseberg and Gokstad, highlighting the perennial problem of dating practical everyday wooden objects. The closest parallels that could be found for the tanged tool handles are from 6th–9th AD century contexts but the style is so functional that it probably changed little over millennia.

In the text above, comparanda for the objects have been drawn primarily from crannogs of Early Historic date, necessarily because these are the only sites producing sizeable waterlogged wood assemblages. There are three items in the assemblage which could be more closely dated to this period, although not unequivocally. If the comparison drawn between the lathe-turned bowl fragment, SF49, and Vessel 5, the E ware jar, is accepted then a *terminus post quem* of the 6th/7th century AD can be ascribed to the bowl. The close similarity in morphology and size between the gaming counters and those from Viking contexts is striking. The Scar counters, with which the Loch Glashan examples compare closely, are of a type which was found throughout the Viking world, most commonly in male graves ranging in date from the 9th to 11th century AD (Owen 1999). Gaming counters of this particular style are unknown before this period (Graeme Wilson *pers comm*) so their presence on the crannog suggests contact with the Viking world, dating them to the early 9th century or later.

CONCLUSIONS

As is clear from the discussion above, there are few wooden objects from the crannog which are entirely unambiguous as to their original function. Indeed, the vast majority of wooden objects found on archaeological excavations probably fall into that category. Until the recent past wooden tools and artefacts were used in almost every aspect of domestic life, in agricultural work and in craft production, many types of which we no longer know about. The ethnographic material presented in the exemplary volume on the wooden artefact assemblage from Elisenhof, an occupation site of the 8th/9th centuries AD in Jutland (Szabo *et al* 1985) illustrates vividly just how ubiquitous wooden objects were. It is, therefore, not surprising that we can no longer identify many objects, more especially when they are broken or fragmented, as they often are on archaeological sites.

This ambiguity of function means that it is difficult to assess the overall nature of the wood assemblage. Does the assemblage represent the remains of domestic activity or small scale manufacturing activity, for instance? The containers, scoops and spatulae and some of the tools could all be domestic plenishings. However, some of the troughs are of a size to have been used for semi-industrial purposes such as dyeing cloth or tanning hides. The size and style of the spatulae and spatulate knives suggest that these tools were designed for delicate work on small quantities of material. They may also have been used in the preparation of skins and/or textile dying. Even the presence of the gaming counters presents an ambiguous picture. One is still in the process of manufacture; were they being manufactured for use/exchange elsewhere or do they represent leisure activities on the crannog?

It is instructive to compare this assemblage with that from Buiston crannog, a site which had all the attributes of a domestic settlement and where the crannog had subsided into the loch, taking with it the house and thus preserving a range of everyday articles which had not been, to all intents and purposes, selectively deposited (Crone 2000). The Loch Glashan assemblage does not have the range of domestic and agricultural tools found at Buiston. In particular, there is little evidence of refuse, in the form of broken tools, lathe-turning and woodworking debris. There are only six finds which could be described as woodworking offcuts, two of which are clearly the result of cutting down discarded timbers (SF61 and SF199). The absence of lathe-turning debris is in marked contrast to other waterlogged wooden assemblages of the Early Historic period. Thirty-two wasters were recovered at Iona (Barber 1981, 335), 20 from Lissue (Bersu 1947, 132), six from Lagore (Hencken 1950, 166), five from Moynagh Lough (Earwood 1993a, 284) and one from Buiston (Crone 2000, fig 92). Bowl roughouts have also been found at Deer Park Farms (Earwood 1993a, 272), Lagore (Hencken 1950, 156) and Buiston (Crone 2000, figs 90 and 91). It is possible that turning was not a craft undertaken by the inhabitants or simply that the debris was burned as fuel. The unused hoops indicate that the occupants certainly repaired, if not manufactured, stave-built containers.

It is a very utilitarian assemblage; there is nothing which has been embellished over and above what was functionally required. Possible exceptions are the

flax scutch, SF119 (figure 20a), with its pronounced head and handle, and the peg, SF112 (figure 23a), with its globular head and collar. Aesthetic consideration went into the design of the gaming counters, too. However, there are none of the decorative pins found at Lagore (Hencken 1950, 161) and Ballinderry 2 (Hencken 1942, 61), or highly decorated artefacts such as the scraper

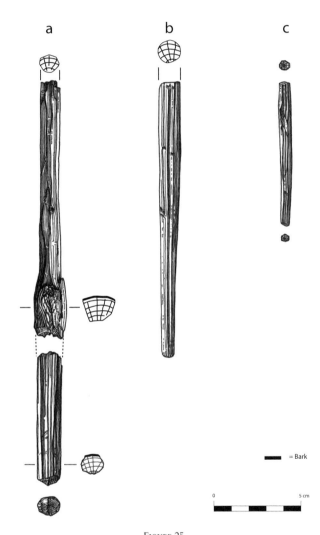

= Bark

Figure 25
Pins/spindles/tapers?: a) SF150/151; b) SF114; c) SF152b

from Buiston (Crone 2000) and the gaming board from Ballinderry 1 (Hencken 1936, fig 90).

The assemblage as a whole may tell us something about the circumstances in which the objects were deposited. They were all found in a remarkably discrete area to the landward side of the crannog (figure 31). There are many complete and functional objects within the assemblage, including most of the carved containers,

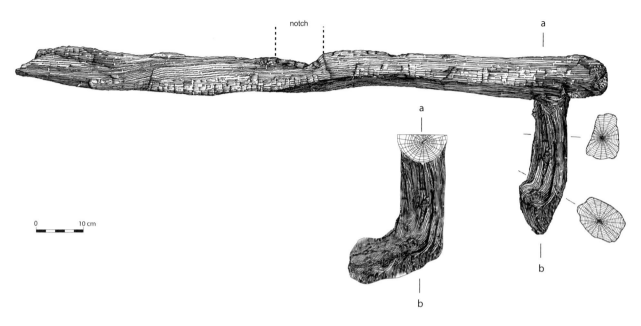

notch

a

a

b

b

0   10 cm

FIGURE 26
Agricultural implement SF45

the tool, SF119 and some of the spatulate knives, and it seems unlikely that these objects would have been deliberately discarded. The absence of evidence for woodworking and lathe-turning debris is also not consistent with the interpretation of the deposits in which the artefacts were found as a midden. In his finds book JGS described some 30% of the wooden finds as charred which would imply that a destruction/disaster event led to the discard of the artefacts. However, charring was not observed on any of the artefacts, or

the structural timbers (Chapter 3.3) during the current study, except for SF119 which was charred on one surface. The woodworm tracks on SF119 suggest that at least some of the assemblage had lain abandoned in a dry environment for some time before final burial in the loch silts. The assemblage may therefore represent the remains of a settlement or settlement/s abandoned abruptly, the debris being swept over the side of the crannog either deliberately when it was re-occupied or by natural action.

## CATALOGUE OF ILLUSTRATED ARTEFACTS

Only those artefacts that have been illustrated are described here; a com-plete catalogue of the entire assemblage can be found in the site archive. The artefacts are described here in order of their Find number. During the excavation two artefacts would occasionally be retrieved together and given the same Find number; in such cases a suffix, *a* or *b* has been given in the catalogue. A small number of objects were also found unnumbered and could not be identified against the excavators original catalogue; these have been listed at the end of the catalogue as Find numbers X1–6. For conversion codes see Crone & Barber (1981).

**SF No:**          **8 (figure 27)**
Description:     paddle
Species:          –
Conv code:      –

This object now measures 1100mm in length although the tip of the blade is broken off and the handle is decayed at the end. Heavy conservation has made it impossible to determine species and type of conversion. The blade is 280mm long and tapers from 100mm at its widest to 80mm at the broken off tip. It is flat on one face but rises to a central ridge on the other. The handle is 40mm in diameter at its junction with the blade but tapers away to a point as a result of decay.

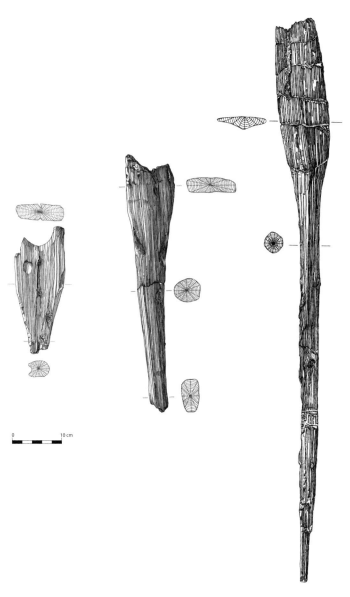

FIGURE 27
Left – rowlocks SF40; middle – rowlocks or oar/paddle SF28; right – Paddle SF8

47

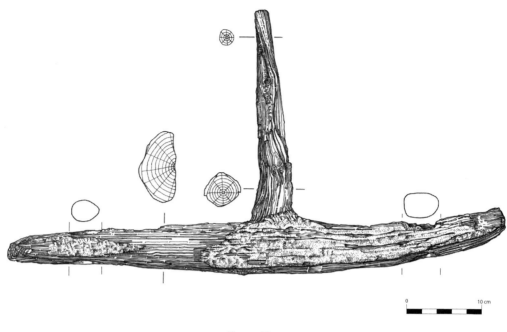

FIGURE 28
Object SF211

There appear to be pressure marks on one side of the handle where something may have been wrapped around it but the conservation method has obscured the detail.

**SF No:**      **15 (figure 11)**

Description:      carved container/vessel
Species:      *Fraxinus excelsior*
Conv code:      A1

This container is now highly fragmented and survives as six relatively substantial and nine small pieces. Many of these fragments are also distorted, probably as a result of compression during burial, but the largest whole piece has an estimated diameter of between 180–190mm. These fragments represent only the walls and rim of the container; there is thus no evidence for its original height nor for the form of the base. The longest surviving fragment is 146mm, providing a minimum height for the container. The container would have been drum-shaped, with very straight sides which varied in thickness from 12mm at the rim narrowing to 8.5mm down the body. The rim itself is plain and flat except in small sections where the external edge has been slightly bevelled.

The container has been carved out of a section of ash log simply by hollowing out the log and trimming its bark surface. It has been carved out assymetric to the centre of the log. A small fragment of bark survives on the largest fragment but the rest of the external surface of the container is dressed. Small axemarks, >25mm wide, probably represent the initial trimming of the log but a knife appears to have been used for the final dressing. The interior of the vessel does not appear to have been so well-dressed but that may be due to conservation. Small axemarks are visible just below the rim on one fragment and below this can be seen small vertical toolmarks, c 11mm wide, bearing striae caused by a nicked blade. These may have been produced by a small chisel.

**SF No:**      **16 (figure 17d)**

Description:      roughout for spoon?
Species:      ?
Conv code:      E

This cog-shaped object has been cut from a thin chord, only 18mm thick, cleft off a branch so that one face is still covered in bark. It is 62mm long and 45mm wide at its maximum points. It has seven angular 'spokes', all irregular in size. These have been created by cutting towards the centre of the object with a knife from two directions and then breaking off the intervening piece, leaving the internal angle rough. Knife cuts are visible between some spokes.

**SF No:**      **23 (figure 21)**

Description:      Handle with tang socket
Species:      *Fraxinus excelsior?*
Conv code:      A

This handle has been simply made by chopping a small, curving branch, 36mm in diameter, to the requisite length and inserting a socket for the tang. The sub-bark surface has not been pared at all. The handle is 65mm long but the the outer end is damaged and it was probably longer – the surviving length is certainly an uncomfortable length to hold. The inner face has been chopped flat with a slight bevel around the outer edge. A socket, 16mm in diameter has been inserted. It is presently 21mm deep but peat has been conserved within it and could therefore be deeper.

**SF No:** **27 (figure 20b)**
Description: tool?
Species: ?
Conv code: D1

This object is complete and has been fashioned from a splinter cleft off the outside of a radially-split plank so that the sub-bark surface survives on one face. It is 227mm long and 25mm wide, and curves very slightly along its length. The tool tapers in thickness from topside to underside; it is 21mm at its thickest on top and tapers to 12.5mm on the underside, giving the impression of a blade. The two narrow faces are cleft and have not been dressed further except for a single facet on the underside which appears to reduce the width of the tip. The two wide faces have been trimmed to reduce the thickness of the blade from 21mm to 14mm.To accomplish this the sub-bark surface on one of the wide faces has been trimmed off by a series of knife cuts. The 'jiggers' across the toolmarks where the knife kept jerking against the grain of the wood are visible. Two large facets, approximately 62mm long, have reduced the thickness at the 'handle' end to 13mm × 8mm and a rectangular hole, 10.5mm × 5mm, has been cut through at this point. There are no signs of wear around the edges of the hole. The very end of the 'handle' is roughly chopped off. The 'handle' sits very comfortably in the hand

with the thumb resting on the widest point of the upper surface.

**SF No:** **28 (figure 27)**
Description: rowlocks or paddle?
Species: *Fraxinus excelsior*
Conv code: A1

The surviving fragment is 510mm long but both ends are broken. The object has been fashioned from a branch at least 92mm in diameter by trimming two opposing faces off the branch leaving a thick plank straddling the centre of the branch. The head is oblong in cross-section, measuring 92mm × 30mm, tapering to 22mm thick at the sides. The head is approximately 160mm long and tapers abruptly to the stem which is hexagonal in cross-section, measuring 45mm × 52mm. The stem then flattens out until it is oblong in cross-section, measuring 65mm × 33mm, with the long axis at right angles to the long axis of the blade. It is very similar to SF40 in size and cross-section at the head but the stem is much thicker and heavier. The top of the head is damaged so that none of the original surfaces remain, but the concave shape of the top suggests that it could have been a rowlock, like SF40. However, it is also possible that it was an oar or paddle.

**SF No:** **29 (figure 22c)**
Description: handle of scoop?
Species: ?
Conv code: D1

This object has been carved out of a radially-split lath the remaining fragment of which is 128mm long, 39mm at its widest and 18mm thick. One end is complete and has been neatly rounded and finished off, while the other end is broken and distorted by a branch scar. Some 12mm before the finished end a distinct projection, oval in cross-section, 31mm long and the same thickness as the 'handle', projects

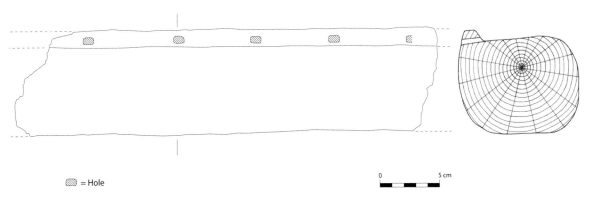

= Hole   0   5 cm

FIGURE 29
Possible frame. Schematic representation of one of the fragments comprising SF155

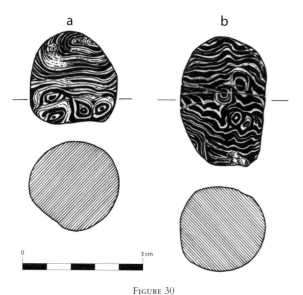

FIGURE 30
a) Gaming piece SF151b; b) roughout for gaming piece SF123

out from the 'handle'. This projection has been broken off and a stump, some 20mm long, is all that remains.

**SF No:** **31 (plate 16)**
Description:       stake?
Species:           ?
Conv code:        A1

This is a large piece of roundwood which had dried out and split prior to conservation. It was at least 90mm in diameter and is 123mm long. It has been chopped towards a point at one end and could be a stake. There are three large holes, 7–8mm across, which are the tracks of a marine bivalve (Richard Sutcliffe *pers comm*).

**SF No:** **40 (figure 27)**
Description:       rowlock
Species:           ?
Conv code:        A1

This rowlock has been fashioned from a branch at least 100mm in diameter by trimming two opposing faces off the branch leaving a thick plank straddling the centre of the branch. The surviving fragment of rowlock is 255mm in length. The sides of the head are relatively straight for 120mm when it then tapers from an oblong cross-section, 100mm × 31mm, to a rectangular cross-section, 36mm × 31mm. At the head, the seat for the oar is a semi-circle, 60mm across and with arms 20mm thick. The base of the seat is well-worn.

**SF No:** **44 (figure 17c)**
Description:       spoon/spatula head
Species:           ?
Conv code:        E1

This spoon/spatula head has been fashioned from a chord of wood and is 3mm thick. It is 46mm long and 37mm across at the widest point. Most of the edge has been trimmed vertical using a knife but around the curved end the edge has been bevelled.

**SF No:** **45 (figure 26)**
Description:       agricultural implement?
Species:           *Quercus* sp
Conv code:        B1

This tool has been fashioned from a half-log and utilizes the natural angle of an attached branch to form the foot. The object is now 1240mm in length, although the upper end in broken off. The beam is 100mm wide and 60mm thick, and 550mm from the broken end a notch has been cut into the upper, cleft face. The notch is 90mm wide and 24mm deep and is steep-sided nearest the foot with a sloping side pointing towards the top of the beam. The other end of the beam has been roughly rounded. Some 75mm in from this end a branch projects from the beam. The junction between beam and branch has been emphasized by chopmarks which have created a distinct right angle. The branch, which is 90mm in diameter, projects for some 250mm before turning at right-angles to the beam. The foot is 195mm long and the tip is very rounded, possibly from wear. However, the foot is very dessicated and split, as is much of the beam, and wear marks are difficult to determine.

**SF No:** **55 (figure 12)**
Description:       trough
Species:           *Alnus glutinosa*?
Conv code:        A1

The rectangular trough has been fashioned from a whole log in such a way that the centre of the original log runs along the centre of the trough. It measures 965mm × 253mm at the rim and stands 143mm high. The end walls of the trough are fairly vertical and the rims curve over to form ledge handles, 12mm and 16mm thick, projecting at right angles from the the walls for a distance of 45mm and 56mm. The side walls are sloping, with simple rounded rims, 13mm thick. The base is rounded and varies in thickness from 33mm at one end to 23mm at the other. Heavy conservation has obscured all toolmarking.

**SF No:** **56 (figure 17a)**
Description:       spatula/spoon
Species:           ?
Conv code:        E1

This spatula/spoon has been fashioned from a chord cleft off a length of roundwood. A small piece of bark is still adhering on the underside. The handle may have broken off the remaining stump looks too narrow to carry the weight of the spoon head. It is possible that the stump is actually a tang for insertion into a handle. The spoon is 99mm long and 40mm

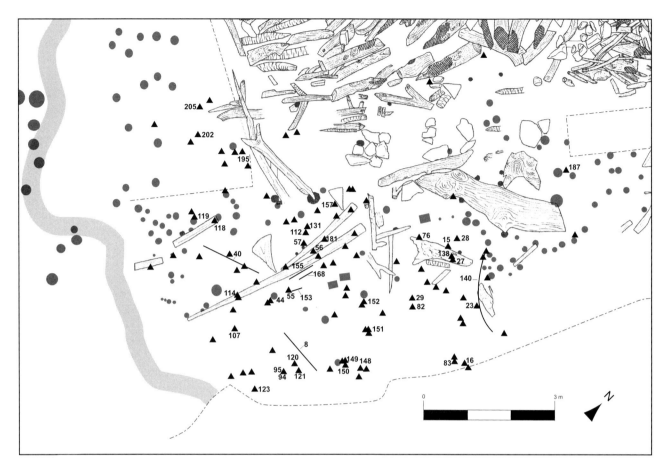

FIGURE 31
Distribution of the wooden artefacts

at its widest point. The tang is 12mm wide at its junction with the head but tapers to 8mm at the end. The spoon is 3mm thick at the tang, thickens to 5mm and tapers to 4mm at the end of the head. It is slightly curved along its length. The edges of the spoon have been cut vertically except at the widest point where they taper to a sharp edge.

**SF No:** 57 (figure 18a)
Description: spatula
Species: ?
Conv code: D1

This object is complete and measures 206mm in length. It has been fashioned from a radially-split lath. The leaf-shaped blade is 112mm long and tapers in width from 29mm to 20mm just below the rounded tip. In cross-section the blade is flat on one face but rises to a central raised ridge on the other. At the apex of the ridge the blade is 8mm thick. The handle is 10mm in diameter but expands to 15mm at the bulbous terminal. It sits comfortably in the grip of the palm.

**SF No:** 76 (figure 23c)
Description: peg ?for loom
Species: ?
Conv code: A1

This peg is now 98mm long but the tip is broken off. It has been fashioned from a length of roundwood, 30mm in diameter. The head is 31mm long, with a rounded top, and its surface is the sub-bark surface of the roundwood. A series of rough knife-cuts abruptly reduces the diameter of the head to a shaft 20mm in diameter. The shaft is faceted and is regular in cross-section down its length.

**SF No:** 82 (figure 14)
Description: dish
Species: *Alnus glutinosa*?
Conv code: B1

This vessel has been carved out of a half-log in such a way that the centre of the original log lies at the level of the rim but is askew to the centre of the vessel. It stands 96mm high

51

and is 306mm × 192mm from rim to rim. The side walls taper from 18mm at the junction with the base to 6mm at the rim but the end walls are much thicker, ie 35mm at one end and 65mm at the end with the handle. The rim is simple and rounded in form. The walls slope outwards from a base which is flat-bottomed but rounded at its junction with the walls. The interior floor of the base is a sharply defined rectangle, 117mm × 170mm, but there is no toolmarking visible within the interior.

The vessel is boat-shaped in plan, with a flattened 'stern' and pointed 'prow'. A handle-like projection at the 'prow' end heightens this impression. The projection is 17mm thick and runs from rim to base. It projects only 15mm from the rim but its outer face is vertical and it projects some 22mm from the base of the dish. It could not have functioned as a handle because it is too small to grip easily and could not have supported the substantial weight of the vessel.

There is clear evidence on the external surface for the manner in which the vessel has been carved out of the log. At both ends the crescentic marks left by the axe are clearly visible and show that the ends of the vessel were roughly shaped by chopping downwards from the bark surface of the original log. The largest and most complete axe mark is 30mm across. At the 'prow' end very small facets, with the striae created by a nicked blade, indicate that a knife was probably used to do the final shaping. The striae show that the direction of cutting was into the centre of the vessel towards the handle-like projection.

**SF No:**       **83 (figure 14)**
Description:       dish
Species:       *Alnus glutinosa?*
Conv code:       B1

This vessel has been carved out of a half-log in a similar fashion to SF82. The dish is flat-bottomed with sloping sides, and measures 371 × 207mm from rim to rim. The rim is a simple, rounded form. The side walls are thin, tapering from 17–22mm at the junction with the base to 5–7mm at the rim. In contrast, the end walls are very thick, tapering from 57mm at the junction with the base to 29mm just below the rim. As a consequence of these thick end walls the internal floor of the vessel is very much reduced in area.

In plan the vessel is boat-shaped and tapers slightly towards one end where the core of the original log rises to create a 'prow-like' impression. There is no toolmarking visible on the interior or exterior of the vessel.

**SF No:**       **94 (figure 17b)**
Description:       spoon/spatula roughout?
Species:       ?
Conv code:       E1

This object has been fashioned from a thin chord cleft off a branch; one face remains covered in bark indicating that the

object was unfinished. It is almost circular, measuring 61mm across and 63mm at its longest point. It varies in thickness from 3mm on one edge to 6mm on the other. The edges are generally vertical but have been bevelled in patches. The object has been damaged at one end so it is not clear whether it was intended to have a handle or not. A fragment of the original edge survives at that end, suggesting that if there was a handle it would have been a narrow one, incapable of holding the weight of such a large head.

**SF No:**       **95a (figure 24c)**
Description:       peg/furniture key
Species:       ?
Conv code:       E1

This object has been fashioned from a length of round-wood, 16mm in diameter and 55mm long, although the tip of the blade is broken off. The sub-bark surface has been pared to form the drum-shaped head, 22mm long. The blade is the same width as the handle in one plane but only 5mm thick in the other and protrudes from the centre of the handle. It is lenticular in cross-section.

**SF No:**       **107 (figure 24b)**
Description:       peg/furniture key?
Species:       ?
Conv code:       A1

This tool is complete and is 91mm long. The handle has been pared along its length and tapers from 15mm diameter at its junction with the blade to 12mm at the end. The 'blade' is 51mm long and has been formed by cutting away two opposing chords off the handle leaving a lenticular cross-section which is the same width as the handle in one plane but only 8mm thick in the other. The blade tapers to only 2.5mm in thickness at the tip.

**SF No:**       **112 (figure 23a)**
Description:       peg/handle?
Species:       *Fraxinus excelsior*
Conv code:       D1

This well-made peg/handle has been fashioned from a radially-split ash lath. It is 100mm long but the shaft is broken off. The head of the peg/handle is almost globular, being 42mm long and 39mm in diameter. It is separated from the shaft by a sharply defined collar or neck, 22mm in diameter and 8mm deep. The shaft itself is 18mm in diameter and is very regular in cross-section down its length. The round head sits very snugly in the palm of the hand and is very well-made.

**SF No:**       **114 (figure 25b)**
Description:       pin/spindle tip?
Species:       *Fraxinus excelsior*
Conv code:       D1

This pin has been fashioned from a radially-split lath and has been carefully dressed to a regular circular cross-section down its length. It is 56mm long but the upper end is broken off. It tapers from 10mm at the top to 6mm at the blunt, flattened tip. The blunt tip precludes its use as a clothes fastener. It is possible that it is a spindle which has broken off above the bulge?

**SF No:**        118 (figure 23d)

Description:        peg – for loom?
Species:        *Quercus* sp
Conv code:        D1

This peg has been fashioned from a splinter off a radially-split plank. It is 63mm long but the tip of the shaft is broken off. The shaft is oval in cross-section, measuring 16mm × 14mm. It expands into a square head, 20mm long and 30mm × 31mm in cross-section. The top of the head appears unfinished.

**SF No:**        119 (figure 20a)

Description:        scutch/beater?
Species:        *Fraxinus excelsior*
Conv code:        E1

This object is complete apart from a fragment broken from one corner. It has been fashioned from a chord of ash and consists of a large ovoid blade with a narrow handle. It is 430mm long overall and the blade is 263mm long and 153mm at its widest. The blade sits assymetric to the handle in such a way that the bulk of the blade lies to one side of the centre line from the handle. The edge closest to the handle is relatively straight while the other edge is curved. This curved edge looks battered and worn in comparison with the straight edge. The objects feels more comfortable in the hand when held with the wider part of the blade pointing downwards so it is possible that the curved edge was working edge. The handle is 167mm long overall and expands in width from 29mm at its junction with the blade to 38mm just before the terminal. At the terminal the handle expands into a circle, 57mm in diameter, which is punctured in the centre by a neatly drilled hole, 12mm in diameter. The handle and blade are roughly the same thickness throughout although the handle narrows from 17mm to 12mm towards the terminal.

One face is partially scorched and woodworm tracks suggest that the object was left dry and discarded for sometime before it was buried in waterlogged conditions.

**SF No:**        120 (figure 13)

Description:        trough
Species:        ?
Conv code:        B1

This rectangular trough has been fashioned from a half-log in such a way that the centre of the log runs along the bottom of the trough. The walls slope outwards from a base, 360mm × 150mm, to maximum dimensions of 430mm × 208mm at the rim. The trough stands 97mm high. The end walls of the trough are thicker than the side walls,

measuring 33mm and 53mm at the junction between wall and base. The rims of the side walls are straight and rounded while the rims on the end walls curve over to form thick ledge handles which project 10mm and 13mm from the walls. The base rotted away in the centre but it clearly varied in thickness from 10mm at one end of the vessel to 19mm at the other. The trough has been heavily conserved and it is consequently difficult to trace toolmarks. A few cut-marks are visible in the angle between base and wall in the interior of the vessel but it is impossible to determine how the trough was roughed out and finished.

**SF No:**        121 (figure 13)

Description:        dish
Species:        ?
Conv code:        B1

This trough has been fashioned from a half-log in such a way that the centre of the original log lies centrally along the vessel at the level of the rim. It is rectangular in plan with rounded corners and measures 620mm × 270mm from wall to wall. It varies in height from 130mm at one end to 100mm at the other and 'sags' in the middle to a height of 95mm. The rim is a simple, flat form varying in thickness from 14mm to 21mm. The walls curve outwards echoing the curvature of the original log. The internal floor has a perimeter sharply defined by knifecuts and measures 495mm × 160mm. A handle projects from either end of the vessel but their positioning is quite different. One handle projects only 16mm out from the rim, is 14mm thick and is square in shape. The other lies some 51mm below the level of the rim and projects some 46mm out from the wall of the vessel. This handle is 18mm thick and is square with rounded corners.

**SF No:**        123 (figure 30b)

Description:        roughout for gaming counter
Species:        ?
Conv code:        –

This is an oval-shaped burr, the surface of which has been highly polished to bring out the ring-markings of the burr. It is 28mm long and 21mm in diameter. Around the middle of the burr are a series of small, very shallow knifecuts, possibly marking out the centre of the burr for cutting in half.

**SF No:**        131 (figure 19c)

Description:        spatula blade?
Species:        *Corylus avellana*?
Conv code:        A1

This object is now in two pieces (which join together) but both ends are missing. It has been fashioned from a small piece of roundwood by paring off opposing faces until a lenticular cross-section, 27mm wide, is left. It appears to reduce in width at one end to a handle or tang which is broken off. It tapers in thickness from 8mm at the 'handle' end to 2mm at the tip.

**SF No:** 138 (figure 19a)
Description: tool/spatula?
Species: ?
Conv code: D1

This object is complete, although slightly damaged on one side of the tip. It is 78mm long and tapers in width from 19mm just above the tip to 15mm at the 'handle' end. The 'handle' end is very slightly enlarged and rounded. It is tear-drop shaped in cross-section at this end, tapering from 8mm to 5mm in thickness, and flattens out along it length until it is only 2mm thick. The 'blade' is slightly curved in cross-section but this may be due to drying. One long edge is much thinner than the other, suggesting that this was the 'working' edge.

**SF No:** 140 (figure 116)
Description: barrel hoop
Species: *Corylus avellana?*
Conv code: E1

This consists of a chord cleft off a withy, with the bark stripped off. It is 660mm long and 36mm wide and tapers in thickness from 17mm thick at one end to 6mm at the other. At the thinner end the width has been reduced to a point by a single chop mark.

**SF No:** 148 (figure 19d)
Description: spatulate knife
Species: *Quercus* sp
Conv code: D1

This tool is complete. It is 218mm long and has been fashioned from a radially-split lath of oak. The handle is oval in cross-section and is slightly bulbous and rounded at the very end. The handle is 19mm wide × 13mm thick. The blade, which is 130mm long, was formed by reducing the thickness of the handle to 5mm but expanding the width to 23mm. The tip of the blade is sloping and rounded.

**SF No:** 149 (figure 15)
Description: turned bowl
Species: *Fraxinus excelsior*
Conv code: –

This is a rim fragment from a turned bowl. It has been carved out of a half-log in such a way that the centre of the original log lies at the level of the rim. The fragment is 58mm wide and 55mm high. Only 30mm of the rim survives so it is difficult to estimate accurately the original dimensions of the bowl. A best projection would give the body of the bowl a diameter of 200mm at its maximum curvature, narrowing to a neck 160mm in diameter. The body of the bowl is 7mm thick but this tapers to 3mm at the rim. The rim is rounded in profile and is enhanced by a single groove just below the rim on the exterior and another groove 2.5mm below the rim on the interior.

The exterior surface of the bowl is very smooth and faint turning marks can only be seen at the point at which the neck begins turning out into the belly of the bowl. On the interior of the rim turning marks can be very clearly seen.

**SF No:** 150 and 151a (figure 25a)
Description: spindle/pin/taper?
Species: conifer – *Pinus sylvestris?*
Conv code: D1

Although these two finds were retrieved separately and cannot be fitted together they have been fashioned from the same type of wood and are so similar in morphology as to suggest that they are one and the same object. Both pieces have been fashioned from a radially-split splinter in such a way that the sub-bark surface is retained down one face. The shaft on 151a has been pared to roughly circular cross-section, 9mm in diameter, which is fairly regular for most of its length. Towards the 'middle' the shaft swells around a natural knot in the wood and is pared to a roughly rectangular cross-section, 12mm × 18mm. Below the knot the shaft tapers away on SF150 to a hexagonal cross-section, 11.5mm × 11.5mm. The tip has been faceted to a blunt point.

**SF No:** 151b (figure 30a)
Description: gaming counter
Species: ?
Conv code: –

This is fragment of burr which has been shaped to rough dome, 21mm in diameter at the base and 22mm high. The 'base' is flattish although this could be a result of breaking off part of the burr. The surfaces are highly polished.

**SF No:** 152a (figure 24a)
Description: peg/furniture key?
Species: *Fraxinus excelsior?*
Conv code: A1

This object is complete and has been made from a small branch, 22mm in diameter and 94mm long. The 'handle' has been shaped by simply paring the sub-bark surface of the branch. The end of the handle has been shaped by small knifemarks and the outer edge is slightly bevelled. The 'blade' is 54mm long and has been formed by cutting away two opposing chords off the branch leaving a lenticular cross-section which is the same width as the handle in one plane but only 7.5mm thick in the other. The end of the 'blade' is rounded.

**SF No:** 152b (figure 25c)
Description: pin
Species: ?
Conv code: A1

This is a finely-made pin, 82mm long, with both ends chopped flat. It is 5.5mm in diameter at the head, tapering to 4mm at the tip, but bulging slightly c 15mm below the head. It has been fashioned from a small twig by vigorously paring away the sub-bark surface. The blunt tip would make it unsuitable for clothes fastening but it may have been used in weaving or lacemaking?

**SF No:** 155 (figure 29)
Description:  structural?
Species:  *Quercus* sp
Conv code:  A1

This find contains three lengths of timber, 350mm, 395mm and 355mm long, respectively. They are clearly fragments of the same object because they are all virtually identical in cross-section and display the same features but they cannot be fitted together, because of damage and shrinkage. The object was fashioned from a small log, approximately 130mm in diameter, which was trimmed to a roughly rectangular cross-section, 100mm × 75mm, and all edges appear to have been deliberately rounded.

A small lip, 17mm wide and 14mm high, projects from one of the narrower sides. This lip is pierced by small, roughly rectangular holes, 9mm wide and 6mm deep, regularly spaced at intervals of between 52mm and 55mm. On one of the lengths there are shallow grooves cut into the surface in front of the holes which may have been caused by a small chisel or gouge used to cut out the holes. There is no sign of wear around any of the holes.

**SF No:** 157 (figure 22a)
Description:  lid handle?
Species:  diffuse-porous
Conv code:  D1

This object has been very carefully carved from a half-log. It is broken at both ends and could be part of a larger object. The fragment is 123mm long and its 'shaft' is 23mm × 21mm. It is almost triangular in cross-section, flattened on one side and rounded on the other two. At the point where the object curves its cross-section becomes larger and squarer, measuring 26mm × 31mm. At this end the surfaces have been carefully smoothed.

**SF No:** 181 (figure 18b)
Description:  spoon/spatula
Species:  ?
Conv code:  D1

Both the handle and the tip of the blade has been broken off this spatula and only 60mm of its original length survives. It is has been fashioned out of a radially-split lath of wood and the surfaces have been smoothed so that there are no visible toolmarks. The blade tapers very slightly from 24mm at the shoulders to 23mm just above the broken end. The blade is lenticular in cross-section, 4.5mm thick at mid-point.

The sloping shoulders tapers to a rounded handle, 9mm in diameter.

**SF No:** 187 (figure 23b)
Description:  stopper/bung/heddle peg?
Species:  *Fraxinus excelsior*
Conv code:  D1

This object has a very distinct, globular head, 48mm high and 45mm wide. The head has been squashed and damaged during burial and is now pear-shaped in cross-section. The surfaces of the head are very smooth and there are no signs of toolmarking. The shaft is 15mm × 17mm in cross-section and is broken, only 53mm of its length surviving. It is very regular in size and cross-section down its length. There are no visible toolmarks on the shaft but the junction between shaft and head is very distinct and could only have been shaped by knife.

**SF No:** 195 (figure 21a)
Description:  handle with tang socket
Species:  ?
Conv code:  A1

This handle is complete and is 66.5mm long. It has been fashioned from a piece of roundwood which has been pared down its length so that it tapers from 25mm diameter at the outer end to 20mm diameter at the socketed end. A socket, 12mm in diameter and 14mm deep, has been cut slightly off-centre. The length of the handle is too short to fit comfortably in the hand.

**SF No:** 205 (figure 19b)
Description:  tool?
Species:  *Quercus* sp
Conv code:  D

This object is complete and is 63mm long. It has been fashioned from a radially-split lath and it tapers in width from 22mm at the 'handle' end to 14mm at the tip. The 'handle' end is slightly bulbous and thicker than the blade which is 7mm thick near the tip. The tool is lenticular in cross-section and one of the sides is much thinner than the other as though this were the working edge.

**SF No:** 211 (figure 28)
Description:  agricultural implement?
Species:  *Quercus* sp
Conv code:  A/B

A split log with a branch projecting at right angles has been utilized to make this implement. The log is 665mm long and 87mm in diameter, and has been cleft in half. The ends have been roughly rounded but the bark has not been completely stripped off, nor has the cleft face been dressed further. The branch, which is 50mm in diameter, projects from the very middle of the log and is faceted to form a stake-like tip 275mm long. Set 80mm and 82mm from each end are two large oval holes, 33mm × 40mm and 38mm × 39mm respectively, which penetrate the thickness of the log. The object was very dessicated prior to conservation and so it is difficult to determine toolmarks and wear patterns but the top perimeter of one hole looks very worn.

**SF No:**     **X6 (figure 16)**
Description:     barrel hoop
Species:     *Corylus avellana?*
Conv code:     E1

This consists of a chord cleft off a withy, with the bark stripped off. It is 910mm long, 35mm wide and 11mm thick. A single facet has cut away the sub-bark surface for some 240mm, reducing the thickness of the hoop to only 6mm. It is very curved along its length but this may be due to drying out.

## 4.2   IMPORTED CONTINENTAL POTTERY

*Ewan Campbell*

### INTRODUCTION

There are 27 sherds of imported pottery, 25 of which can be confidently assigned to five individual vessels (vessels 1–5; figure 32), either by joins or by the distinctive nature of the fabric. The remaining two small sherds may or may not belong to these identified vessels. The vessels all belong to the same general tradition of Continental white gritty wares and can all be broadly classed as Thomas's Class E ware (Thomas 1959), though some of the forms and fabrics fall outside the normal range of variation of E ware. The fabric and other general details of this ware have been described elsewhere and will not be repeated here (Peacock & Thomas 1967; Campbell 1991, 448–70). Five vessels is a medium number of vessels to be found on a site, and in fact only eight out of the 65 known E ware sites have produced more than five vessels, most producing just one or two vessels. The number of vessels, as opposed to the number of sherds, has been shown to correlate accurately with other indicators of the status of sites producing E ware (Campbell 1991).

### PROVENANCE

Detailed studies by Campbell (1991) have confirmed an origin for E ware in coastal western France, and this is likely to have lain somewhere between the Loire and the Gironde estuaries. E ware in general can now be seen from the Whithorn evidence to begin to be imported in the mid 6th century, but the main period of importation, as determined by a variety of lines of evidence, was the late 6th and 7th centuries (Campbell 1997). These dates are confirmed by the radiocarbon dates obtained from the charred residues on the Loch Glashan E ware (Chapter 5.2). It is not known if E ware or its successors continued to be imported after this period. Certainly the trading system which brought it appears to have collapsed by around AD 700, perhaps due to competition from the emerging *wics* of southern England (Campbell 1996a, 88). However, in western Scotland there are some white gritty imports which, on typological grounds, appear to date to the succeeding centuries (Laing 1974, fig 3; Campbell 1991, 170), suggesting continuing sporadic contact with the same area of France. Vessel 5 belongs to this later group.

### TYPOLOGY AND CHRONOLOGY

The vessel forms are mainly jars or ollae, defined as form E1, but *Vessel 4* is unusual and may be a bowl or small globular pot, or possibly the base of a pitcher. *Vessel 3* has suffered slumping in production or in the kiln, making its profile rather unusual, but it was probably intended to be an E1 jar, and there is a similar globular form from Dunadd (Campbell 1991, 361; Craw 1930, fig 10, 18), perhaps suggesting they were part of one batch of imports. The base of the vessel is a slight pedestal, a feature unique in E ware, but appears to be derived from a crude attempt to cut the pot off the wheel rather than a deliberate design feature. *Vessels 1, 2* and probably *3* belong in the main tradition of E ware, and were dated on typological grounds to the 7th century in the original draft finds report before the radiocarbon dates were obtained. *Vessel 1* is almost identical to one from Dinas Powys, South Wales (Alcock 1963, fig 29, 5). *Vessel 5* shows some signs of belonging to a later development of vessel form, as it has a higher shoulder, less globular shape, and almost triangular flat-topped rim (plate 17). This rim form is somewhat similar to some Late Saxon wares such as Chester ware (cf McCarthy & Brooks 1988, fig 111), though this may not be significant. In France, globular forms with sagging bases became the norm by the 10th century (Hodges 1981, 62), so the Loch Glashan form must predate this major change. This vessel may therefore date to the 8th or 9th centuries. *Vessel 4* cannot be dated typologically.

Given the suggested late dating of *Vessel 5* compared to the other E ware, it is interesting that this vessel was found standing upright on the surface of the crannog when the site was first discovered (Chapter 1). Even though the position may not be undisturbed (see below), the completeness suggests that it could have been in use when the crannog was abandoned. All the other E ware sherds were found either on the very edge of the crannog mound or in the brushwood layer outside the piling (figure 33). The pottery would therefore support a date for occupation of the crannog during the 7th and 8th centuries AD, with an outside possibility of occupation ranging from the 6th to 9th centuries.

FUNCTION

The function of E ware vessels has been a matter of debate. Although Thomas originally suggested the vessels were 'kitchen ware', Campbell has produced evidence that the jars were in fact originally containers for exotic goods, including certainly dyestuffs and possibly spices, nuts and honey (Campbell 1996b). Many E ware jars, including *Vessels 3* and *5*, do not have the basal sooting which would be expected if these were cooking vessels, though they show signs of wear on the interior and lid-seats. *Vessel 3* has a purple stain on some sherds, similar to that found on vessels from Dunadd, Buiston crannog, Dundonald Castle, and Teeshan crannog (Co Antrim). Analysis has shown these stains to be caused by members of the *Rubia* group of plants, and those from Teeshan are certainly from the exotic dye plant madder (see below). Whether the E ware vessels were used for transport of the dyestuff, or for the dyeing process, is difficult to decide. However, this primary use of E ware as a storage and transport vessel for exotic goods was often followed by reuse in a variety of ways, and the Loch Glashan vessels show examples of this. For example *Vessels 1* and *2* have basal sooting indicating use for cooking functions, and *Vessel 4* has had a more complicated history of use. After it was broken in use, the basal part was trimmed down and reused, perhaps as a lamp or a shallow cooking vessel, as shown by the external sooting and internal carbonized deposits which run over the broken edges (plate 18). Attempts to identify the organic residues in the interior have not produced definitive results (Appendix 7.1).

STATUS

Campbell has shown that the exotic commodities transported in the E ware vessels were controlled by aristocrats from high status sites, with smaller amounts

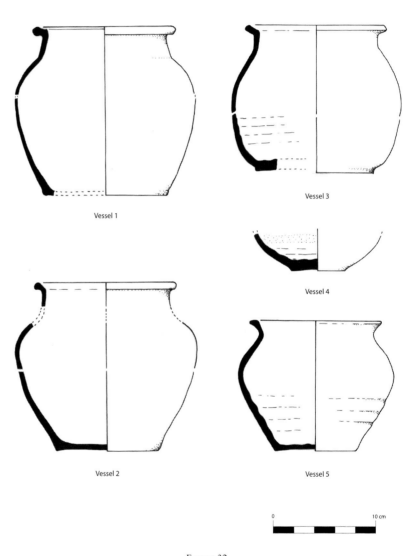

FIGURE 32
Profiles of E ware vessels 1–5

being redistributed to surrounding client sites from these key import centres (Campbell 1996a). Dunadd was the major import site in this area (in fact it has the largest number of E ware vessels of any site), and the E ware from Loch Glashan almost certainly was brought from there rather than being imported directly. As already noted, the total of five E ware vessels at Loch

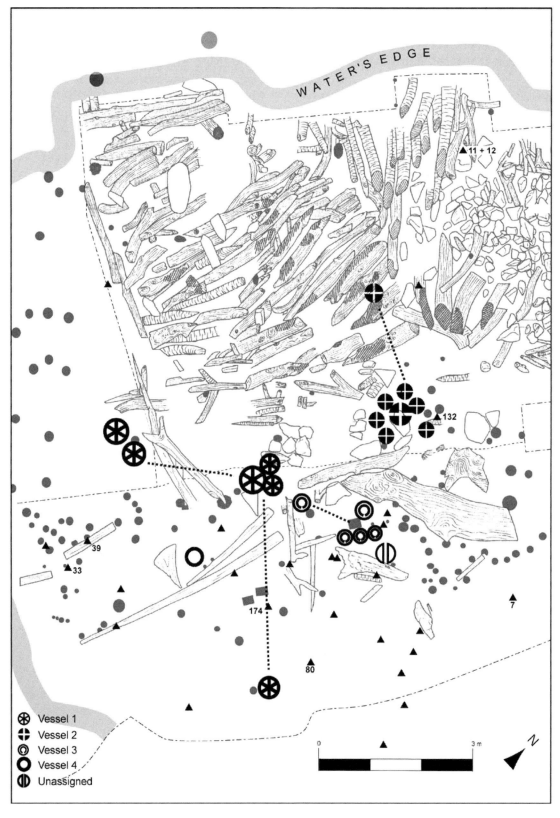

FIGURE 33
Distribution of E ware sherds and other inorganic artefacts

Glashan is in the medium range, and is comparable with other important sites such as the royal crannog of Lagore (Co Meath), which also has five, and the royal sites of Dumbarton Rock and Clogher (Co Tyrone), with three and five respectively. In contrast, the two Atlantic roundhouses in Argyll with E ware, Ardifuir and Kildalloig, have only one vessel each, despite both being totally excavated.

Whether the vessels were originally brought to the site empty or not is impossible to say, though the supposition is that it was the contained goods which were important as gifts rather than the pots themselves. Several factors point to a close connection between Loch Glashan and Dunadd in relation to the pottery. The presence of purple staining on E ware at both sites, otherwise found at only two other sites, and close similarities of form between some of the vessels, strongly suggests that the E ware from Loch Glashan came from the Continent via Dunadd. It has been suggested that the leather work from the site may have been one of the commodities traded in exchange for imports which came with E ware (Campbell 1991, 165). There are therefore strong indications that Loch Glashan was a client site of Dunadd, or possibly even a site used by the kings at Dunadd, as crannogs at this period in Ireland are often of high status and associated with nearby royal sites (Warner 1988).

TAPHONOMY AND CONTEXT

The study of the taphonomic processes which lead to the deposition and retrieval of pottery has been shown to be crucial in any understanding of the significance of ceramics, both in chronological and social terms (Bradley & Fulford 1980; Moorhouse 1986; Campbell 1991, 50–4; MacSween 2003). A study of the taphonomy of E ware shows that the Loch Glashan assemblage has unusual characteristics (Campbell 1991 165, illus 131), and provides an interesting insight into the depositional processes at work on the site. *Vessels 1–4*, which were derived from stratified contexts, provide the best evidence. Analysis of maximum sherd size, a key indicator of the degree of degradation and mixing of deposits, shows that the Loch Glashan E ware is

unusually 'unbroken', with few small sherds, and a low sherd to vessel ratio (figure 34). It seems that most of the recovered sherds were never trampled after breakage, as can be seen by comparing the sherd size curve with that of a site where vessels are known to have been trampled (*ibid*). In a normal depositional context this would indicate the E ware vessels were close to being

PLATE 17
E ware Vessel 5. (*E Campbell*)

'primary refuse' in the terminology of Schiffer (1976), and could therefore be used as an indication of the area of use of the vessels. However, other evidence suggests that this is not the case. While enough of the vessels survive to enable complete profiles of most of the vessels to be drawn, in all cases substantial sections of the vessels are missing. This in itself shows that there has been disturbance of the 'primary' deposit. It seems most likely that the broken vessels immediately on breakage were quickly swept up towards the side of the site, as the broken sherds would have considerable 'nuisance value' (Sommer 1990, 53), and then discarded by throwing over the edge of the palisade. Similar patterns of disposal have been reported in ethnographic studies (Haydn & Cannon 1983), and can be seen in other early medieval sites such as Kildalloig Dun, Argyll (Campbell 1991, illus 172). The unusual environment of the crannog then prevented any further degradation of the pottery, in contrast to the normal processes at work on a dryland

PLATE 18
E ware Vessel 4. See colour frontispiece.

site (Campbell 1991, illus 126). This interpretation of the pottery as a secondary deposit is supported by a study of the relative abrasion of the sherds, with some joining sherds from the same vessel being fresh and others abraded, suggesting different depositional trajectories for different parts of the vessels.

Confirmation of this pattern comes from the positions of *Vessels 1* and *2*, which were found just inside the palisade (figure 33), but share the same sherd size curve as those outside the palisade. This suggests the possibility that midden material was initially allowed to accumulate at the edges of the palisade, and then periodically thrown over the palisade. It is significant that one sherd from *Vessel 1*, most of which lies just inside the palisade, was found in the densest part of the brushwood layer, as were all the sherds of *Vessel 3* (figure 33). The importance of this patterning is that it might suggest that the majority of the artefacts from the brushwood layer are the result of deliberate disposal of rubbish, rather than being a deposit washed off the surface of the crannog as part of its post-occupational degradation. It might be argued that the E ware *Vessels 1 and 2* were left behind on the crannog because the final dump of midden material was never thrown over the side of the crannog due to abandonment, but this might be pushing the evidence too far.

The distribution evidence also raises the question of where the pottery was used, if the place of deposition was not the place of use. Initially, Clay 1 and 2 were thought to be hearths (Scott 1961, 21), and so it seemed possible that the E ware vessels were associated with cooking and could be primary refuse. However, the lack of burning, and reconsideration of the stratigraphy of the crannog (Chapter 3.5), suggest only a coincidental association. The one clue to the place of use comes from the small sherd LG6, which came from the interior of the crannog, inside the area of flattened timbers initially regarded as a rectangular building (figure 33). This sherd is likely to have been left behind as 'micro refuse' caught in an artefact trap (Sommer 1990, 53–4) during the sweeping up process, a situation which can paralleled at other early medieval sites (Campbell 1995, fig 3).

*Vessel 5* was recovered from the surface of the crannog by Roy Ritchie before the excavation, but the excavator was sure from questioning the finder that it came from the same area as *Vessels 1* and *2* (Scott in litt). Despite the lack of a precise findspot, this vessel has characteristics which tell us something of the process of abandonment of the site. Firstly, it is almost complete, by far the most complete E ware vessel in Britain or Ireland. Secondly, it was found standing upright on the surface of the crannog when it was first exposed, though it may have placed in this position during the period after the crannog was exposed in 1959 (Chapter 1). These two factors suggest that it was abandoned where it was in use, either as primary refuse or more likely left behind on abandonment of the site as 'de facto' refuse (Schiffer 1976). Given its suggested dating to the 8th/9th centuries, this gives a *terminus post quem* for the date of abandonment of the crannog. This is also a likely indication of the actual abandonment date, as ethnographic studies have shown that vessels like this have fairly short lives.

Finally, the stratigraphy of the pottery has to be considered. All the sherds except LG11, 12 and 14 were found above the brushwood layer, where the majority of wooden and leather finds were recovered. This might be seen as support for the early radiocarbon dates for the wooden objects. The three sherds from the brushwood (and the two metal objects) could have fallen through gaps in the brushwood to the position where they were recovered. Whatever the explanation, it seems that at least some of the pottery was in use at the final period of use of the site.

One other find has to be discussed in relation to the E ware, namely SF149, the turned wooden bowl. It has been claimed (Earwood 1992, 156) that this vessel is a copy of an E1 jar. She also claims that other wooden vessels from Early Historic sites are similarly skeuomorphs of E2 beakers and E3 bowls. I believe this is unlikely, as the profiles bear only a general resemblance to these forms, or are markedly different, as in the 'E2' bowl from Lissue (*ibid*, fig 3, 3). The supposed E1 forms such as the Loch Glashan vessel lack the shoulder characteristic of E ware jars, and seem at least as likely to be derived from high status metal or glass prototypes as these lower status containers for transporting goods. The footrings of Earwood's Type 1 bowls (*ibid*, fig 1, 1) are likely to have this derivation, as the overall forms are not similar to Radford's A ware (*contra* Earwood 1992, 154). It follows that the forms of the turned wooden bowls have no specific chronological significance.

DYESTUFF ANALYSIS ON E WARE POTTERY
*Penelope Walton Rogers*

*Analytical procedure and results*
The pinkish purple staining on the inner surface of E ware Vessel 3 was most apparent on sherds 1 and 2, with minor traces on sherd 3. The colorant was first investigated by a method successfully applied to

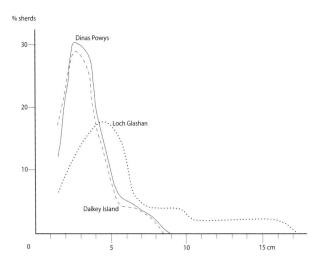

FIGURE 34
Size distribution of E ware sherds from Loch Glashan in comparison with sherds from Dinas Powys and Dalkey Island (after Campbell 1991)

stained potsherds from other sites (Walton Rogers 1999), which consists of swabbing the coloured area with an alcohol-acid mix and then analysing the swabs by a system developed for dyes in textiles (Walton & Taylor 1991). No dye could be detected in swabs from the first sherd, but a more aggressive method of removing the colorant, by soaking and warming all three sherds simultaneously in the alcohol-acid mix, allowed a small trace of a madder-type dye to be detected by absorption spectrophotometry (for details of the analysis, see archive report).

Madder-type dyes can be obtained from a number of different plants of the family Rubiaceae. The dye from cultivated madder, *Rubia tinctorum* L, can usually be distinguished from the wild madders and bedstraws by chromatography, but in the case of the Loch Glashan sherd the concentration of the dye extract was too weak to allow chromatographic separation. Nevertheless, the analysis has shown that the inner face of the vessel has at some stage been in contact with a red madder or bedstraw dyestuff.

*Other dye-stained vessels*
Better preserved remains of madder-type dyes have been identified on E ware sherds from Teeshan, Co Antrim; Dunadd, Argyll (sherd GP240); and Buiston, Ayrshire (sherd HV140). In the case of the Teeshan sherd, chromatography showed the main chemical constituent of the dye to be alizarin, with purpurin as a minor component, indicating that the source of the dye is cultivated madder, *R. tinctorum* (Walton unpubl

a). On the Dunadd and Buiston sherds, however, only purpurin was detectable, which indicates either that the source is wild madder or bedstraw, or that the mineral content of the clay has caused the dye constituents to be taken up differentially into the fabric of the pot (Walton unpubl b).

In England, there are further examples of madder-stained pots. The earliest is a tall jar made in a native Kent fabric, from Christ Church College, Canterbury, and dated to the second half of the 8th century (Walton Rogers 1999). The Canterbury dye proved analytically to be similar to the Teeshan madder, with alizarin predominating over purpurin. Further examples have been recorded from cooking pots of different wares from late Anglo-Saxon London (Taylor 1991, 169–70) and Thetford (Cole in Rogerson & Dallas 1984, 167), Anglo-Norman Winchester (Walton Rogers unpubl c) and medieval Norwich (Walton unpubl d). The alizarin-purpurin ratio has not always been recorded, but where it has, alizarin dominates, indicating cultivated madder, *R. tinctorum*.

Except for the Canterbury vessel, which was a narrow jar, the English pots were mostly about 300mm diameter and often had sooting on the outer face, which suggests that they were used to heat small quantities of liquid dye. Some of the E ware sherds also display sooting, although the vessels they come from are smaller than the English ones, having a maximum body diameter of 220–260mm (E Campbell *pers comm*). The amount of fibre or yarn that could be dyed in pots of this size is relatively slight and Campbell (this volume) has suggested that the E ware vessels were in fact used to transport the raw dye.

Some sort of trade in madder in the 7th and 8th centuries seems credible in the light of recent research into the dye's history. The plant, *R. tinctorum*, is a native of Asia Minor, the Caucasus and parts of southern Europe. The dye, which was transported as chopped roots or powder, was widely traded in the Roman empire and when it is detected in textiles made in Roman Britain, it is probably because imported dye had become available to native weavers. Once the Romans depart from Britain, alizarin-based madders disappear from the archaeological record and are replaced by purpurin-based dyes, which probably derive from indigenous plants such as bedstraw, *Galium verum* L, or wild madder, *Rubia peregrina* L. These are a less rich

source of dye and were used mainly in small items such as braids (Walton Rogers 2001a; 2001b).

Alizarin-based madder re-appears in the 7th century, in textiles from high-status sites (Whiting 1983), and by the late Anglo-Saxon period it is commonplace in a full range of fabrics (Walton 1988). Written sources refer to the cultivation of madder in late Anglo-Saxon England and extensive remains of the *R. tinctorum* plant, soil drenched in madder dye and madder-dyed textiles have been recovered from 10th century deposits at Coppergate, York (Walton 1989, 397–401; Walton Rogers 1997, 1766–70). There is less available evidence for dyeing in Scotland and Ireland, but a purpurin-based madder-type dye was identified in a textile from the Early Christian rath at Deer Park Farm, Co Antrim, N Ireland (Walton unpubl e), while alizarin-based (cultivated) madder was found in some of the textiles from Viking Age Dublin (Walton 1988).

All of this suggests that there was a shift from the use of native species to cultivated madder over the 7th to 9th centuries in the British Isles. It is possible, however, that in those parts of France which were closer to the heart of the Roman empire, the cultivation of *R. tinctorum* had already been introduced (Wild 1970, 81) and had survived the collapse of the empire. Certainly, in this region, unlike Britain, Roman looms continued in use into later periods (Walton Rogers 2001c). The cultivation of madder on Charlemagne's estates is mentioned in *Capitulare de Villis* (paras 43 and 70, see Loyn & Percival 1975, 64–9), and, in the second half of the 9th century, a forged charter appeared, purporting to show that northern French merchants had rights over the trade in madder dating back to the 7th century (Pertz 1874, 140–1; Dhondt 1962, 217–18). Although this is a spurious document, some earlier trade in madder may have formed the basis of the claim.

If, as Campbell suggests, E ware vessels originate in France, then the alizarin-based madder on the Teeshan sherd may well represent a raw dyestuff imported from the same region. The dyes on the Dunadd, Buiston and Loch Glashan sherds provide less effective support for this theory, because alizarin was not detected and wild madder or bedstraw cannot be discounted. Nevertheless, they show an association between E1 vessels and madder-type dyes at a time when red dyes were a valuable and comparatively rare commodity.

## CATALOGUE OF ILLUSTRATED ARTEFACTS

Dimensions:
RD – Rim diameter; BD – Basal diameter; MD – maximum body diameter; H – Height; T – thickness of wall; V – volume; W – width; MS – Maximum sherd size (chord measurement).

**Vessel 1 (figure 32)**
Seven sherds forming most of profile of $E_1$ jar. Rim everted at almost 90°, slightly thickened and bevelled, with lidseat. Sharp neck/shoulder carination. Broken just above base. **Use:** inside edge of lidseat worn. Exterior sooted on lower part. **Condition:** some sherds very abraded, others fresh. Unabraded 5 joins abraded 14. **Colour:** buff/grey. **Dimensions**: RD 14cm, MD 18cm, BD c 12cm, H c 16cm, V 2240cc, MS 10 + 5 + 4 + 1cm, 9cm, 7cm, 6cm. **Reg. Nos**: LG5, 13, 14, 18.

**Vessel 2 (figure 32)**
Eight sherds forming most of profile of $E_1$ jar. Rim everted at 45°, rounded and thickened. Neck vertical. No internal rilling. **Use:** base burnt and sooted. **Condition:** badly abraded. Fabric normal E ware with abundant iron ore of various colours, one large quartz 7 × 4mm, one rounded rock fragment. **Colour:** off-white. **Dimensions**: RD 14–16cm, BD 10cm, MD 17cm, H c 16cm, MS 6cm, 5cm, 5 + 5 + 3cm, 4 + 4 + 3cm. **Reg. Nos**: LG6, 7, 8, 10, no No.

**Vessel 3 (figure 32)**
Eight sherds forming most of profile of $E_1$ jar. Rim everted at 60°, simple, angular profile, with lidseat. Neck vertical, upper body globular. Lower body not joining, globular, sagging over base, which is thick and badly formed with slight pedestal. Internal and some external rilling. Base dried on coarse sand leaving impressions around edge. **Use:** no sooting, but there is a black ring around lower 2cm of wall, perhaps firing mark. Slight purple stain on two sherds. **Condition:** unabraded. Fabric normal E ware with a few sandstone grains, a few carbonized organic inclusions, brown iron ore. **Colour:** grey/off-white. **Dimensions**: RD 13cm, MD 16cm, BD 11cm, H c 14cm, MS 14 + 8 + 3cm, 5 + 5 + 3 + 3 + 3cm. **Reg. Nos**: LG1, 2, 3, 4, 9, no No.

**Vessel 4 (figure 32)**
Basal part of globular vessel. Internal rilling, basal string cut-off. **Use:** base sooted on exterior. Interior with carbonized organic material on upper part. Heavily burnt, and edges abraded and sooted over breaks. The base of this vessel has been trimmed down after breakage and reused as a lamp or shallow cooking vessel. Fabric too burnt to make out. **Colour:** black. **Dimensions**: BD 5.5cm, MS 12cm, MD ?13cm. **Reg. No:** LG12.

**Vessel 5 (figure 32)**
Almost complete $E_1$ vessel, about one-third of upper side missing. Rim triangular, flat-topped. Neck flaring, body high-shouldered with internal and external finger rilling. There are firing cracks on the upper body and the base where the present piece is missing. Surface uneven, lumpy. **Use:** no sooting, some wear in interior. **Condition:** unabraded. Fabric normal E ware with red and brown iron ore and clay pellets up to 8mm. **Colour:** grey-buff/orange and grey. **Dimensions**: RD 13cm, MD 15cm, BD 8cm, H 12.3cm, V 1120cc, MS 15cm. **Reg. No:** no No.

*Unassigned sherds*
Two unassigned bodysherds. **Dimensions**: MS 10cm, 2cm. **Reg. No:** LG11 and no No.

## 4.3 INDUSTRIAL CERAMICS

*Ewan Campbell*

The two fragments of crucible, SF11 and SF12, were found close together, and belong to the same vessel (figure 35). This was a lidded crucible of sub-triangular shape, having an upright vertical lug on the lid. The general type is characteristic of early medieval Celtic sites with well-known examples from Dinas Powys in Wales, Lagore and Garryduff in Ireland, and Dunadd. It was classified by Tylecote as Type E1. There are differences between these lidded crucibles however. Those from Dinas Powys all have rounded cylindrical lugs (Alcock 1963, fig 31) as do those from Lagore (Hencken 1950, fig 60). However, those from the 7th-century metalworking deposits at Dunadd have rectangular-sectioned lugs, and are identical to the Loch Glashan example. The fabric of the Dunadd crucibles was also similar to the Loch Glashan crucible, suggesting they were made from the same source of clay. The Dunadd type was classified as Type C at that site (Lane & Campbell 2000, illus 4.40) and was the commonest crucible form at Dunadd. The type may be an adaptation of the long-lived sub-triangular form of the local Iron Age, with an added lid.

At Dunadd, metallurgical analysis showed that Type C crucibles were used mainly for casting silver/copper alloys (Lane & Campbell 2000, 206, table 5.5). The XRF metallurgical analysis of the Loch Glashan crucible (Appendix 7.2) also shows that it was used for melting silver (with smaller amounts of copper present), supporting the conclusion that this closed form of crucible was specially designed for use with silver. Presumably, the lid would help prevent oxidation of the silver melt. The use of silver is particularly relevant in determining the status of the site. This will be discussed further in Chapter 6.3, but what is clear is the very

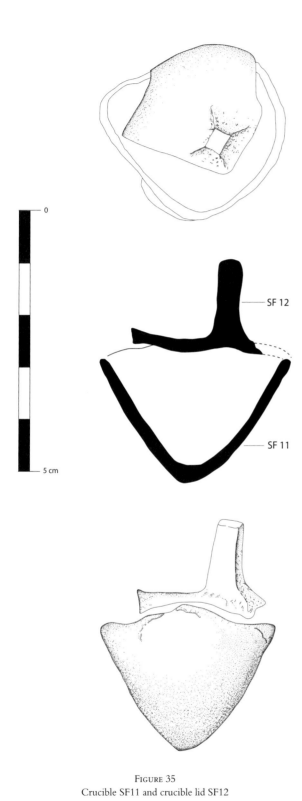

0

5 cm

SF 12

SF 11

close similarity between the metalworking practices at the site and those at Dunadd.

Lidded crucibles are also known from contemporary sites in Scandinavia, such as Helgö in Sweden (Lamm 1977, fig 1), but there the knob is usually on the side, and the body seems to have been formed differently, more like Dunadd Type D. At Ribe in Denmark Type 5 crucibles are stated to have a lug on the lid, and were also used for silver, but no clear examples are illustrated (Madsen 1984, 27). It is not clear if these Scandinavian examples represent an independent convergence of form relating to function, as seems likely, or illustrate some form of contact between the two areas in the 6th or 7th centuries.

The Loch Glashan crucible was found in an area of the crannog with few other finds (figure 33). It is perhaps surprising that no mould fragments were recovered, but there are several possible reasons. The waterlogged environment may not have been conducive to the preservation of poorly-fired ceramics such as moulds, or they may not have been recognized by the excavators. Irish crannogs with important metalworking, such as Moynagh Lough, show the metalworking debris confined to discrete areas (Bradley 1993, fig 8.3). It is possible that significant metalworking deposits exist in the unexcavated margins of the site, but this is impossible to prove. On the other hand, only two crucibles were recovered from the 19th-century excavations at Buiston crannog, and none from the recently excavated areas (Crone 2000, 151), illustrating that large-scale fine metalworking was not a constant feature of these sites.

FIGURE 35
Crucible SF11 and crucible lid SF12

## CATALOGUE OF ILLUSTRATED ARTEFACTS

**SF11 (figure 35a)**

Complete lower part of lidded crucible, conical section, sub-triangular shape. Well formed with thin walls. Traces of clay luting of lid all round except near spout. Fabric grey, with abundant quartz, some mica. **Use:** Lower half of interior with black and brown slaggy dross. No vitrification on exterior. **Dimensions:** Height 26mm, size 33 × 35mm, T 2–3mm.

**SF12 (figure 35b)**

Sub-rectangular lug and part of lid of crucible showing open edge, joining No 11. Lug blackened to the front.

## 4.4   THE BROOCH

*Ewan Campbell*

DESCRIPTION (figure 36 and plate 19)

SF80 is a small, copper-alloy penannular brooch and pin, complete, with decorated terminals and hoop panel. The brooch hoop is circular, diameter 34mm. It is of D-shaped section, width 4–5mm, thickness 1–2mm. The hoop is finely polished, and very regular in shape. Towards the terminals it increases in thickness to form a cusp, preventing the pin sliding over the terminals. The hoop panel is sunken and oval shaped, with a central circular setting. The surface of the panel has chased hatched decoration. The central circular setting has a cabochon amber setting, diameter 3.5mm, held in place

by peening over the edges of the setting. The circular setting overlies the hatching of the panel field. The back of the hoop has been filed flat. There are a few scratches, but no inscription or decoration visible on this side.

The terminals are sub-square and quadri-lobate, with central settings of amber. Each is slightly differently decorated. The central circular settings have ribbed collars forming a rosette, and as in the hoop, appear to overly the hatched decoration of the terminals. The cabochon amber setting remains in the right terminal, but is missing in the left. There is a conical pit in the centre of the setting below the missing amber. The points of three of the lobes have similar conical pits to those on the pin, but the lobe adjoining the hoop is a solid boss. The decoration consists of a band of single line transverse hatching around the margins of the lobes, with the central area of each lobe left blank. There is no roughening for enamel on these fields.

The pin is bent over the hoop loosely, allowing it to slide over the hoop panel. A patch of wear on the inner side of the end of the hoop beside the right-hand terminal indicates that the pin was worn horizontally, pointing to the left. It is bent where it crosses the left-hand of the hoop. The pin is 57mm long, 3mm wide, with the head 6mm wide. It is decorated halfway along the shank, and on the head. The shank decoration consists of an elongated lentoid area of single line transverse hatching within a border, with dots formed from conical pits at each end. The pin head decoration is

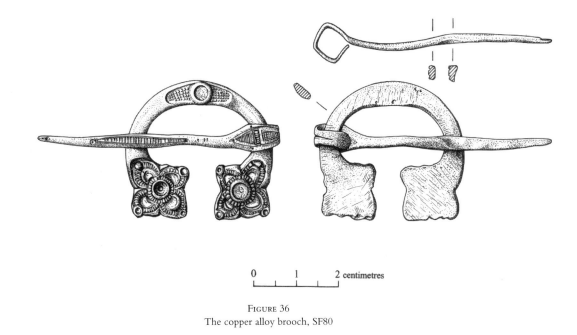

0          1          2 centimetres

FIGURE 36
The copper alloy brooch, SF80

PLATE 19
a) Front view of the brooch with pin in position; b) back view of brooch
[See colour frontispiece.]

a rather fatter lentoid, with similar transverse hatching, but with a double border, and divided asymmetrically in two by a band of longitudinal hatching. Four dots, of similar conical pits, flank the hatching.

The brooch is in excellent condition. Found in the brushwood layer (figure 33).

DISCUSSION

*Technology*

The composition of the brooch is a quaternary alloy of copper, zinc, tin and lead (Appendix 7.3), with no traces of gilding. In this respect it is unlike most of the analyses of metalworking debris from Dunadd, and more like Anglo-Saxon or Norse metalwork analyses. There are few analyses of Pictish copper alloy objects available for comparison, as most of the brooches are of silver/copper alloy (Wilson 1973, 174–5). There is one pin from Dunadd with a similar composition (Lane & Campbell 2000, table 5.8, no. 44), though it is not known if it was manufactured there

The means of production of the brooch can be seen on the SEM microphotographs (plate 35). The decoration of the brooch has taken place in three stages. Firstly, an outline of the undecorated brooch has been produced, possibly in wax before being cast in lead. This undecorated lead model was then chased with small chisels to create the hatching of the hoop and the other transverse decoration of the terminals. This has been done fairly crudely, with numerous double strikes and misaligned strokes. This suggests that a lead, rather than wax, die was being used at this stage otherwise mistakes could have been rectified. Finally small cylinders were placed in the centre of the terminals and hoop panel to act as stone settings. These can be seen to be secondary to the hatching which runs underneath them. It could be argued that the last two phases took place on a cast copper alloy blank. However, two points argue against this. Firstly the chisel used is exceptionally fine, in some cases having a breadth of 0.5mm, and a thickness of 0.2mm. Such a fine tool could only be used on a soft material such as lead. Secondly, where the central settings overlie the hatching there is no trace of solder, showing that these features were cast into the copper alloy brooch rather than being added later. It is just possible that the central settings were emplaced as solid cylinders then drilled out, rather than being cast as empty cylinders, as there is a small conical hole in the centre of the setting under the missing amber on the left side.

It seems as if the chased cross-hatched decoration on the hoop panel is intended to copy the chip-carved interlace of the St Ninian's Isle brooches (Wilson 1973, plate xxxiib). There has been some debate on whether the detailed interlace decoration found on these early medieval brooches was cast in (Stevenson 1974, 19 n 8), or engraved after casting (Wilson 1973, 97). A highly decorated mould from Dunadd has shown that such detail could be cast (Lane & Campbell 2000, 117, illus 4.20, 653), but the detail on the Loch Glashan brooch shows how difficult it can be to distinguish tool marks on the die from those applied directly to a cast blank. Without the evidence described above that the circular settings *overlay* the hatching, it would have appeared that the chased work was the final stage in the production of the brooch, applied to the cast copper alloy brooch rather than the die.

The brooch, while not having complex interlace, is clearly modelled on more elaborate brooches which do have this decoration. Being cast in copper alloy rather than silver suggests that it is of lower status, but it is a surprisingly accomplished piece of work given that it was not a precious or costly item. Settings for amber or glass were however used on other copper alloy pins and brooches, such as the Dunipace brooch-pin (Youngs 1989, 105).

*Chronology*
A date in the 8th or early 9th century is usually assigned to this style of brooch and the parallels quoted (Youngs 1989, *passim*). However it should be cautioned that there is little hard evidence to support the date of manufacture (as opposed to deposition) of any of these brooches.

*Status*
The Loch Glashan brooch is not an especially large or highly decorated brooch compared to many others of the period. The size is much smaller than other brooches of the St Ninian's Isle series, but is close to the Type G brooches manufactured in some quantity at Dunadd (Lane & Campbell 2000, 106). It cannot be considered to be indicative of high status, especially as it has no gold or silver component, metals which seem to have been restricted to higher echelons of society if the Irish Laws can be believed (Nieke 1993; Kelly 1988, 114). On the other hand it is very well made compared to other copper alloy brooches of the period, and is clearly something over which considerable care has been taken in production. The use of amber is indicative of a certain status, and is a rather puzzling usage alongside low status material such as copper alloy. The use of a quaternary copper alloy, rather than simpler copper/tin alloys, would have imparted a brassy colour rather similar to gilding, and may indicate that the brooch was intended for someone of elevated rank, or even that quaternary alloys had a higher status than we might suspect.

*Affinities*
The Loch Glashan brooch is clearly related to the St Ninian's Isle series, and was listed as such in the definitive publication of the type (Wilson 1973, 89). It shares the features of oval hoop panel with central setting, the bent-over pin with lentoid decoration on the head and shank, and the quadrilobed terminals. The design is derived from the tri- or quadri-lobate bird-headed terminals of brooches such as St Ninian's Isle No 27 (Wilson 1973, pl xxxva), but tending towards the square terminals of brooch No 19 (*ibid*, pl xxxiia). The form of the lobes however cannot be exactly matched, and is perhaps closer to those of the Rogart (*ibid*, pl xxxviid) and Croy (*ibid*, pl xxxviiic) brooches. It differs in the more pointed shape of the lobes, and in having the small settings at the point of the lobes rather than in between, as in the latter two brooches. It is also notable that the brooches from St Ninian's Isle all have flattened hoops, unlike the D-shaped section of the Loch Glashan brooch. The use of hatching, rather than interlace, is seen on a few other brooches, for example the large silver-gilt brooches from Croy (*ibid*, pl xxxviiia), and Ervey crannog, Co Meath (Youngs 1989, 88) the latter being influenced by the Pictish series. Ervey is the only other brooch with a pin having transverse hatching on the shank, and the overall pattern of decoration is the closest to the Loch Glashan brooch. The use of crosshatching on the hoop panel is interesting, as all the other St Ninian's Isle brooches have interlace. However the Aldclune brooch (Youngs 1989, 113) has imitation chip-carved grid pattern on the hoop, and Ervey has a mesh pattern on the cusps, and it seems likely that this type of design was the model for the Loch Glashan brooch.

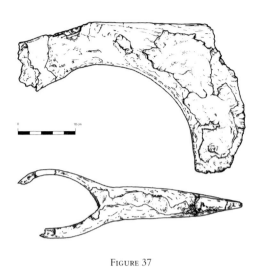

FIGURE 37
The iron axe, SF174

These close parallels lie in southern Pictland or Ireland, rather than the north, and may represent aspects of a regional school in the southern Highlands, rather than a specifically Pictish milieu. The concept of the St Ninian's Isle type as culturally 'Pictish' has been questioned (Lane 1984, 55; cf Graham-Campbell 2001, 34–5), and is a product of the culture-history model which equates material culture with ethnic groups in a way which has been shown to be unsustainable. For example, while many of the moulds from Dunadd have square-ended hoop panels, supposedly characteristic of 'Irish' manufacture, at least one mould and a trial piece have rounded ends (Lane & Campbell 2002, 122); in another case Anglo-Saxon types of brooch have been adapted to 'Irish' brooch styles (ibid, 117). In a period of extremely fluid interaction in art styles (Campbell & Lane 1993), cultural attribution of brooches is probably a misplaced activity.

## 4.5   THE IRON AXEHEAD

### Colleen Batey

Only two supposed iron objects were recovered from Loch Glashan, both from the brushwood layer, and X-ray examination has shown that one of these is not an artefact at all. SF7 is a tubular object in several fragments, which was found to be composed of iron pan or heavy mineralization possibly originally formed around a long bone fragment. This may therefore represent the only other evidence of bone recovered from the site apart from the cattle teeth found in the same deposit (Chapter 3.3).

SF174 is an altogether more significant find. It is a socketed bearded axe head found deep in the brushwood layer. X-ray examination indicates that the metal content remains high. The axe head has a broken shaft and a flattened top side or upper edge which expands towards the shafting area and is tapering towards the broken blade (figure 37). The outer edge of the blade is damaged but appears to be curved, ending in the blunt edge, ie the 'beard' (Goodman 1964, 29). There is some distortion in the shafting area, with the longer part cracked and slightly incurving which gives the impression of a more oval hafting, but this is misleading and the compression may have been caused at least in part by hammering during the hafting process. The tail of the axe has been simply folded over and secured (probably by welding) to one face of the axe to form a loop for the socket or shaft.

A similar method of construction was used in the manufacture of a shafted axe from the 8th-9th century raised rath at Deerpark Farms, Co Antrim, although the blade is a different form (Scott 1990). The hafting loop has been created by folding over the tail, although the blade itself was formed by the forging out and folding back on itself of the metal. The manufacture of this item is at variance with other examples studied from that period where the metal has been completely folded over on itself to form the hafting loop and both cheeks of the axe and an insert has been added to reinforce the blade (ibid, 131–3, plate 5.3.23).

The majority of surviving medieval axes are variants of the bearded type (Goodman 1964, 29). Such axes are invariably depicted as woodworking tools rather than as weapons. It is a general purpose tool which would certainly have served efficiently to hew wood and trim such substantial timbers as were recorded in the structure of the crannog. However, its blade would have been too big for shaping wooden artefacts such as the trough (Chapter 4.1).

The range of axe heads which have been identified probably owes as much to refinements in working techniques as it does to specific dating. A useful sequence of head forms is published in relation to finds from the Viking and later site at Novgorod, Russia (Khoroshev & Sorokin 1992, 129 fig IV.20) which indicates blades of the type found at Loch Glashan in the earlier stages of a sequence spanning the period 10th-15th centuries. A broad or bearded axe was found in Viking deposits at Coppergate, York (Ottaway 1992, 527). Other very similar axeheads have been found in northern Ireland, where they have been defined as Class 7, dating to the 9–11th centuries (Bourke 2001, fig 1, 7).

There appear to be few earlier antecedents for this axe type. At least one bearded axe was found at Lagore, although it has a much more substantial hafting socket (Hencken 1950, 107–8). Unfortunately, the example was an unstratified earlier find from the site. A hoard of Anglo-Saxon woodworking tools from Hurbuck, Co Durham includes several different axes, but none are of the form discussed here, the nearest parallel being the T-shaped axe (Wilson 1976, fig 6.1, 257; Wilson 1981, 82–3).

## 4.6  METALLURGICAL WASTE

### *Effie Photos-Jones*

### INTRODUCTION

Pieces of metallurgical waste (slag) were found on the surface of the crannog during removal of the stone horizon. They were sampled as SF6 and SF13, SF6 consisting of two separate bags which are referred to here as SF6.1 and SF6.2. Ritchie also reported that he found iron slag on the surface of the crannog when he visited (Chapter 1) but nothing further is recorded about the whereabouts of this material.

### SEM-EDAX ANALYSIS OF BLOOMERY IRON SLAG

Metallurgical slags contain a number of distinct mineralogical phases, which become apparent when the sample is prepared as a polished block and examined under reflected light. These include dendrites of wustite (FeO), long or broken-up needles of fayalite $(2FeO.SiO_2)$, angular grains of hercynite $(FeO.Al_2O_3)$ and a glassy phase that grows interstitially within the other phases. The interstitial glass may itself, in the process of cooling, precipitate fine grains of fayalite and/or wustite. Not all phases that are present within the smelting slags are seen in the smithing slags, iron oxides (magnetite and wustite) as well as fayalite being the main constituents of the latter.

SEM-EDAX analyses are undertaken first on the entire surface of the polished block, and subsequently on each of the different mineralogical phases. Both sets of analyses need to be reported. The first type (taken over a mean of three) represents area or bulk chemical analysis and is considered to be representative of the composition of the sample as a whole. As such, it identifies the slag as metallurgical of the ferrous or non-ferrous variety. The second type is aimed at establishing the composition of each of the mineralogical phases within and so at identifying the process that generated it. In brief, spot analyses are aimed at establishing whether the slags are of the smithing or smelting variety and provide information on the environment, temperature and conditions within the furnace in question.

### RESULTS

#### SF6.1

This was an amorphous brown black slag, mildly magnetic, showing porosity only on section. Area analyses at two different sections of the sample showed the composition to be primarily a manganese-rich iron oxide. Spot analyses of the iron oxide and the interstitial material revealed a glassy phase and that of fine dendrites of iron oxide (plate 20). The glassy phase incorporates, apart from manganese, small amounts of barium, phosphorus and sulphur.

The sample appears to be bloomery iron slag of the smelting or bloom smithing variety (billet formation) on the strength of its high manganese content and the minor inclusions like phosphorus, barium and sulphur present within the glassy phase.

#### SF6.2

This sample consists of two sub-samples, SF6.2a and SF6.2b. Both are amorphous brown black slags, mildly magnetic, showing porosity only on section (c 3–4cm long axis). Area analyses showed the composition of each to be primarily an iron silicate, rich in alumina. Spot analyses were undertaken on four phases: a) the iron oxide, b) the fayalite, c) the hercynite or aluminium-iron oxides and d) the glassy matrix (plate

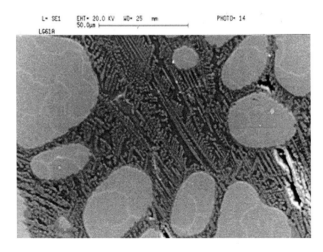

PLATE 20

SEM-BS image of a section of SF6.1. Well-rounded dendrites of wustite in a matrix consisting of two phases, a finely dendritic one, also of wustite and a glass (Bar = 50 microns)

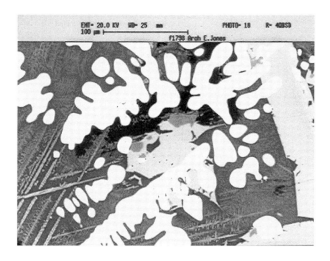

PLATE 21
SEM-BS image of section of SF6.2b showing dendrites of wustite, angular (dark grey) grains of hercynite, long needles of fayalite (light grey) and interstitial glass (dark grey with feathery fayalite within) (Bar = 100 microns)

21). Small amounts of barium, phosphorus and sulphur were detected in the glassy phase.

The two sub-samples of sample SF6.2 are fragments of smelting iron slag on the strength of the high alumina phase, hercynite, found within. They are, together with SF6.1, suggestive of iron making practices on site.

*SF13*
Amorphous brown black slag mildly magnetic, showing porosity only on section (c 3cm long axis).

Area analysis at one section of the sample showed the composition to be primarily of an iron oxide

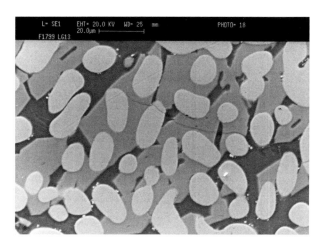

PLATE 22
SEM-BS image of SF13 showing dense dendritic growth of iron oxide; also fayalite and glass. The well-formed crystals of both wustite and fayalite suggest slow cooling (Bar = 20 microns)

with an alumino-silicate rich glass. Spot analyses were undertaken on all three phases: a) the iron oxide, b) the interstitial glassy matrix and c) the fayalite (plate 22).

The glassy phase incorporates calcium, sodium and potassium as well as small amounts of phosphorus. The manganese component is low in this sample in comparison with that of SF6.1 with which it is chemically more closely similar. Variations in manganese content are indeed expected depending on the amount of manganese nodules within the bog ore used as the ore source. Occasional fine metallic iron grains (prills) have also been detected. Metallic iron is usually conspicuously absent from most of the bloomery iron slags of the Scottish Highlands bloomery mounds. This suggests that conditions within the furnace allowed the slag to be free running at a relatively low temperature, a task not difficult to achieve given their high iron and manganese content. Both oxides are natural fluxes reducing the melting point of the slag, and therefore allowing good separation between metal and waste.

DISCUSSION

Bloomery mounds (small mounds of metallurgical waste usually measuring about 1m high, 3m wide and 5m long) have been found in association with low shaft bloomery furnaces as well as bloomery hearths in the Scottish Highlands dating primarily to the late medieval period (Photos-Jones *et al* 1998; Atkinson & Photos-Jones 1999). The slag found on the crannog may have derived from such a mound since it is almost certain that even a single smelt would have produced more waste than the amount recovered. In this context it is pertinent to recall that a bloomery site with a hearth was located about 800m to the north of the crannog on the eastern shore of the loch (Chapter 2.3; figure 1b).

The raw materials were the widely available local bog iron ore or iron oxyhydroxides, a poorly crystalline form of goethite (Hall & Photos-Jones 1998) while the fuel used was usually oak or alder charcoal. In the bloomery furnace, metallic iron was reduced from its ore while in the solid state, ie the iron was never intentionally molten. The numerous slag impurities trapped within the iron mass had to be hammered out, resulting in a billet that was subsequently shaped or forged into the desired artefact. These slag inclusions which are carried over into the metal artefact bear testimony to the bloomery and by extension provenance the source of the raw material.

Bloomery slags have been traditionally classified as 'tapped' and 'non-tapped' on the basis of the method of their removal in the course of the smelting operation. When tapped they acquire the characteristic drip-like surface texture. The Loch Glashan slag is amorphous. Smelting and smithing slags have been traditionally differentiated on the basis of their morphology, primarily the presence or absence of smithing hearth bottoms, but this is at best a first level classification. Chemically, slags of the smelting or smithing type are iron-rich (with up to 60–70% iron oxide), crystalline, spongy, dense and brown-black in colour. Mineralogically they tend to be similar, but it is on the basis of fingerprinting elements that a distinction between the two stages can be achieved. However, in the absence of fingerprinting elements there is little chance for a definitive answer apart from that which can be extracted from associated evidence like metallurgical ceramics, remains of furnaces and related features and artefactual evidence.

The Loch Glashan slag is of the typical Highland bloomery type with regards to the manganese and phosphorus contents. While iron making at the basic level of production of metal artefacts for everyday use is a recurrent theme in the Highlands, the co-existence of iron making with non-ferrous metal working, as exemplified by the silver-rich contents of the crucible (Chapter 4.3 and Appendix 7.2) raises questions regarding the broader range of expertise of local 'smiths'.

*Addendum*

One other piece of evidence from the crannog is relevant to this discussion. SF9 was also found on the surface of the crannog during removal of the stone horizon and was tentatively identified by JGS as a piece of pumice. However, examination has revealed that the object is not pumice but is composed mainly of quartz, with some feldspar and lithic fragments (Anthony Newton *pers comm*). It is probably fused sand, the partial melting of the grains caused by proximity to a fire, and as such could be related to the metalworking activities that the slag and crucible fragments represent.

## 4.7 THE SEGMENTED SILVER-IN-GLASS BEAD

### *Ewan Campbell*

DESCRIPTION (plate 23)

This is a cylindrical segmented bead of opaque white and colourless glass, broken in half lengthways. There are four segments formed by crimping the drawn tube, with a slight collar between segments. Both ends are broken off, but it is not clear if these are original breaks, where the bead has been separated from its neighbours, or of more recent origin. The bead appears to be drawn, with marked longitudinal layering in the core. Colour appears to be a pale green with a pearly sheen. On close inspection however, the core is of opaque white glass full of bubbles, with an external layer of colourless transparent glass. The outer layer is thicker on one side, as if the glass has dripped, and this thicker metal is broken off on three of the segments. The metal is of good quality with no signs of decay. There is some black discolouration at one point between the two layers of glass, indicating decay of a metallic silver layer. Length 20mm, overall diameter 6–7mm, Diameter hole 1–2mm. Recovered during post-excavation conservation in peaty packing around a wooden artefact.

DISCUSSION

*The source of the bead*

The analysis of the bead (Appendix 7.4) confirms that this is a silver-in-glass (or silver-foil) segmented bead, a highly specialized type well-known in Scandinavian contexts (Callmer 1977, 88–9, Group Ea). However, beads of similar manufacture, though often with gold foil rather than silver are known from the Roman and early Anglo-Saxon periods in western Europe (Boon 1977; Guido 1978, 93–4; Guido 1999, 78–80; Brugmann 2004, 75, type 8.2.3), and the type in general can be described as metal-in-glass. A notable example of the gold-in-glass type is from the well-known site of Dinas Powys, Glamorgan (Alcock 1963, fig 41, 5), where it was found in a 7th-century context (Campbell 1991, 432). Others from a necklace in a burial overlying the forum in Wroxeter, may be of 6th century date (Boon 1977, 199). Originally described by Harden as 'Coptic', Boon considered on distributional evidence that they were also manufactured in the late and post-Roman period in the Rhineland (Boon 1977, 201), while Guido suggested a wide spread of sources from around Gdansk to Dacia (1999, 79).

More recent work has shown that the type was certainly manufactured in the eastern Mediterranean, with a 5–7th century Byzantine workshop being excavated in Alexandria (Rodziewicz 1984, 242). There is a likelihood that they continued to be produced into the Islamic period, as the glass analyses are similar to those of Islamic glasses. There appears to have been a change from the use of gold foil to silver at some time around the 8th century. In Scandinavia

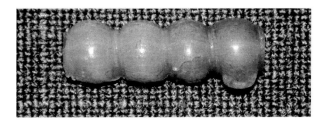

PLATE 23
The silver-in-glass bead. See colour frontispiece.

they are commonest in the early Viking period, and occur along with other segmented beads of a variety of colours, including blue and yellow. Recent work on the well-stratified deposits at Ribe, Denmark, has shown that the metal-in-glass beads there are all silver-in-glass beads, and that they are confined to the late 8th and early 9th centuries at that site (Sode & Feveile 2002, fig 3). It had previously been considered that these were manufactured in Scandinavia, due to the numbers of deformed beads found at sites such as Birka, Kaupang and Helgö, but the analyses and technological details of the beads from Ribe show that they were probably manufactured in Alexandria (Sode & Feveile 2002, 12). Segmented beads, of the silver-in-glass type as well as blue and yellow types, are also found in Scandinavian contexts in Britain. One of the best known assemblages is the necklace of 44 of these beads from a female burial at Cnip, Isle of Lewis (Wellander *et al* 1987, illus 6, 169–70). A 10th-century date was originally suggested but this has recently been revised to the 9th century (Batey & Graham Campbell 1998, 74). In summary, an 8th- or 9th-century date for the bead seems likely, though an earlier date cannot be ruled out.

The question must remain as to the route by which this bead reached Argyll, with two possibilities presenting themselves. Firstly, it could be of Scandinavian derivation (if not manufacture), and have reached Scotland as the result of Norse contact with the Gaels of Dál Riata in the late 8th or 9th century. This would be early for a Norse to native (rather than native to Norse) transaction, but not impossible. The less likely alternative is that the bead came via the western trade routes which linked Atlantic Britain to the Continent and Mediterranean in the 6–8th centuries (Campbell 1995; 1996), and which are so prominent at the nearby royal site of Dunadd (Lane & Campbell 2000, 98–103). This matter is discussed further below (Chapter 6.3).

*Technology*
The technology of the bead deserves some comment. Examination by Sode and Feveile (2002) has shown

that a complex series of operations were required to produce the silver-in-glass beads, and the technical examination of the Loch Glashan bead (Appendix 7.4) supports their results. The clear glass core was first formed as a tube drawn from glass full of tiny bubbles which make it appear opaque. This tube would have been formed on a metal wire which could be removed on cooling. The tube was then dipped in molten silver (actually a silver/arsenic alloy). Next this tube was inserted inside another tube which had a larger diameter perforation. The two beads were then reheated to enable the outer and inner tubes to fuse, and then crimped together by rolling in a stone mould such as those found at Alexandria (Rodziewicz 1984, fig 265; pl 72). In the Loch Glashan bead the outer layer of glass has melted and run to one side, making it look as if the silver-covered tube has been dipped in molten glass. This is technologically unlikely, and is merely the result of the difficulty in gauging the correct temperature of the furnace in the reheating process. Comparison with the Cnip beads shows an identical mode of formation, though the core of the Cnip beads is not generally opacified by bubbles. However, there is much variation and opaque cores are found on some Scandinavian beads. Both the Cnip and Loch Glashan beads have clear outer layers, but some of the Scandinavian beads have less commonly amber or blue outer layers. Some of these have been described as gold-in-glass beads, but no evidence of the use of gold has been found in Norse period beads, with the apparent gold sheen of some silver-in-glass beads being due to optical effects (Sode & Feveile 2002, 7; cf Wellander *et al* 1987, 164). The production of these complex beads requires a set of skills and techniques which are unlikely to have been copied by craftworkers in north-western Europe, suggesting that they were all made in the continuing tradition of glass manufacture in the Near East.

## 4.8   THE LEATHER ASSEMBLAGE
### *Clare Thomas*

INTRODUCTION

The finds book records at least 90 items of leather; the number is not precise because some entries are not specific, merely mentioning 'pieces'. The situation is also complicated by the deterioration of the leather since it was excavated, which has undoubtedly led to further fragmentation. Several of the small finds contain more leather than is recorded. The finds book entries

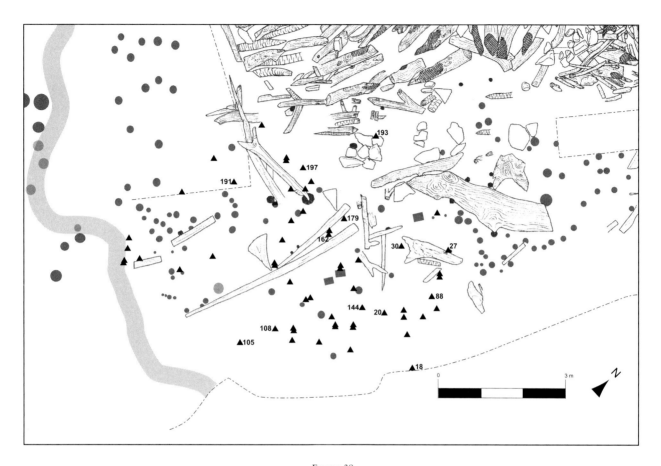

FIGURE 38
Distribution of leather artefacts

include one 'jacket', five shoe fragments, one sheath and three straps, as well as a 'decorated piece'.

Forty-four fragments, from 35 finds numbers, can no longer be accounted for. Eleven of these may be represented by the unlabelled leather. The missing items include potentially significant pieces such as 'part of leather sole' and 'larger piece of sole leather', as well as two 'straps'. However, it should be noted that these descriptions may not necessarily be reliable, as the 'strap' from SF20 is an offcut.

In all, 74 separate items survive and were examined as part of this study. As some small finds numbers contained several fragments each fragment has been given its own number, L1, L2, etc. SF105, the collection of fragments originally described as a jacket, or jerkin has since been re-interpreted as a satchel (Chapter 4.9) and it is discussed separately (Chapter 4.10). The rest of the assemblage is described below by category.

The leather had been conserved soon after retrieval using PEG (for details see Chapter 4.9) and while this served to stabilize the condition of the leather the waxy

coating that resulted may have obscured details which were more obvious at the time of excavation. The assemblage was not examined until 1997 by which time it was in a very desiccated and fragmented state. It should be noted here that it is not the conservation of the leather which prevented species identification; the bulk of the material was very worn (see below) and this had removed the diagnostic grain surface and hair follicle pattern that is characteristic of freshly tanned leather.

The findspots of the leather objects are shown in figure 38.

SHOES

The original finds book refers confidently to several shoes. The surviving evidence is, however, more ambiguous. Only ten items can be attributed to shoes, and doubt exists over several of these. Two of these [L2 and L3] appear to be vamps, the front section of a shoe upper covering the toes and part of the instep (figure 39a, f and g); however, it is also possible that

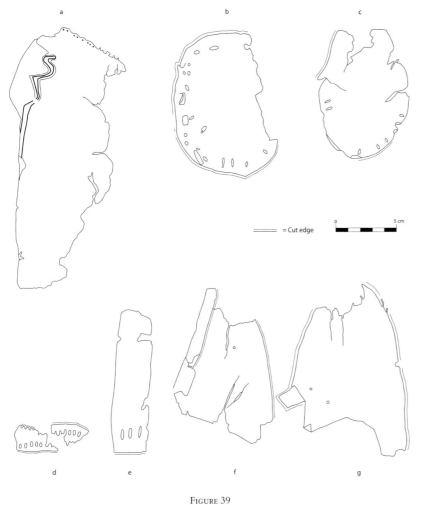

a = Cut edge
0          5 cm

FIGURE 39
a) L3 (sole/upper); b) L10 and c) L11 (clump soles); d) L9 and e) L8 (upper frgs); f) and g) L2
(top layers delaminated vamp/sole)

when other identifiable shoe features do not. It is very probable that these shoes had integral sole and upper units, as found in 'hide-shoes' from Irish peat bogs (Lucas 1956). This may explain the apparent absence of soles. If not still attached to their uppers, such soles would have no defining stitching channels and would just appear to be scraps.

The possibility that these are 'hide-shoes' is reinforced by the presence of continuous rows of slots for wrap-around thongs, as on six items [L4–L9]. Such slots are found on both Irish and Continental hide-shoes (Lucas 1956, 374–78, Types 3 and 4, 383; Lucas 1972, 204–5; Hald 1972). Lucas's Types 3 and 4 have been made out of a broad half-oval of leather (figure 41). Type 3 has one seam up the centre of the vamp and another at the rear of the quarters. Thongs have usually been used for these seams, resulting in rows of thong-holes. Only four shoes of this type have been dated – three to AD 200–500, one to 'before the 9th century'. Type 4 is similar, but has no seam up the vamp. Instead, there is a continuous line of thonging from one side of the quarters to the other, which when pulled tight forms a shoe and holds it on the foot. There is usually a short thonged seam at the rear of the quarters, although on some examples this is replaced by a projecting tab from one side of the quarters that fits into a slit on the other side. None of these shoes came from dateable contexts (Lucas 1956, 374–8; Lucas 1972, 204–5).

The two fragments with long rows of thong holes [L4 and L7] are most likely to belong to Type 4 shoes. L8 is too short to determine whether it is from a Type 3 or 4 shoe. The situation is not so clear with three other items. L 5 and L6 have two different rows of thong holes. Large irregularly spaced holes lie next to a cut edge, while a second row of smaller, neater holes are positioned 20–70mm from the first row. It is possible that the row next to the cut edge is for the type of thong described by Lucas, while the second row might be for a decorative thong. However, it is also conceivable that these items are not from shoes at all. Similarly, L9 has

they could be sole fragments, or combined sole/upper fragments of one-piece shoes. Six other items [L4–L9] have slots for thongs and are probably parts of uppers (figures 39d and e, and 40). On the other hand, it is not inconceivable that they could be from garments. The only definite sole fragments are two clump, or repair, soles [L10 and L11] (figure 39b and c).

It is unlikely that these clump soles could be soles with thonged sole-upper seams; such soles have tunnel holes at right angles to the sole margin, not parallel. They are also spaced much more closely together. Furthermore, the effect of pulling the thong tight is to leave a continuous rib between the lines formed on either side of a tunnel hole (Thornton 1990, 591, 592, fig 159, no 1859). In addition, no lasting margins have been recognized but this could be the result of wear and tear. On the other hand, lasting margins are usually very recognisable and seem to survive even two parallel rows of small slits; again, this suggests a different arrangement.

Comparable material from Scotland includes the shoes from Iona, Dundurn, Buiston, Dowalton Loch and two unprovenanced shoes in the Museum of Scotland. However, none of these provides close parallels for the Loch Glashan examples. The Iona shoes, dating to the late 6th–early 7th centuries, have uppers cut to a pattern similar to Lucas's Type 1, but with separate soles, which means that in terms of both construction and style they are quite different from the Loch Glashan examples (Groenman-van Waateringe 1981, 318–28). The Dundurn shoe, which is probably of 7th century date, is of one-piece construction, with seams at the toe and at the rear of the quarters (Alcock *et al* 1989, 217, microfiche 2, 3:A8). It is decorated all over with oval punch-marks contained in horizontal bands, and with vertical bands from toe to vamp throat and on the vamp wings. Its cutting pattern resembles that of Lucas's Type 1. Thus, it too differs significantly from the Loch Glashan

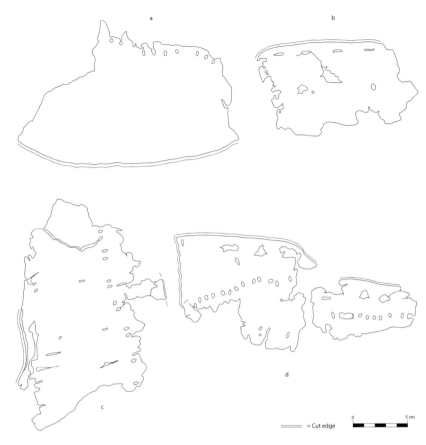

FIGURE 40
Leather shoes – upper fragments: a) L4; b) L7; c) L5; d) L6

examples. The two Buiston shoes, of early 7th century date, are of one-piece construction and have slots for a thong on the vamp wing (Groenman-van Waateringe 2000, 128–33). A seam up the centre of the vamp, as well as at the rear of the quarters, means that they resemble Lucas Type 3. A very distinctive feature of these two shoes is the gathered, or folded, nature of the central vamp seam. The two unprovenanced shoes in the Museum of Scotland are very similar to the Buiston examples. One of these has been radiocarbon-dated to the 6th/7th centuries (NMS TA 11–1350 ± 100 BP GrA-821). The fragment from Dowalton Loch is decorated in a style similar to the Dundurn shoe. It is almost certainly of one-piece construction, with a thonged seam at the rear of the quarters. It is probably of 5th to 6th century date (1440 ± 40 BP OxA-6804) (Alison Sheridan *pers comm*).

There are few recorded 'hide shoes' from England. The nearest chronological parallels are from Sutton Hoo, but all the evidence there points to turnshoe construction, with separate soles and uppers joined by an edge-flesh seam (East 1983, 792–4). Five shoes of

one-piece construction were found at York, dating to the 9th to 11th centuries. Only one of these bears any resemblance to 'hide-shoes' (Mould *et al* 2003, 3275–8, shoe 15357). It is most probably an elaborate version of Lucas' Type 3, with a notch to allow for a neat seam at the quarters, and an oblique, rather than central, vamp seam. Three shoes may be a variant of Lucas' Type 2, while a fourth has a sole with a central seam (Mould *et al* 2003, 3275–81, shoes 15354, 153456, 15353, 15355). Continental examples of hide-shoes are much more numerous. Hald, for instance, records many from Denmark and elsewhere, dating from Bronze Age times onwards (Hald 1972). Most of these have a seam up the centre of the vamp, as seen on the Buiston shoes. Such shoes were also found at Novgorod, where they are called 'porshni', but those illustrated are of 12th- to 14th-century date (Brisbane 1992, 183–84). Other possible parallels of 8th- to 10th-century date were found at Haithabu (Groenman-van Waateringe 1975, 24; 2000, 133).

The shoe fragments are all worn, with no surviving grain pattern; furthermore, the presence of clump

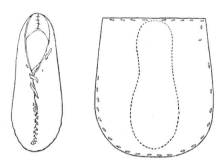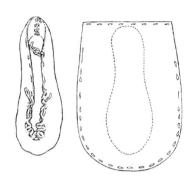

FIGURE 41
Reconstructions of hide shoes (after Lucas 1956): left – Type 3; right – Type 4

soles indicates repair work. However, shoes from archaeological contexts usually are worn, especially examples with a single sole, such as medieval turnshoes. Shoes of one-piece construction are even more vulnerable, and harder to repair. Soles could be patched, but once the sole portion began to break away further repair was not possible.

### THE SHEATH

The sheath [L12] is of very simple construction, consisting of a single piece of leather folded once and secured on the open side by a thong threaded through slots (figure 42a). There are no traces of any decoration.

Sheaths of this type frequently form part of medieval leather assemblages. Vince, for instance, describes 10th-century sheaths from London of similar construction, except that his examples appear to have been stitched with thread (Vince 1991, 210–11). Thornton, on the other hand, illustrates a 10th-century example from Winchester which is formed of two pieces of leather fastened together with a thong threaded through both long edges (Thornton 1990, 863). Later medieval sheaths, of 12th century or later date, are usually of a slightly more complicated construction, where the leather is folded twice and stitched up the centre of the reverse with a butted edge-grain seam (Thomas, forthcoming; Cowgill *et al* 1987, 34–9).

Most medieval sheaths are decorated, usually with incised lines and stamped patterns. (Thomas, forthcoming; Cowgill *et al* 1987, 40–4). Vince notes with surprise the absence of decorated sheaths at Haithabu (Vince 1991, 211). However, plain sheaths do exist; four from Perth High Street include one of late 12th to mid-13th century date with thonging up the side (Thomas, forthcoming), while another from

Durham, of 10th–11th century date, has a single side seam, though it is not clear whether this was made with thread or thonging (Carver 1979, 28–9).

### BELTS AND STRAPS

One fragment [L13] with a faint trace of stitching and with irregularly positioned slits may be part of a belt, possibly with a buckle or other metal fitting (figure 42d). [L14] is a strip which has been knotted by being threaded through a slit in itself, and is probably part of a strap (figure 41e).

Belts and straps had an infinite variety of uses, including adjustment of shoes and clothing, carrying of tools, equipment and weapons and horse tack.

### FRAGMENTS WITH SLITS OR TRACES OF STITCHING – POSSIBLE GARMENTS

One item with three rows of slits or oval holes [L19] and another large piece with stitching [15] are possibly parts of garments (figure 43). Six fragments with traces of stitching [L22–L27] and two large items with no indication of any seams [L20–21] are also probably remnants of either clothing or shoes. Unfortunately, it is not possible to be more specific.

### MISCELLANEOUS

L16 is a small, approximately circular fragment with a toothed edge and several holes in the middle (figure 42b). It may be a washer.

### WASTE MATERIAL

The bulk of the leather assemblage consisted of waste material, 31 offcuts and 18 scraps [L17 (figure 42f), L18 (figure 42c), L28–L74]. The offcuts all have at least one cut edge while the scraps have neither cut edges nor stitching. One fragment with three straight edges and a curved concave edge [L18], all cut, is probably waste from cutting out a sole or vamp of upper, albeit unusually wasteful. Triangular offcuts could be remnants from shoe manufacture, although none have the concave edges of typical sole-cutting waste [L30, L32, L34, L37, L41, L44, L46 and L51]. At least 19 offcuts are worn, while another nine have at least one torn edge, suggesting that most are a by-product of reuse of other items. Similarly, 15 scraps are worn, which implies that they too are fragments torn from larger, re-used objects.

Waste material was also found at the sites mentioned above. At Buiston, for example, it comprised primary offcuts, from the cutting of new leather, as well as scraps both with and without stitching (Groenman-van Waateringe 2000, 129). The Iona report mentions waste material, but does not distinguish between primary and secondary working (Groenman-van Waateringe 1981, 318). Dundurn produced seven offcuts but again no further definition is made (Alcock *et al* 1989, fiche 2, 3:A8). The York report distinguishes between primary, secondary and tertiary waste: their primary waste consists of trimmings from the whole hide; 'secondary' waste is similar to the triangles mentioned above, while the tertiary waste comprises thin, irregular strips from final trimming. However, most of the York material is of much later date (Mould *et al* 2003, 3245–6).

CONCLUSION

The highly fragmentary condition of the shoes makes them a very tantalizing group, especially given the frustrating shortage of construction details. The ambiguous nature of the evidence prevents more than a suggestion of style. The closest parallels are the shoes from Buiston and the two unprovenanced shoes, but their gathered vamp seams are not evident in the Loch Glashan assemblage. The resemblance to the Irish parallels, especially to Lucas Type 4, is most striking.

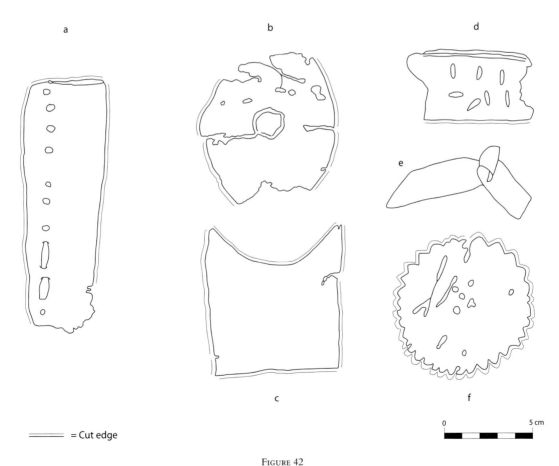

======= = Cut edge

0       5 cm

FIGURE 42
a) L12 (sheath); b) L16 (washer?) c) L18 (offcut); d) L13 (belt fragment); e) L14 (strap); f) L17 (offcut)

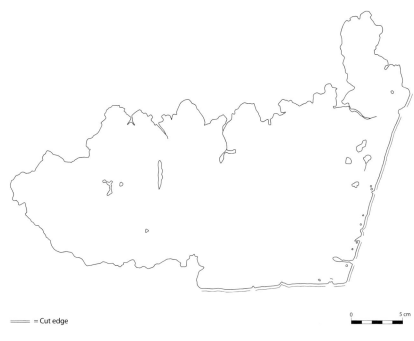

= Cut edge

0                    5 cm

Figure 43
L15 (frg garment)

The Continental parallels indicate that this type of shoe construction was widespread, and not just an oddity of Ireland and the west of Scotland. Overall, the existing comparanda indicates that this type of one-piece shoe had a currency certainly from the Bronze Age until at least the 7th or 8th centuries AD so their usefulness for indicating a chronological horizon at Loch Glashan is limited.

The value of the leather assemblage lies in the evidence it displays for the nature of leatherworking on the crannog. None of the fragments displayed the clear grain pattern indicative of freshly tanned leather. Rather, the worn nature of the offcuts and scraps, and that of virtually all the rest of the leather assemblage, suggests that the activity involved mainly the re-use of old leather items. This interpretation is supported by the evidence that has emerged from the re-examination of the satchel (Chapter 4.9). It seems likely that the thonging in the seams was cut and the satchel was dismantled into its component parts. Larger items, such as the satchel and the clothing fragments, may have been kept for re-use, in particular for patching. Even as recently as the mid-1980s, a cobbler in the Skinnergate in Perth was buying old handbags and belts for use in repair work.

It is not possible to judge whether leather was being worked on a domestic or commercial scale. Before the introduction of modern alternatives such as plastic and vinyl, leather was used for a very wide variety of purposes. Scrap from reuse was almost certainly very common.

## CATALOGUE OF ILLUSTRATED ARTEFACTS

Only those artefacts that have been illustrated are described here; a complete catalogue of the entire assemblage can be found in the site archive. Numbers in brackets are small finds numbers followed by Kelvingrove Museum accession numbers

**L1. Satchel (SF105; A6046dy) (figures 43 and 44)**
Front, back and sides of a satchel. Also includes a number of small unidentified fragments accessioned under the same number.

Fragment 10, the largest of the fragments, is roughly rectangular. Three edges have a row of slots each for attaching the fragments together by a thong, although the most worn edge has none, suggesting the actual size is larger, possibly by as much as a third more, than what remains.

Surviving height c 610mm; width c 440mm; thickness c 1mm.

Probably back of satchel, also forming top and flap at front.

The second largest fragment, Fragment 13, is also roughly rectangular, and again, there are three edges with a row of slots each, and a missing edge where the leather has deteriorated. Based on the size of the previous fragment, it would appear that the overall dimensions are reasonably well represented by the maximum height and width of what remains. A double row of slots runs c 60mm above the bottom edge. This appears to have been used to pinch a fold in the fragment, a thong securing the fold, creating a right angle which forms the base of the satchel and the front. The bottom left corner has become detached since excavation.

Surviving height c 610mm; width 403mm at bottom, 370mm at top, thickness c 1mm.

Probably front and base of satchel.

Third fragment, fragment 11 (including detached fragment 11B), is ovate with a narrower straight edge, and a wider rounded edge. The fragment is in two parts, with a small gap between them. The three straighter edges each have a row of slots, and there is also a double row of slots c 30mm apart from each other two thirds of the way up the fragment, the bottom row being worn appreciably. This is suggested to have supported a strap. The rounded edge appears to have folded inwards.

Surviving length 425mm; width at wider end 150mm, at narrower end 60mm; thickness c 1mm.

Probably side of satchel.

The fourth fragment, fragment 2, is similar to the third, being very roughly ovate, although considerably more degraded, having a number of missing areas, as well as being delaminated. There two side edges are better preserved, each having a row of slots, while the bottom and top edges are both similarly degraded. Where the third fragment has a double row of slots, this fragment has a missing area of leather.

Surviving length c 400mm; width 100–160mm.

Probably side of satchel.

There are, in addition, a number (17) of smaller fragments, some of which appear to attach onto the above fragments, but many of which are laminated and do not appear to relate to the satchel. Fragment 1 in particular, is considerably thicker than the leather of the satchel, and appears to be an off-cut. At least four of the fragments – fragment 6, 12, 15 and 21 – have slots.

**L2. Vamp of upper or forepart of sole (SF20; A6046ay) (figure 39g)**

Two exceedingly delaminated irregularly shaped fragments, resembling a vamp. One has three straight edges, possibly cut, but more likely split; fourth edge torn. Dimensions c 115 × 47 – 88mm. Second has two slightly curved edges and a third edge which appears to have been cut in the shape of a vamp throat. Dimensions c 138 × 100. No trace of any stitching. These two fragments almost certainly are delaminated layers of the same item, either a vamp or the forepart of the sole of a one-piece shoe. Also, three small fragments, with split or cut edges, possibly part of same item but not illustrated.

**L3. Combined sole and upper fragment? (SF144; A6046ar) (figure 39a)**

Irregularly shaped fragment, with traces of one stitched edge, which appears to have been part of a closed seam. One long edge cut or more probably split along an irregular line – rest torn. A curved double line has been cut along the worn grain surface; this may be accidental. Exceedingly worn, torn and delaminated. Length 210mm, width 80mm.

Possibly part of one-piece shoe, comprising sole and upper with seam from either front of vamp or rear of quarters.

**L4. Fragment of upper? (No identifying number) (figure 40a)**

Approximately oval fragment of leather with row of oval slots parallel to one edge, similar to thong holes on fragments of satchel. Edge above slots has probably been cut, others torn. Probably fragment of upper of one-piece shoe with horizontal thong. Worn, partially delaminated and badly desiccated. Length 200mm; width 95–127mm; length of edge with thong holes c 110mm.

## L5. Fragment with two rows of thong-holes? (SF20; A6046ay) (figure 40c)

Irregularly shaped fragment, all edges torn. One edge cut, along an irregular line. Immediately above it, traces of large, irregularly spaced thong holes. These holes have been distorted but are approximately 5 × 5mm and 25–30mm apart. Approximately parallel with this cut edge and c 75–90mm above it, there is a horizontal row of small, neat slits, in pairs, forming tunnel holes. Slits are 4.5 × 2mm, and 7mm apart, centre to centre. Pairs are irregularly spaced, 18, 16, 17, 14, 18 and 10mm apart. Leather extends c 45mm above this row. Extremely worn and almost completely delaminated. Maximum dimensions c 205 × 133mm.

This item is almost certainly related to the next item. Their function is not clear. The larger thong holes may represent repair, which might explain their irregular shape and spacing.

## L6. Two fragments with two rows of thong-holes? (SF20; A6046ay) (figure 40d)

Two irregularly shaped fragments, possibly originally one piece, each with a cut edge with traces of large, irregularly spaced thong holes next to it. These holes are now distorted but are approximately 7 × 7mm and 20–30mm apart. There is a second row of thong-holes, 20–40mm above the first. These consist of small, neat pairs of slits, which form tunnel holes. Slits are 3 × 2mm and are 5–6mm apart, with 7–11mm between pairs. Larger fragment has traces of a stitching channel, which could be either hemstitch or edge-flesh, at right angles to the cut edge. Short length of thong is still attached to smaller fragment. Leather extends c 60mm beyond this row. Both fragments and thong are worn, torn and delaminated. Dimensions: 130 × 95mm and 95 × 55mm; thong: 15 × 5mm.

The cut edges and the two distinct rows of thong-holes are very similar to those on no. 9. Possibly these are from a shoe, with the cut edges and the larger holes forming the top edge, and the lower row of slits holding a decorative thong. On the other hand, perhaps these are remnants of an item of clothing.

## L7. Fragment of shoe with slits for thong? (LG27) (figure 40b)

Irregularly shaped fragment, with one cut, slightly curved edge. Other edges torn. Parallel to cut edge, row of widely spaced slits. Slits are 9mm long, up to 2mm wide and 25–30mm apart, centre to centre. Possibly trace of row of holes almost at right angles with cut edge – remains of stitching? Very worn and delaminated. Surviving length c 145mm, width 83mm.

Possibly part of shoe with slits for thong and with sewn quarters seam.

## L8. Fragment of shoe with slits for thong? (SF193; A6046n) (figure 39e)

Rectangular fragment with three oval slits. Two long and one short cut edges, and one short torn edge. Parallel to short cut edge, row of three oval slits, 9 × 1mm, 7 × 1mm, 7.5 × 1mm. Worn and delaminated. Dimensions 116 × 26–30mm.

Probably part of shoe with slits for thong.

## L9. Two fragments of shoe with slits for thong? (SF30; A6046at) (figure 39d)

Two tiny fragments, each with two parallel rows of small slits. Slits are 3 × 1mm, and are 5mm apart, centre to centre. Rows are 15mm apart, centre to centre. Worn and partially delaminated.

Possibly part of a thonged shoe.

## L10. Clump sole? (LG27) (figure 39b)

Approximately oval fragment, with pairs of holes forming tunnels adjacent to perimeter, and with three fragments of thong in place. Holes are either round, diameter 2mm, or oval, 2 × 4mm, and are approximately 5–8mm apart; pairs are c 13mm apart. Edges adjacent to holes cut; one edge torn. Dimensions c 115 × 85 × 2mm.

Clump sole or repair patch, most probably for forepart.

## L11. Clump sole fragment (SF117) (figure 39c)

Fragment of clump sole, probably for seat. Pairs of holes forming tunnel holes for thong. Exceedingly worn and completely delaminated. Length 103mm, width 75mm.

## L12. Sheath (SF179) (figure 42a)

Folded fragment of leather, held together with thong threaded through pairs of slits, which form tunnel holes. Fragment has cut edges at top and down the side; bottom edge, which is narrower than top edge, is torn. Slits are 4 × 2.5mm, and are 5–9mm apart, with 7–15mm between pairs. Four fragments of thong survive; each is 5mm wide, lengths vary between 5 and 38mm. Fragment is worn and delaminated.

Length 137mm; width 34–45mm; width available for knife 25–30mm.

This is a sheath for a slender knife with a narrow blade. It is of very simple construction, with the leather folded only once, and with the two thicknesses fastened together with a thonged side seam

## L13. Belt (SF191; A6046) (figure 42d)

Approximately rectangular fragment, now in two pieces, with two long cut edges and with two torn short edges. There is a suggestion of stitching parallel to one long edge, but not penetrating through to the other side. In middle of fragment, seven slits, each c 10 × 2mm. No apparent pattern to slits. Dimensions c 70 × 38 × 2mm.

Possibly, fragment of belt, with slits for attachment of buckle or other fastening.

### L14. Knotted strap? (SF18) (figure 42e)

A narrow strip of leather, knotted through a slit in itself. Worn, torn and delaminated. Length 115mm; width 15–17mm.

Possibly part of a strap.

### L15. Fragment of clothing? (SF88) (figure 43)

Large piece of leather, now in two sections. Two straight cut edges at approximately 60 degree angle to each other. Other edges torn. Tiny holes and small impressions near cut edges might just conceivably be traces of stitching. Exceedingly worn, torn and delaminated.

Length 355mm; width 258mm; length of cut edges 190 and 145mm.

Possibly part of garment.

### L16. Circular fragment with toothed edge (SF162; A6046aq) (figure 42b)

Circular fragment with irregular toothed edge and with several small holes in centre. Diameter c 75mm; thickness c 2mm.

Possibly a washer.

### L17. Offcut? (SF197; A6046l) (figure 42f)

Approximately oval fragment, with cut outer edge and with round central hole. Torn at both ends, and with two other tears, as well as several small holes. Delaminated. Dimensions c 80 × 75mm.

### L18. Offcut (SF108; A6046p) (figure 42c)

Approximately rectangular fragment, with curved concave edge and with three straight edges, all cut. Worn and delaminated. Dimensions 68 × 77mm. Possibly waste from cutting out a sole – but wasteful.

## 4.9 THE HISTORY, CONSERVATION AND RE-INTERPRETATION OF SF105, THE SATCHEL

*Rob Lewis*

HISTORY

When SF105 was uncovered during the excavations at Loch Glashan, JGS recorded in the site notebook that

PLATE 24
The satchel, SF105, as it was displayed on the manikin. Left – back view; right – front view

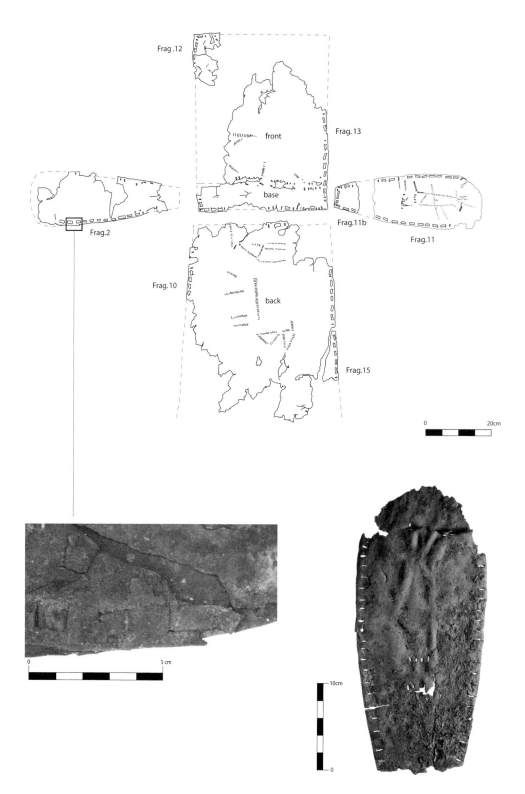

FIGURE 44

The components of the satchel were stitched using leather thonging inserted in and out of slits cut at right angles to the edge of the piece.

Top – shows an exploded layout of the satchel components; the sequence in which the thongs were inserted into the slits is shown.

Left – remains of the leather thong *in situ*. Note the cut end of the thong.

Right – Fragment 11, one of the side panels showing the slits around the edges and in the centre for the attachment of the strap. Note the creasing characteristic of a bag hung from its side strap.

'... the greater part of a leather jerkin ...' had been found. This interpretation of the collection of leather fragments that constituted SF105 was not questioned and after conservation they were accordingly mounted on a manikin and displayed as a garment for the next 40 years (plate 24). The chosen form of display helped to perpetuate the interpretation (for latest published reference see Alcock 2003), as did the manner in which the fragments had been mounted. Many of the smaller fragments were in 'floating' positions on the manikin, ie mounted several inches apart from where they would have joined, thus presenting an 'exploded' view of the artefact, as it were. Had the fragments been joined, the implausibly narrow waistline and cuffs, and overly high neckline would have been noted. Furthermore, there had been a great deal of selectivity about which fragments were mounted, only those fragments which had not delaminated (see below) being displayed on the manikin. Consequently, the second 'sleeve', which was more fragmentary, had been mounted separately in Perspex, leaving the object on the manikin more incomplete than it actually was and impeding re-interpretation.

JGS was himself perplexed by certain features of the object, in particular the row of lacing near the base of the front, and Matson (1998, 14), in her study of the leather assemblage, realized that it could not be a jerkin, but it was Dr Colleen Batey, Curator of Archaeology for Glasgow Museums 1990–2002, who raised the possibility that the fragments might constitute a bag of some sort rather than a jerkin. In order to re-examine the leather more closely and identify it objectively the fragments were removed from the manikin and all the fragments that comprised SF105 were re-treated so that they could be handled and recorded fully. A full report on the procedures and methodology employed can be found in Lewis (2003).

CONSERVATION

The leather fragments comprising SF105 had been treated with polyethylene glycol (PEG), a polymer of ethylene oxide, available in a range of chain lengths which afford a variety of physical properties. In current conservation, it is used primarily for the conservation of waterlogged wood, where the variety of chain lengths allows the treatment to match the condition of the wood. In its early use however, it was applied to a wider range of organic material, including leather. Though its use with leather would serve (and for highly degraded leather, still continues to serve) the most basic function of allowing the leather to be

removed from a waterlogged state without appreciable shrinkage, the resultant leather would be brittle, darkened, and unacceptably stiffened; the molecular weight of the PEG molecules likely to have been used do not permit the flexibility that is required of leather.

Although with the benefit of hindsight, the use of PEG was a poor choice, it has not been deleterious in terms of the general stability of the artefact. The leather was stiff, brittle, dark, and glossy but it has not obviously deteriorated greatly since treatment, although the inflexibility of the leather has caused some physical damage.

The fragments were mapped while on the manikin and then removed for closer examination. Once the re-interpretation of the fragments had been verified they were all re-treated so that they could be displayed in a different form, if required. One of the reasons PEG is used is its solubility in water, which means waterlogged material can be immersed straight into baths of PEG. The implication for the removal of the PEG is that it can be simply washed out, returning the fragments to a waterlogged state. With the PEG removed, a new bulking agent could be added which would be more sympathetic to the leather. The standard agent used in conservation is glycerol, which has similar properties to PEG in the bonds it forms, but is of a lower molecular weight. Glycerol treated material is far more flexible, as well as lighter in colour and weight. The treatment involves immersing the fragments in a bath of glycerol, after which the fragments are frozen – the glycerol at this stage acts to prevent damage to the leather from the formation of ice crystals. Once frozen, the ice is removed from the leather by freeze-drying, which causes sublimation, turning it directly from a solid to a gas – this avoids problems with surface tension that can occur with water leaving the leather as a liquid. Once the water is removed from the leather, the fragments are gently humidified, allowing them to attract a small amount of moisture. Organic materials do this naturally, to maintain equilibrium with their environment. The humidification of the leather allows the leather to return to its original shape, preserving more of the form which the artefact took during its use.

RE-INTERPRETATION

Each fragment was numbered and fully mapped; as well as the more obvious signs of manufacture, features such as wear marks and creases were recorded (figure 44). Worn leather retains a 'memory' of its original function,

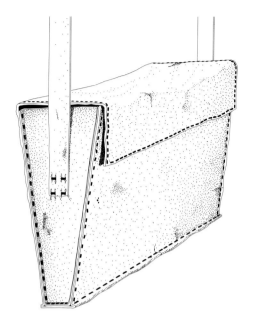

FIGURE 45
Reconstruction of the satchel

but because the fragments had been pressed against the mount, original creases were less clear, and new creases had been created based on the shape of the manikin. The fragments were then treated like jigsaw pieces until a position of best fit was found.

The double row of slots on Fragment 13 was first examined. A distinct crease is present running between the slots, with the slots themselves being almost exactly symmetrical on either side of this crease. The crease was clearly made by folding the leather and then cutting the slots just behind the newly-formed edge. A leather thong would then be passed through the slots, effectively making a right angle in the leather panel. This would have formed the base of the satchel.

It then became clear that the width of the straight 'base' of Fragment 11B was almost exactly equal to the width of the base as formed by the row of double slots on Fragment 13. Furthermore, the slots along each edge matched up exactly. Though the base of Fragment 2 was missing, it was considered a reasonable assumption that, since Fragment 2 was similar in shape to Fragment 11, it would also join Fragment 13 at its base.

Since it has already been established that Fragments 2 and 11 join the 'base' area of Fragment 13, it seemed probable that the long sides of Fragments 2 and 11 would then join the upright sides of Fragment 13. The most conclusive evidence for this came from the matching of the slots cut along the edges. Since each was

individually made, and the distance and positioning of them irregular, it was possible to match up the slots on the fragments where they joined. The order that resulted is laid out in figure 43 and is clearly a bag, or satchel, a reconstruction of which is presented in figure 44.

That Fragments 2 and 11 are indeed the side panels of a bag is confirmed by other features. Fragment 11 has a double row of slots at exactly the point where one would expect the strap attachment, the bottom row of which are torn and the leather in this area decayed. The leather is altogether missing from this area on Fragment 2. It is suggested that the repeated application of weight on this area would have worn the leather, accelerating the degradation, thus explaining the torn slots and the absent areas of leather. A heavy bag, hanging from a strap secured at these points on the side panels would have incurred these patterns of wear. Further support for this interpretation comes from the crease patterns on Fragment 11, which had vertical, concertina-style creases, consistent with carrying a heavy object, rather than the horizontal creases one might have expected on a sleeve (figure 44).

The components of the satchel were laid flesh-to-flesh and the seams secured by threading thongs of leather through slots cut at right angles to the edges. The wear marks on the leather record the sequence in which the seams were threaded; this is illustrated on figure 44, the rectangles indicating over-threading. There is some evidence that this threading was also used for decorative effect. On Fragment 12 it appears to run around a corner which can only have formed the edge of the flap or the edge of the front panel (as it is shown on figure 45). The threading appears to continue on up the sides of the back (see Fragment 10 and 15) beyond the point at which it would have been necessary to secure the back to the side panels. The threading along the front edge of the base is suggestive of a decorative effect, too. There is no evidence for the means of fastening but it is possible that the flap was secured by thongs attached to the threaded front edge. The strains that this would have caused at this point of attachment would have worn the leather and might explain why there are areas of leather missing along the double row of slots (figure 44).

The thong has survived *in situ* in only one place (figure 44) which is surprising in itself, given the overall survival of the leather. The end of the surviving fragment is sharp, as though it has been cut rather than frayed or worn. The strap attachments indicate that the satchel was very worn and it is possible that it had already been dismantled into its component parts so that the usable fragments could be recycled.

SUMMARY

Of the 21 fragments recovered as SF105 (Lewis 2003) only seven can be definitely ascribed a place within the reconstructed satchel (figure 44). A further two fragments have slots but no other diagnostic features which allow them to be placed. It is also possible that there are other unidentified components of the satchel within the leather assemblage.

SF105 can now be confidently described as a satchel but the nature of its contents is less easily ascertained. The satchel could, of course, have contained a multitude of objects but the care taken in creating a flat base and in shaping the tapering side panels suggest it was made with a specific object in mind. The likely Early Historic date of the context in which the satchel was found together with its shape raises the attractive possibility that it was intended for carrying books. The fore-edge of the book would have been inserted into the satchel first, with the spine then being at the top of the satchel, thus accounting for the tapered shape of the side panels. With this interpretation in mind, it is possible to suggest the maximum size of a book which could have been contained within a satchel of this size (measurements are taken from within the area bounded by the stitch holes, but a margin of error of at the very least 5mm should be allowed to account for other factors such as shrinkage of the leather);

Thickness of spine approx. 120mm
Thickness of fore-edge approx. 50mm
Width of book approx. 370mm
Height of book approx. 370mm

## 4.10 BOOK SATCHELS IN MEDIEVAL SCOTLAND AND IRELAND

*Bernard Meehan*

INTRODUCTION

The identification of a leather satchel in an Early Historic context at Loch Glashan has stimulated this summary of surviving comparanda and contemporary literary and visual references to their use. There is no doubt that the use of leather satchels for storing and carrying books was a widespread practice in medieval Scotland and Ireland. The major evidence of this comes from frequent references to book satchels in literary sources. The word normally used in medieval Irish for a book satchel or a carrying-case for relics was *tiag*, from the Latin *theca*. In Hiberno-Latin, the word used was *scetha*, from the Late Latin *scheda*, a loose

sheet of parchment, the expansion of the meaning to 'satchel' perhaps coming from the practice of wrapping a loose sheet of parchment around books to protect them (Sharpe 1985). Only four medieval book satchels are however known to survive from Ireland, in collections at Trinity College Library, Dublin, the National Museum of Ireland, and Corpus Christi College, Oxford. Unambiguous depictions of book satchels are uncommon. Five Pictish stones show clerics carrying satchels. There are only two images of book satchels in insular manuscripts – and these are by no means certain – and no unequivocal images on Irish high crosses. It is not clear whether the Loch Glashan satchel was made specifically to carry books. If it was, it is the earliest surviving example.

SURVIVING BOOK SATCHELS

Surviving medieval leather satchels are not common. Those associated specifically with books are particularly uncommon. The standard commentary (but not a wholly accurate one) is by Waterer (1986). He identified three:

1. The Book of Armagh satchel (Trinity College Dublin MS 52★★★; plate 25) probably best dated to the 15th century, and associated with the early 9th-century Book of Armagh (Ryan 1983, 178–9). This satchel, at $320 \times 290 \times 57$mm, is considerably bigger than the manuscript and was clearly intended originally for a different book or books.

2. The satchel (measuring around $190 \times 140 \times 57$mm) for a 12th-century Irish missal which retains its original binding (Corpus Christi College, Oxford, MS 282; plate 26).

3. The Breac Moedóc (National Museum of Ireland, P 1022), associated with St Moedóc of Ferns. This may have been used for books originally, but later it was used to hold a house-shaped reliquary which was too big for the satchel and caused it some damage. It measures $267 \times 222 \times c\ 80$mm (all measurements across the centre).

Single hides were used for the body and flap in both the Breac and Corpus satchels, with the gussets separate, while the Armagh satchel is made from a single skin throughout. All three satchels have carrying straps, and all have elaborately tooled decoration, though the Corpus satchel is now so heavily abraded that it is

PLATE 25
Book of Armagh satchel (15th century) is the largest and most decorated surviving book satchel.
For photographs and graphic reconstructions of patterns of decoration in the Armagh satchel and the Breac Moedóc, see Waterer (1968).
(*Reproduced courtesy of the Board of Trinity College Dublin*)

difficult to read the decoration with the naked eye. The Armagh satchel and the Breac Moedóc have both been dated recently to the 15th century (Hourihane 2003, 148–52). The resemblance of the decoration of the Corpus satchel to the Breac Moedóc should be noted in support of the view that it has a similar date.

To Waterer's examples should be added a large late 10th-century cowhide (?) leather satchel from Fishamble Street, Dublin, excavated in 1978 (National Museum of Ireland, Fishamble Street I, E141: 5213). This has been greatly deformed, and measures in the region of 500–600 × 300–400 × c 130mm. On the back, it has the tooled decoration of a cross with bifurcated arms, set within a tooled border, and as a consequence can be identified as a satchel for books or other ecclesiastical artefacts. The front of the satchel has a tooled border. A cross was identified on the front as well as the back (Wallace & Ó Floinn 1988 no 449), but this is no longer clear.

Other notable artefacts from the Dublin excavations include a leather fragment with a small stamped cross, perhaps from a book cover (NMI, Fishamble Street II, E172: 2748); a small leather bag with flap and side pocket found at High Street (NMI E71: 15581), dated to the late 12th century (Lucas 1973, 43); and a large leather container, like a kit bag in appearance, from Fishamble Street (NMI, E172: 1666), which may have been used to carry milk or water (Wallace & Ó Floinn 1988). Although so few book satchels have been identified, it is likely that there are other survivals from sites like Fishamble Street in a fragmentary or unrecognized form.

It was not uncommon for leather work in early medieval Ireland to be tooled. Examples include an early medieval leather bottle from Clooncose, Co Leitrim (NMI 1928: 12), and a decorated leather bottle from Ballymoney, Co Antrim (Ulster Museum 1919, 304: Raftery 1941, 151, pl 105/2).

The 7th-century text, the *Hisperica famina*, contains two references to book satchels. It instructs the monks to:

*Hang your white booksacks on the wall, / set your lovely satchels in a straight line, / so that they will be deemed a grand sight by the rustics.* (Herren 1974, 85)

It also describes the making of a book satchel:

*This white satchel gleams, / it has thick bristles that provide a rather small cover; / the aforesaid container is sewn in the shape of a square; / the upper rim surrounds a single opening, / which is closed by a tight covering with many-angled turning knobs, / then is bound by twelve cords, / and the curved load is born [sic] on the necks of the scholars. / I shall describe the excellent construction of this book satchel: / not long ago it protected the fattened flesh of a sheep; / a butcher flayed the hairy hide with a sharp knife; / it was stretched on the wall between thick stakes / and dried with fiery smoke. / A proud craftsman cut out the aforesaid container, / drew taut the skin covering with tight laces, / fashioned the four angles, / and finished the leather container with a choice strap.* (Herren 1974, 105–7; O'Neill 1997, 69–79, 78–9).

Several references to book satchels occur in saints' lives. Adomnán's Life of St Columba of Iona (c 521–97), written c 700, contains two accounts in which book satchels were ruined by water but those of their contents which had been written by St Columba remained intact because they were written by the saint (Sharpe 1995, 160–1).

The Life (9th century) of St Ciaran of Clonmacnoise (6th century) describes an incident in which a book satchel was dragged along the ground on the foot of a cow. While the satchel suffered as a result, the gospel book within it was found to be dry and white and undamaged, as though it had been kept on a bookshelf (Sharpe 1985; Reeves 1857, 116–17).

In a Homily on the life of St Columba from the Leabhar Breac (c 1394), it is said of St Columba that 'it was his wont to make crosses and satchels and wallets for books and all church equipment'. Columba is said to have blessed 'three hundred victorious crosses, three hundred wellsprings that were swift, an hundred booksatchels, with an hundred crosiers, with an hundred wallets' (Stokes 1877, 115).

References in, for example, the lives of St Comgall, or St Cainnech (died c 599), a contemporary of St Columba, suggest it was customary for an ecclesiastic to carry a book satchel. The life of St Ciaran indicates that the satchel was carried on the shoulder: 'accipiens cethas suas cum libris in humeris suis'. St Carthage of Lismore was said to have placed two satchels full of books on his shoulders: 'duas scethas libris plenas suis humeris imposuit', thus indicating that the satchel, like a modern-day schoolbag, was designed to carry more than one book. The *Vita S Kennechi* seems to refer to the flap of the satchel: 'expande et aperi cetham librorum nostrorum' (Sharpe 1985, 152–3; Reeves 1857, 116–17).

The Calendar of Oengus (c 800) provides an account of Longarad, a 'master of study and jurisprudence and history and poetry', who offended St Columba by hiding his extensive collection of books on an occasion when Columba visited. When Longarad died, 'the book satchels that were in the cell where Colum cille dwelt fall. All are silent at the noisy shaking of the books'. It was said in an allied text that all the book satchels of Ireland fell down on that night (Stokes 1905, 199).

In the Tripartite life of St Patrick (c 10th century), St Patrick encounters six Irish clerics heading to Rome on pilgrimage, with an equal number of their children, carrying codices hung on their belts. Seeing this, Patrick offered them a skin on which he had been in the habit of lying and standing in celebration of Mass for twelve years and suggested they use it to make a satchel for carrying books (Reeves 1857, 116–17).

The sarcophagus built in 1484 for the body of St Columbanus (died 615) in Bobbio in north Italy has five compartments showing incidents from his life. In the first compartment Columbanus is shown carrying a book satchel, according to Margaret Stokes (1892, 158). In her sketch, however, the object looks more like a purse than a satchel.

The use of book satchels was not unique to Ireland and Scotland. The 7th-8th-century Cuthbert [Stonyhurst] Gospel of St John, now held in the British Library, was kept at Durham cathedral in the 12th century in three bags of red leather (Raine 1835, 199). It was reported that the manuscript was hung around the neck of William Fitzherbert, Archbishop of York, as a special honour, when he came to inspect the tomb of St Cuthbert in the 1150s. William showed the manuscript to his household and hung it around their necks (*ibid*, 198). The wearing of sacred texts is paralleled in other cultures: the Judaic wearing of phylacteries (Deuteronomy 6.8) is one example (Brown 2003, 70).

A 19th-century sketch allows us to imagine how satchels might have been disposed around an Irish monastic cell. In 1837, Robert Curzon visited the half-ruined

Coptic monastery of Souriani, in a region north-west of Cairo (Curzon 1849, 94–8, and see plate 27). The monastery had given refuge to a group of 'Abyssinian eremites … [as] black as crows; tall, thin, ascetic looking men of a most original aspect and costume … Over their shoulders they had a strap supporting a case like a cartridge-box, of thick brown leather, containing a manuscript book'. In the company of an 'increasing number of these wild priests', Curzon was taken to the 'college or consistory' of the monks, which also served as their library. Beneath a wooden shelf, 'various long wooden pegs projected from the wall; they were each about a foot and a half long, and on them hung the Abyssinian manuscripts, of which this curious library was entirely composed'. Curzon described the manuscripts as 'enclosed in a case, tied up with leather thongs; to this case is attached a strap for the convenience of carrying the volume over the shoulders, and by these straps the books were hung to the wooden pegs, three or four to a peg, or more if the books were small: their usual size was that of a small, very thick quarto'. Similar, though unsophisticated and battered, examples of such Ethiopian manuscripts in satchels are in the collections of Trinity College Library, Dublin (TCD MSS 10597, 10729).

Three of the beehive huts on Skellig Michael, Co Kerry (cells 'A', 'E' and 'F'; plate 28) have projections on the exterior which extend into the interior and may have served similarly as pegs for hanging book satchels (de Paor 1955, 185; Henry 1957, 124).

It is difficult to be certain whether an object which is represented as suspended around a neck is a satchel, a reliquary, a book shrine or a rational (an item of episcopal dress). In the field of insular manuscripts, only one book satchel was identified in a recent iconographic survey (Ohlgren 1986, 44). This manuscript, the Cadmug Gospels (Fulda, Landesbibliothek MS Bonifatianus 3), was written in Ireland, or by Irish monks on the Continent, in the 8th century (second half). The evangelists are shown with a bifurcated rod

PLATE 26
Corpus Christi College, Oxford, MS 282, with its satchel. In a photograph in Buckley (1915) the tooled decoration is visible to a greater extent than it is in the present day. The extent to which the tooling has disappeared from view since this photograph was taken is remarkable

in their right hands and what may be a book satchel with a flap – though without a carrying strap – in their left (Braunfels 1968; plate 29). This identification is not certain, as the 'satchel' might just as easily be identified, in the conventional way, as a gospel book. Such an identification is made by Alexander (1978, 228). On folios 1v and 85v of the 9th- or 10th-century Book of Deer (Cambridge University Library Ii.6.32), probably from Scotland, evangelist figures carry objects on straps around their necks. Their frontal positioning suggests that they are probably not satchels (ibid, 70; but see Marner 2002, 3).

There appear to be five examples of book satchels in Pictish stone art:

1. A cross at Meigle Museum, Perthshire, shows an ecclesiastic carrying a book satchel. Set within crosses, the image is clearly Christian (Stuart 1867, pl VII), and can be dated 8th–9th century.

2. St Vigeans, Angus, stone 07: cross with two ecclesiastics, one of them carrying a book satchel (Allen 1903, fig 278).

3. NMS, Edinburgh, IB 46. Cross-slab from Papil, Isle of Burra, Shetland. This shows four monks, two of them carrying book satchels (plate 30). Papil may have been an important Columban site (Allen 1903, figs 6–9).

4. NMS, Edinburgh, IB 109. Cross from Culbinsgarth, Isle of Bressay, Shetland. Both faces of the cross feature facing pairs of ecclesiastics with crosiers and book satchels (Allen 1903, figs 4, 4A).

5. The Papil shrine panel, discovered in 1943. Here, three figures with croziers process towards a high cross; a fourth figure is on horseback; while the final figure carries a satchel in addition to a crozier (Moar & Stewart 1944).

On these stones, the satchel seems clearly to identify the figure carrying it as an ecclesiastic. In the case of 2, 3 and 5, Isabel Henderson has pointed out that the satchel is with the figure to the rear, who thus seems to be denoted as 'a designated bearer of the text' (*pers comm*). This leads to a possible reinterpretation of a relatively common Pictish symbol, the horizontal rectangle, which appears in 17 instances on Pictish stones (Mack 1997, 13). They mostly have the appearance of containers with flaps, as Charles Thomas (1963) has pointed out. While they might denote writing tablets, it is possible, given their general resemblance to the objects carried by the evangelists in the Cadmug gospels, that they represent satchels and so perhaps indicate the presence of ecclesiastics.

INTERIOR OF THE ABYSSINIAN LIBRARY, IN THE MONASTERY OF SOURIANI, ON THE NATRON LAKES.

| Abyssinian monk clothed in leather. | The dining table. | The blind abbot leaning over the author. | Abyssinian monk. | Coptic monk. | The books hanging from wooden pegs let into the wall. | The Author's Egyptian servants. |

PLATE 27
Book satchels hang from pegs in the library of the Coptic monks of Souriani, as depicted in Curzon (1849).
(*Reproduced courtesy of the Board of Trinity College Dublin*)

PLATE 28

Skellig Michael, Co Kerry, beehive hut, cell E interior, with modern camera case. Projections within cells A, E and F may have been used for hanging book satchels. (*Reproduced courtesy of Michael Ryan, Grellan Rourke and Dúchas*)

There appears to be no unequivocal depiction of a book satchel on Irish high crosses. On the south base of the north cross at Ahenny, Co Tipperary, the figure to the rear of a funeral procession seems to be carrying a satchel (Harbison 1992, 12 and fig 11). This figure may perhaps be compared to those on the Pictish stones noted above. It has been suggested that the figure to the right of the cross at Carndonagh, Co Donegal, carries a book satchel suspended from his shoulder (Mullarkey 2000, 58; Harbison 1992, fig 87). The objects hanging from the neck of Christ on the east face of the cross at Kilfenora, Co Clare (Harbison 1992, 116, fig 375), or on the west face of 'St Patrick's cross' at Cashel, Co Tipperary, are more enigmatic (*ibid*, 35, fig 905). On Muiredach's cross at Monasterboice, Co Louth, David has a bag for stones over his shoulder (*ibid*, 140, fig 738). On the east face of the Cross of the Scriptures at Clonmacnoise, a travel bag can be seen on the back of a figure on the east face (*ibid*, 49, 133). The satchel carried by Zacharias on his back on the south side shaft of the Tall Cross at Monasterboice seems to be the closest in shape to surviving book satchels, though the stone is greatly eroded (*ibid*, 149, fig 492).

Examples of the sculptural depiction of leather bags occur in the later Middle Ages. For example, a tomb at Jerpoint, Co Kilkenny, of an Irish layman, Thomas, dated to the first half of the 14th century, shows a figure with a 'large rectangular bag or wallet' over one shoulder (Hunt 1974, pl 52).

Among other small metalwork figures on the ferrule of the Lismore Crozier (National Museum of Ireland L.1949:1), which was made c 1100, is one figure who carries a book satchel or reliquary (Mullarkey 2000, 59–60).

THE LOCH GLASHAN SATCHEL

The recent history of the satchel is presented in Chapter 4.9. Its interpretation as a satchel was verified after examination by this author. The satchel was very worn and had clearly had a long use life. It may already have been dismantled into its component parts ready for re-cycling as scrap. The deposits in which the satchel was found have produced evidence of episodic activity from the 2nd–4th centuries AD to the 9th century AD and the satchel, or rather its dismantling, could have been associated with any one of the episodes (Chapter

PLATE 29
Cadmug Gospels, 8th century. See colour frontispiece.

6.1). This makes it by far the earliest surviving insular satchel. Whether it was used specifically for books is not known, for the purpose of a satchel will always be difficult to verify unless it is possible to peer inside and view the contents. However, the overall design of the bag argues for its use for carrying a bound codex or codices, spine uppermost. As a medium for the transmission of the Christian message, the codex had a widespread popularity from the 4th century. In the context of Argyll, it is likely that the first codices in the area followed Columba's foundation of monasteries

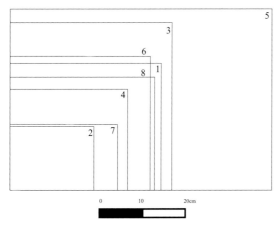

0        10        20cm

1. Armagh satchel
2. Corpus satchel
3. Loch Glashan satchel
4. Breac Moedoc

5. Fishamble Street satchel
6. Lough Kinale book shrine
7. Book of Durrow ( leaves)
8. Book of Kells (leaves)

FIGURE 46
Sizes of other satchels, book shrines and book leaves, in comparison
with the Loch Glashan satchel

on 'Hinba' (perhaps Canna) and on Iona after c 561 (Meehan 1994b, 90).

The absence of tooled decoration is inconsistent with surviving satchels, though consistent with Pictish representations of satchels, none of which is decorated. Lewis (infra) has suggested that the thonging around the edges of the base and flaps was a form of embellishment.

The Loch Glashan satchel is a large container, larger than both the Breac Moedóc and the Armagh satchel (figure 46). Its internal dimensions (around $370 \times 370 \times 50$–$120$mm) would make it an unusual shape for a single book, but it was not unusual for more than one book to have been carried. Its almost square shape (though it may have changed to some extent due to weathering) accords with the description of book satchels in the *Hisperica famina*: 'sewn in the shape of a square' (Herren 1974, 105). It may be noted, though whimsically, that the Book of Kells (TCD MS 58), whose leaves now measure around $330 \times 250$mm in their trimmed state, is one surviving book which could have fitted into it with a reasonable degree of comfort.

If the Loch Glashan satchel had an ecclesiastical function, it might equally have been as a container for a reliquary or a book shrine. It was not uncommon for shrines and reliquaries, as well as books, to be placed in leather satchels. Examples include the 15th-century satchel, with a St Andrew's cross stitched on to it, for the 10th- and 15th-century Corp Naomh bell shrine, from Templecross, Co Westmeath (NMI 1887: 145). The 8th-century Lough Kinale shrine (NMI 1986: 141), probably made for a book, has external dimensions of $345 \times 280 \times 110$mm, and internal dimensions of $335 \times 225 \times 96$mm (Kelly 1994). A shrine of this size could have fitted into the Loch Glashan satchel.

## 4.11   THE QUERNS

*Ann Clarke*

INTRODUCTION

As described in Chapter 1, all of the querns discussed below, with one exception, were removed from the crannog prior to the excavation. In 1977, Stuart Dobbin, an undergraduate at Glasgow University reported on the quern assemblage for his undergraduate dissertation and catalogued 18 stones, labelling them LGQ1–18 (Dobbin 1977). However, investigation of the site archive as part of the publication project revealed that there were another three stones which

Table 1    Characteristics of the rotary querns from Loch Glashan. All measurements in mm.

| LGQ | Upper | Lower | Breakage | MD | MTh | DCH | DHH | Rind slot | Dim RS |
|-----|-------|-------|----------|-----|-----|-----|-----|-----------|--------|
| 1 | | ★ | AC | 445 | 26 | 20 | | | |
| 2 | ★ | | AC | 410 | 37 | 58 | 9–20 | | |
| 3 | ★ | | AC | 365 | 55 | 70 | 8–23 | ★ | 25 × 25 × 15 |
| 5 | ★ | | HS | 600 | 86 | 100 | | ★ | 60 × 35 × 18 |
| 6 | | ★ | F | 480 | 33 | 50 | | | |
| 7 | ★ | | F | | 70 | | 18 × 18 | | |
| 8 | ★ | | F | 400 | 87 | | | | |
| 9 | ★ | | F | 370 | 102 | | | | |
| 10 | ★ | | F | | | 65 | | ★ | 44 × 25 × 14 |
| 11 | ★ | | F | 560 | 70 | 65 | | ★ | |
| 12 | ★ | | F | 720 | 75 | | | | |
| 14 | | ★ | F | | 46 | | | | |
| 16 | ★ | | F | 550 | 33 | | 15 | | |
| 19 | ★ | | C | 460 | 30 | 68 | ★ | ★ | 28 × 20 × 8 |
| 20 | | ★ | C | 494 | 56 | 15 | | | |

KEY: Breakage AC almost complete; HS half surviving; F fragment; C complete MD maximum diameter; Mth maximum thickness; DCH diameter of central hole; DHH diameter of handle hole; Dim RS dimensions of rind slots

Dobbin had not seen and these have subsequently been catalogued as LGQ19-21. The only quern found during the excavations was given a find number, SF39 but it is referred to throughout the text by the catalogue number ascribed by Dobbin, LGQ2.

The present study has determined that, of the 21 possible quern stones retrieved from the crannog only 16 can be described as such. These are all rotary quern stones and consist of four lower stones and 12 upper stones. A further three stones (LGQ4, LGQ17 and LGQ21) have different characteristics to the rotary querns but may also have been used for grinding and are discussed separately below. The remaining two items in the assemblage may never have had any specific function.

RAW MATERIAL AND CONDITION

The geological identifications were undertaken by Dobbin (1977) and Alistair Gunning, of Glasgow Museums. All of the querns have been made from the metamorphic rocks that are local to the area including epidioritic hornblende schists, mica-schist, phyllite and schistose grit. The largest quern, LGQ5, is made of felsite, which outcrops as an igneous intrusion just 4km to the north-east of the site (Dobbin 1977).

Three querns, two upper stones and one lower stone are complete, though two of these, LGQ19 and LGQ20,

a probable pair (see below) are damaged along an edge (figure 47 and see plate 32). A further three querns are almost complete though one, LGQ 1, is made from conjoining fragments whose staining patterns indicate that the quern must have been broken in antiquity (see below). Fragments, some with evidence for rind slots and handle holes, represent the rest of the querns.

THE ROTARY QUERNS

These are all disc querns and their characteristics are summarized in table 1. The four lower stones are all thin discs, three of which retain a small central hole that has been perforated all the way through (figure 51) allowing the spindle to be adjusted from below to alter the space between upper and lower stone.

The features of the upper stones are described individually below.

*Handle holes*

LGQ2, LGQ3 and LGQ16 have upright handle holes worn through to the base, which are conical in cross-section and made about 20mm in from the edge (figures 48 and 50b). LGQ2 and LGQ3 have crescentic notches on their perimeter, indicating the position of earlier handle holes since removed by wear and breakage. These two querns are some of the smallest in the assemblage (table 1) but the broken handle holes indicate that they

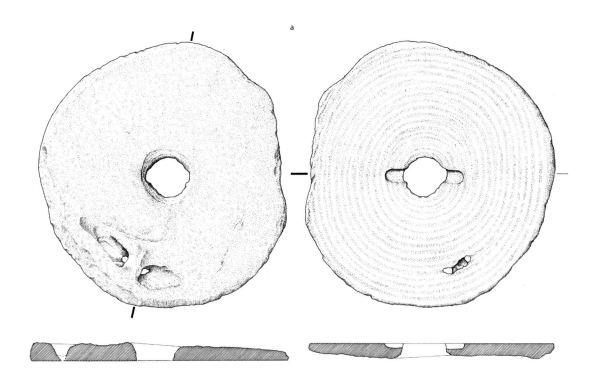

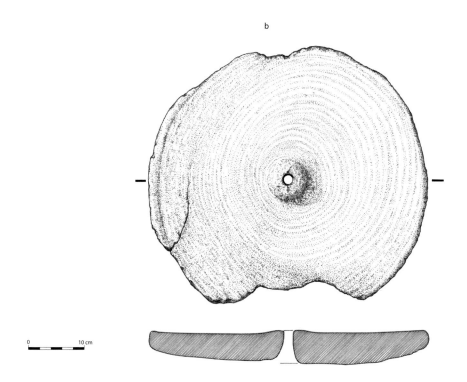

FIGURE 47
a) upper quernstone LGQ19; b) lower quernstone LGQ20

must have been at least 20mm-30mm larger in diameter when first made. The handle has more leverage the further it is from the centre of the quern but this makes the handle holes particularly vulnerable to breakage.

A fourth quern, LGQ7 (figure 50c), has a square upright handle hole worked 30mm from the edge.

The handle hole on LGQ19 is significantly different to the others in the assemblage (figure 47a). A tangentially-aligned, V-shaped channel has been cut in from the upper surface of the quern leaving two holes some 32mm apart on the surface. There are what appear to be erosion hollows stretching out behind each of the holes. As the base of the quern has worn down the base of the V has eventually been worn away and the channel has broken through to the base of the quern revealing a sharp-edged groove between the holes. The design of this handle hole immediately suggests the use of a cord looped through the channel but it is difficult to see how such an arrangement could provide a very effective handle for spinning the quern. The battering to knuckles would have been wearisome and the wear on the cord in the channel would have meant frequent replacement. There must surely have been some other arrangement, such as a metal frame in the channel supporting a rigid upright handle above (Adam Welfare *pers comm*).

*Rind slots*
Rind slots are present on five querns, LGQ3 (figure 48b), LGQ5 (figure 49a), LGQ10 (figure 50d), LGQ11 (figure 50a), and LGQ19 (figure 47a). They occur in opposing pairs and usually have a rectangular cross-section, although the one on LGQ10 is concave in cross-section. The two rind slots on LGQ5 lie at right angles to each other indicating that four rind slots were originally made on this quern. One pair may have been cut to replace the other but as this is a particularly deep quern it is possible that the extra rind slots were needed for a wider spindle on which to balance the upper stone.

Since many of the querns are fragments it is not possible to determine whether they all originally had rind slots but LGQ2, which is virtually complete, has no rind slots indicating that not all the upper stones were spun in this manner.

*Central hole*
The diameter of the central hole would appear to be related to the presence of rinds, since there needs to be room for the grain to pass between the rinds to the working surface below. The five Loch Glashan querns with rind slots have central holes of 65mm–100mm in diameter whilst LGQ2, the only complete quern with

no rind slots has a smaller central hole with a diameter of just 55mm.

LGQ3 and LGQ5 have slightly raised collars around their central holes which may have been non functional. Iron staining is present on the upper face of LGQ3 forming two regular circles 120mm and 130mm in diameter concentric with the collar and central hole (plate 31). It is possible that this staining represents the remains of a detachable hopper, either made of metal or, more likely, of wood or leather which would have trapped iron residue from the water and soil whilst it decayed (Mandy Clydesdale *pers comm*).

*Context and deposition*
As described in Chapter 1, all but one of the querns were collected from the surface of the crannog prior to the excavation. Their findspots are not recorded but it is assumed that they were collected from amongst the horizon of large stones which covered the crannog. LGQ2 was found with the bulk of the artefacts, in the brushwood layer in amongst the piling (plate 13 and figure 33). Many of the querns are just fragments. The staining on alternate faces of the fragments which comprise LGQ1 indicates that it was broken and redeposited in antiquity. Either it was thrown down and broken immediately or post-depositional processes have tumbled the fragments.

It is not known whether LGQ19 and LGQ20 were found as a pair but they fit together very snugly (plate 32) and they have both sustained similar damage along part of the circumference (figure 47) suggesting that were together when this damage was caused. This implies that the quern was still in use up to the point of abandonment or at the very least, that the whole quern had been stored, stones together, in a safe place.

*Condition*
As well as the fragmentation of much of the assemblage there are features which indicate that this was a collection of well-used querns which may have been at the end of their useful life. The thinness of many of the stones, the relict handle holes on the edges of LGQ2 and LGQ3 and the fact that all handle holes had worn through to the base of the stone are all indicative of heavy wear-and-tear. Only one quern, LGQ5, does not appear to have been used, its base still rough and displaying the peck marking used to shape it (figure 49a). However, this quern also displays rind slots at right angles to each other, a feature which often signifies re-cutting of the rinds because they have worn down (Adam Welfare *pers comm*). It is possible

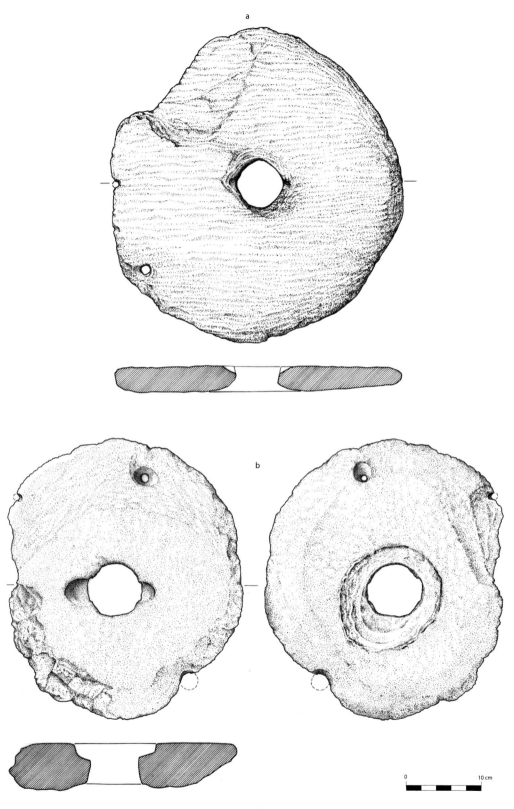

FIGURE 48
Upper quernstones; a) LGQ2; b) LGQ3

Table 2   Comparison of quern diameters between Dunadd and Loch Glashan

| Diam mm | 0–50 | 50–100 | 100–150 | 150–200 | 200–250 | 250–300 | 300–350 | 350–400 | 400–450 | 450–500 | 500–550 | 550–600 | 600–650 | 650–700 | 700–750 |
|---|---|---|---|---|---|---|---|---|---|---|---|---|---|---|---|
| Dunadd | | | x | | | | xxxx | xx | xxxx xxxx | | | | | | |
| Loch Glashan | | | | | | | | xx | xxx | xx | xx | x | x | | x |
| Querns with collars and/or concentric grooves | | | | | | | | E | B S S | P D | | | L | | |

KEY: E Edinburgh Castle; B Bayanne; S Scalloway; L Loch Glashan; P Pool, D Dunadd

that this was a used quern which had just been re-surfaced but the lack of a worn surface, together with its thickness, suggests that this quern has never been used for grinding.

It is possible that it broke during manufacture as several veins run through this stone which would have caused inherent weakness in the quern.

PLATE 31
Quern LGQ3 showing the concentric circles of iron staining around the central hole on the upper surface.
(*Reproduced courtesy of Glasgow Museums: Kelvingrove Art Gallery and Museum*)

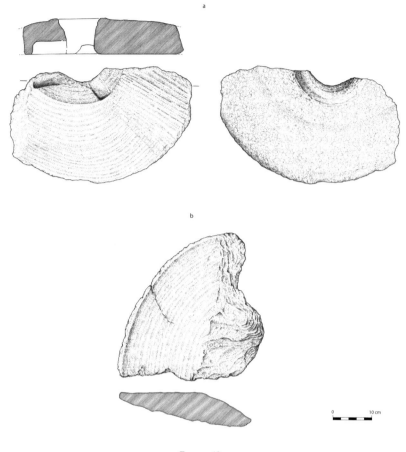

FIGURE 49
Upper quernstones; a) LGQ5; b) LGQ12

*A shield former?*

LGQ5 differs from the other querns in the assemblage in several respects; at 600mm in diameter it is one of the largest present (figure 49a); it is the only one to have been made from felsite, a stone which had to be brought some distance to the site; and it displays little evidence of wear (but see above). JGS was not convinced that it was a quern and pursued alternative theories for its function (see site archive). He suggested that it may have been used as a former in the preparation of the outer leather skins for wooden fist shields and that it was mounted, exactly like a quernstone, on a spike embedded in a wooden block pivoting on a cross-piece (rind) resting on the spike and raised or lowered at will. Thus a skin could be worked on the former, which could be spun around as necessary. It seems unlikely that a large central hole and the raised collar would have been necessary on a leather former and furthermore, it would have been less time-consuming to make a wooden former. However, it remains an interesting idea in view of the other evidence for leatherworking on the crannog (Chapter 4.8).

OTHER POSSIBLE GRINDING STONES

Three of the stone objects collected from the crannog surface may have had a grinding function but are not rotary querns. They are discussed here.

LGQ4 and LGQ17 (figure 52) are both fragments which has made it difficult to assess their original function. LGQ4 has a much larger central hole (150mm-170mm diameter) than is commonly found on rotary querns and, moreover, it is funnel-shaped (though since the top surface has sheared off this is not a firm observation). The surviving face has been pecked flat to a rough finish and there is no smoothing wear on this face; instead there is a polish around the edge of the central hole. LGQ17 has no central hole surviving but the upper face, which has been pecked to shape has a shallow slope leading down to, presumably, the centre of the piece. No function can be ascertained for either of these pieces and there are no known parallels from other Early Historic sites.

LGQ21 is a large slab of quartzose grit which was found in several fragments (figure 53). The conjoining pieces most likely make up the bulk of the original slab, which is 820mm in length and about 380mm wide. It has been shaped to form an upper working face which slopes downwards from an outer edge some 100mm high to the lower edge just 25mm in thickness. The outer edge is broadly curved in plan and forms a lip to the smooth, concavely worn face that is worn to an offshoot at the lower edge. One of the fragments has a very smoothly worn face but the conjoining pieces, though shaped, are rougher in feel. This could mean that the slab was broken in antiquity and one of the fragments re-used. However, if this were the case then one would expect the outer edges to be more worn than they are when in fact the breakage still looks rather fresh. Alternatively, the slab may have broken and the various fragments subjected to depositional processes that differentially affected the surface.

The function of this item remains obscure. JGS thought that it might be a hearthstone or a very large lower quernstone though the latter is unlikely given its sub-rectangular form and wear traces. Given the smooth concave face that has been worn on the surface it seems most likely that it was used for grinding or rubbing. It would appear likely that the worker knelt over the slab from the higher side and worked downwards and outwards towards the lower edge. In this respect it is similar to a saddle quern though it is rather large for such a piece. Another possible use might be as a washing stone with the downward slope taking away the excess water.

DISCUSSION

Rotary querns have a long history of use being introduced into Britain round about 3rd to 4th centuries BC and developing through the centuries from the smaller bee-hive and bun-shaped forms through to the bigger and flatter disc rotary querns of the brochs and later Iron Age (MacKie 1987, 7). The use of disc querns continued in Scotland up to, and beyond the Industrial Revolution and on the Atlantic fringes of Scotland, disc querns were even used within living memory (Curwen 1937; MacKie 1987, 5). The shape of the rotary quern and the various morphological developments in handle holes and mechanisms for the adjustment of the amount of grinding space have undergone considerable changes throughout this time and the technical details are well summarized by Curwen (1937; 1941) and MacKie (1987, 7). However, despite the visible changes in quern technology and their potential for dating, there are three main problems that beset their use as chronological indicators. The first is that many querns, both rotary and saddle types are found in secondary contexts, often re-used, or deliberately incorporated, as building materials in floors and walls. For instance, at Aldclune the rotary querns were placed in the floors of the Iron Age round houses (Hingley *et al* 1997). Their incorporation in structures means that the secondary deposits can provide at most a *terminus post quem* for their use on site. Secondly, the querns are often found as fragments, many of which do not bear those characteristics which are most useful for identifying the technological level of the quern, ie rind slots or handle holes.

Finally, the study of the chronology of rotary querns has to a certain extent become frozen by the concentration of the debate over the introduction of disc querns and the development of brochs (Armit 1991, 190). However, almost a thousand years passed between their introduction in Scotland and their use at Loch Glashan and with more recent excavations of later Iron Age and Early Historic structures, elements of quern style and period of use can now be explored (table 2).

At Pool, Orkney there are at least seven rotary querns from Iron Age and later phases but the only rotary quern with evidence for a rind slot was found in a 7th-century AD context (Clarke forthcoming a). At 595mm in diameter it is as large as, though thinner, than LGQ5. A distinctive feature of LGQ5 is the raised collar around the central hole. Disc querns with collars are dated to the 6th century AD at Pool (Clarke forthcoming a) whilst collared querns with additional encircling grooves are dated to 650–900 AD at Scalloway (Sharples 1998) and at Bayanne, Shetland (Clarke forthcoming b). However, collars are not always indicators of a later date; a bun-shaped quern from an earlier Iron Age phase at Edinburgh Castle also had a collar (Clarke 1997).

Upright handle holes are traditionally used on disc querns but occasionally other methods of spinning the quern have been used. At Dunadd an 'elbow-shaped' perforation was made on the side of the cross-marked quern, which was described as an early medieval feature (Campbell 1987). Another quern from Dunadd had a protruding knob on the perimeter of the upper stone which may have been turned with the use of a cord (Lane & Campbell 2000). These examples suggest that experimentation with methods of spinning the quern was not uncommon in the Early Historic period and it is, perhaps in this context that the V-shaped handle hole on LGQ19 should be viewed. Unfortunately, the rarity of these handle hole variations makes them unreliable as chronological indicators.

MacKie has noted that querns that were in use in Scotland up to the present day were about 450mm–600mm in diameter and that the lower stone was completely perforated to make it adjustable (MacKie 1987, 5). The querns from Loch Glashan have a similar size range to these modern querns (table 2; it should be remembered here that two of the smaller querns would originally have been at least 20–30mm larger in diameter making most of the querns over 400mm in diameter) and the three lower stones are completely perforated. For comparison, none of the querns from Dunadd exceed 500mm in diameter (table 2).

On size alone then, there is a case to be made that the Loch Glashan querns are of a later date than most of the Dunadd querns. There are a number of other features on the Loch Glashan querns that also support a later, medieval date for the querns. The square hole on LGQ7, the V-shaped handle hole on LGQ19, and the evidence for a hopper on LGQ3 are all indicators of increasingly sophisticated design, and suggest that the querns are typologically late in the development of quern technology (Adam Welfare *pers comm.*).

This proposed chronology would mean that the actual form of the rotary quern remained very similar for as much as a millennium. This conservatism in quern style could be compared to the blackhouse pottery, which is found on similar settlements and also remained unchanged over the centuries, consequently making it chronologically undiagnostic (MacSween *pers comm*).

*Taphonomy and deposition*

The taphonomy of the querns is of considerable interest. With one exception, they were all found in and amongst the stones covering the surface of the crannog (Chapter 1). One argument put forward in Chapter 3.5 was that they were part of a conflation deposit of settlement debris, implying that the querns had been used throughout the occupation of the crannog. While this remains a viable explanation there is another possible explanation for this concentration of querns. The use of the hand mill was outlawed in 1284 AD in order to force tenant farmers to bring their grain to the water-powered mills then being built by local lairds, who could then charge for the milling (MacKie 2002, 91). It is possible that the querns were dumped on the by-then abandoned crannog to prevent their use. Lane & Campbell (2000, 237) have proposed a similar explanation for the large numbers of querns found at Dunadd, although they suggest that the querns may have been seized to enforce the use of an earlier innovation, horizontal water-mills. Thus, the presence of the querns at Loch Glashan may not necessarily reflect the agricultural activities of its inhabitants.

PLATE 32
Querns LGQ19 and LGQ20 assembled together for display. Also included in the display are, clockwise from left, wooden artefacts SF55, SF121 and SF119.
(© *Crown copyright: RCAHMS Jack Scott collection*)

## CATALOGUE OF ILLUSTRATED ARTEFACTS

Numbers in brackets are Kelvingrove accession numbers.

### LGQ1 (A6046fe) (figure 51a)

Lower stone of disc quern. Green micaceous schist. Three fragments form an almost complete stone. Iron pan staining is present on one face of each fragment, but it is on the reverse side of the large piece suggesting that the quern must have been broken, or at least disturbed prior to final deposition.

The worked face is worn smooth to a concave cross-section and is raised to a shallow cone-shape around the central hole that is fully perforated and funnel-shaped.

D quern c 445mm
T at central hole 26mm
T at perimeter 21mm
D central hole 20mm

### LGQ2 (A6046ga) (also SF39) (figure 48a)

Upper stone of thin disc quern. Micaceous phyllite. Almost complete with central hole and handle hole surviving. The worked face is pecked to roughen and then worn to a slightly concave cross-section. The handle hole is upright and conical in section and fully perforated and made 20mm from the perimeter of the quern. A previous, but broken, handle hole is evident as a notch on the quern's perimeter.

D quern 410mm
MT 37mm
D central hole 58mm
D handle hole 20mm top and 9mm bottom

### LGQ3 (A6046fd) (figure 48b)

Upper stone of disc quern. Schistose grit. Almost complete with central hole and handle hole surviving. The base is worn very smooth, particularly towards the outer edge. A pair of rind slots has been pecked onto the base. The handle hole is conical in section and fully perforated and made 21mm from the quern's perimeter. Two previous, but broken handle holes are evident as notches on the quern's perimeter. Two circles of iron staining are concentric with the central hole on the upper face and this may be the remains of a hopper made either of iron or, more likely an organic material such as leather that has caused iron pan formation during deposition.

D quern 365mm
MT 55mm
D central hole 70mm
D handle hole 23mm top and 8mm top
D iron stains 120mm–130mm
Rind slots 25mm long, 25mm wide, 15mm deep

### LGQ4 (A6046fg) (figure 52)

Fragment of green epidioritic schist. Part of one face survives but it looks as if the opposite face has sheared off. The surviving face is pecked flat but it is rough and this may mean that it has not been used as a quern or else it has been weathered. However, there is a 'polish' around the central hole here, which the putative weathering has clearly not destroyed so the rough base is most likely an original feature. The central hole is much larger than other disc querns and a different shape, being wider at the surviving face than the top. Taking into account, the lack of a worn face, the 'polish' around the central hole and the wide 'funnel neck' then this

101

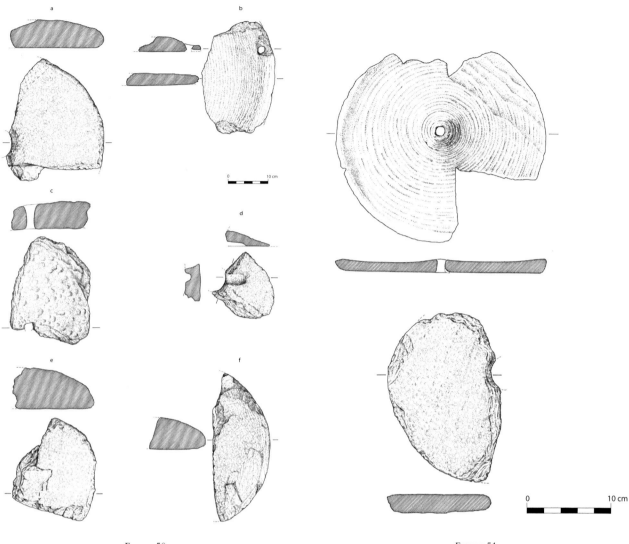

FIGURE 50
Fragments of upper quernstones: a) LGQ11; b) LGQ16; c) LGQ7;
d) LGQ10; e) LGQ9; f) LGQ8

FIGURE 51
Lower quernstones: top – LGQ1; bottom – LGQ6

does not conform to the characteristics of a disc quern and may be a larger millstone.

No measurements because of breakage but minimum thickness is 70mm

D central hole top 170mm and bottom 150mm

**LGQ5 (A6046fl) (figure 49a)**

Upper stone of disc quern. Felsite. Broken down length truncating central hole. The base has been pecked flat but the surface remains rough. Remains of two rind slots are made at right angles to each other implying that there were another two that originally formed a cross. On the upper face there is a raised collar formed around the central hole. The evidence of the rough base would indicate that this quern had not been used. Perhaps the piece had broken in manufacture or first

use since veins of quartz run through the rock, which would cause lines of inherent weakness.

D quern c 600mm
MT 86mm
D central hole 100mm
Rind slots 60mm long, 35mm wide, 18mm deep

**LGQ6 (A6046ff) (figure 51)**

Lower stone of disc quern. Epidioritic schist. Fragment, truncating central hole. The upper worn face is concave in section and is raised around the central hole, which is completely perforated.

D quern c 480mm
D central hole c 50mm
MT 33mm

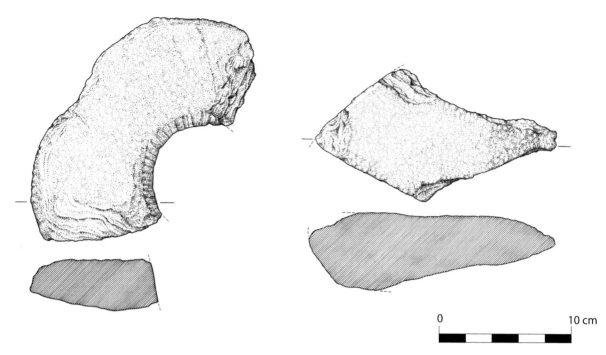

FIGURE 52
Possible millstone fragments: top – LGQ4; bottom – LGQ17

### LGQ7 (A6046ex) (figure 50c)

Upper stone of disc quern. Green schist. Fragment of edge survives with truncated handle hole. Worked base is pecked and roughened with slightly concave cross-section. The upright handle hole is square in plan and made 30mm in from the quern perimeter.

No measurements because of breakage (though Dobbins estimates diameter to be c 600mm)

MT 70mm
Handle hole 19mm wide

### LGQ8 (A6046fa) (figure 50f)

Upper stone of disc quern. Green micaceous schist. Fragment of edge surviving. Base is flat and pecked to roughen it.

D c 400mm
MT 87mm

### LGQ9 (A6046ew) (figure 50e)

Upper stone of disc quern. Epidioritic hornblende schist. Fragment of edge survives. Base flat and worn smooth.
D quern c 370mm
MT 102mm

### LGQ10 (A6046fc) (figure 50d)

Upper stone of disc quern. Green schist. Fragment truncating central hole. Base is flat with a pecked surface. A rind slot survives which is concave in cross-section.

No measurements for diameter or thickness because of breakage

D central hole c 65mm
Rind slot 44mm long, 25mm wide and 14mm deep

### LG11 (A6046ey) (figure 50a)

Upper stone of disc quern. Schistose grit. Fragment truncating central hole. The base has been pecked then worn flat and smooth, particularly around the outer edge. There is a rind slot truncated by breakage.

D quern c 560mm
MT 70mm
D central hole c 65mm

### LGQ12 (A6046gb) (figure 49b)

Disc quern. Epidioritic schist. Fragment with no handle hole or central hole surviving, but probable upper stone. The worn face has been pecked to roughen and shape and then worn smooth particularly around the outer edge.

D quern c 720mm
MT 75mm

### LGQ16 (A6046fh) (figure 50b)

Upper stone of thin disc quern. Chlorite schist. Fragment with handle hole surviving. The base has been pecked to roughen it and worn flat. Upright handle hole made on upper face 19mm from quern's perimeter.

D quern c 550mm

MT 33mm

D handle hole c 15mm

### LGQ17 (A6046fm) (figure 52)

?Quern. Fragment. A flat face has been prepared by pecking. No central hole survives; rather this face has been shaped to form a shallow slope down to the centre. One original edge is straight. The lower face is very rough.

MT 95mm

### LGQ19 (figure 47b)

Complete upper stone of disc quern. Metamorphic grit. Part of the perimeter is damaged and is straight for about 240mm. From the top view the central hole is notched where the rind slots are cut from below. A V-shaped perforation has been made on the upper face by cutting two holes approximately 30mm wide and 32mm apart which were angled diagonally towards each other. The holes on the upper face have worn away while the base of the perforation has become exposed on the lower face through wear. The base appears flat and worn and two rind slots have been cut from the central hole.

D quern 455mm

D central hole 68mm

T at central hole 30mm

T at perimeter 18mm and 30mm

Rind slots 28–30mm long and 20mm wide

### LGQ20 (figure 47b)

Complete lower stone of disc quern. Epidiorite. Part of perimeter is damaged presenting an irregular edge for 240mm. The base appears flat and worn. The central hole is fully perforated.

D quern 594mm

D central hole 15mm

T at central hole 56mm

T at perimeter 30mm

### LGQ21 (ARCH NN 2699 and 2700) (figure 53)

A large, worn slab of quartzose schist. Described by JGS as a 'hearthstone'. It comprises three large conjoining fragments which most likely make up the bulk of the original slab. It has been shaped to form an upper working face which slopes downwards from an outer edge some 100mm high to the lower edge just 25mm in thickness. The outer edge is broadly curved in plan and forms a lip to the smooth, concavely worn face that is worn to an offshoot at the lower edge. One of the fragments has a very smoothly worn face but the conjoining pieces, though shaped, are rougher in feel. This could mean that the slab was broken in antiquity and one of the fragments re-used. However, if this were the case then one would expect the outer edges to be more worn than they are when in fact the breakage still looks rather fresh. Alternatively, the slab may have broken and the various fragments subjected to different depositional processes that would affect the surface.

ML 820mm; MW 380mm. MT at lip 102mm; MT at lower edge 25mm

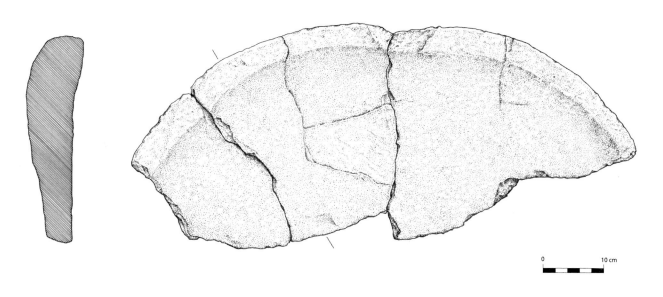

FIGURE 53
Possible hearthstone LGQ21

## 4.12 THE COARSE STONE FINDS

*Colleen Batey*

### INTRODUCTION

In all some 22 stone objects were retrieved during the excavation. Some went missing soon after excavation and have never been examined while some have subsequently been discarded as artefacts after closer examination of the assemblage. In all 16 objects are described below according to interpretative category. Their findspots are illustrated on figure 33.

### SLINGSTONES/GAMING PIECES

Five small rounded pebbles described by the excavator as sling stones were found either on or near the surface of the brushwood layer (SF2, SF3 and SF4) or within the brushwood itself (SF93 and SF129). None of them were found together. All the stones are local in origin and have not been modified in any way (Alastair Gunning *pers comm*). However, they all fall within a narrow size range of 20–30mm in maximum diameter, suggesting that they were clearly selected and introduced to the site.

Small selected pebbles of a similar size were found at Scalloway, in Shetland (Clarke 1998a, 178–80). Clarke suggested that the size range of these pebbles, c 20–29mm, indicated use as gaming pieces or counters rather than slingstones which would probably be of a larger size. Similar finds have been noted from the Howe in Orkney (Ballin-Smith 1994, 188–9, 191) and Clickhimin broch in Shetland (Hamilton 1968, 80, 86, 120 and 143) where they are described universally as slingstones. Either interpretation has equal validity but the identification of gaming counters amongst the wooden artefacts from Loch Glashan (Chapter 4.1) suggests that board games may have been popular with the occupants.

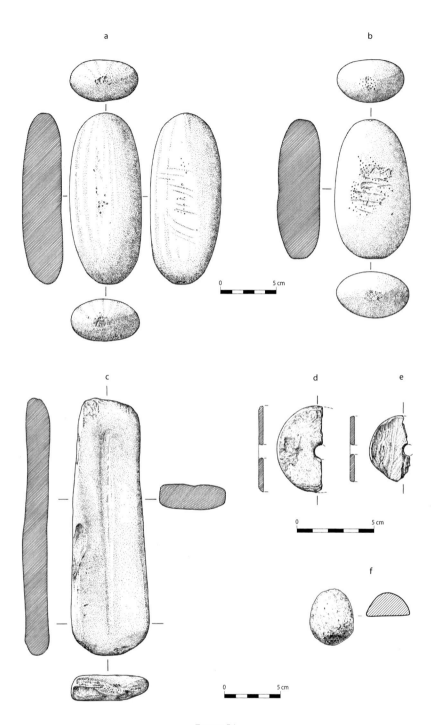

FIGURE 54
a) Pounder/anvil SF131; b) Pounder/anvil SF132; c) Hone SF21; d) spindlewhorl SF5; e) spindlewhorl SF77; f) slickstone SF113

### POUNDERS/HAMMERSTONES

Three finds fall within this category, SF131, SF132 and SF219. SF131 and SF219 were found on or near the surface of the brushwood layer which SF132 was found on the surface of the sand-and-gravel horizon.

SF131 is an elongated pebble with minor use at the short ends and slight pecking on the flat faces and it appears to have smoothing caused by wear on one of the long faces (figure 54a). SF132 has wear at both ends and extensive percussion damage mid way along one of the flat sides (figure 54b). SF219, a quartzite pebble, has wear at the tapering narrow end only. While SF219 seems to have served only as a pounder or hammerstone, SF131 and SF132 may have served multiple functions, being used as anvil stones as well as pounders. The additional smoothing on SF131 may also indicate use as a rubbing or smoothing stone, perhaps in the working of wood or leather.

In describing similar material from the Howe, Ballin-Smith (1994, 196–7) distinguished grinders, pounders and hammerstones. The Loch Glashan examples fall within the grinding category, with traces of percussion and little shattering at the end faces. Clarke classes this type of tool more generally as 'cobble tools' and has discussed them extensively in relation to the Iron Age assemblage from Scalloway (Clarke 1998b, 140–4). In common with the Loch Glashan examples, mid-face pitting and glossing, as well as end trauma are recorded on the Scalloway assemblage.

Such finds date from the prehistoric period onwards and are not particularly chronologically sensitive.

WHETSTONES/HONES

Ritchie recorded that he found four whetstones on top of the crannog (Chapter 1) but they have never been located. However, drawings of three of these whetstones have recently been found and these are reproduced here (figure 55). There were three items in this category found during the excavation, SF1, SF21 and SF135, all in or on the brushwood layer. They are all probably hone stones, indicating opportunistic selection of local material rather than specific selection of stone suited to the task.

SF1 is a square-sectioned rectangular stone which could have served as either a hone or a rubber, as it has one very flat and smoother side. SF21 is an elongated and tapering piece with an irregular flat surface which seems to have been used for sharpening (figure 54c). One edge is also slightly battered which could suggest a dual purpose tool, as with SF1. This duality of purpose was also noted at Dunadd (Lane & Campbell 2000, 178) and reinforces the idea of opportunistic use of resources rather than a considered collection. SF135 is highly laminated and fractured.

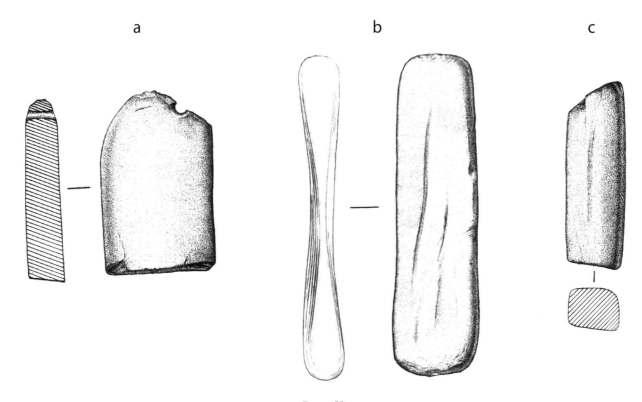

a                    b                    c

FIGURE 55
Three of the whetstones found by Roy Ritchie on top of the crannog: a) SF X7; b) SF X8; c) SF X9

It has a modern notch at one point and its intact end is slightly rounded in shape. Both flat faces may have served as honing surfaces. Without examination, all that can be said about the three whetstones from the surface collections is that they are not diagnostic of any period, though the pierced example, SF X7, is likely to be Norse to medieval in date.

SPINDLE WHORLS

Three spindle whorls were recorded during excavation, SF5, SF77 and SF164, but the latter is now missing. SF5 was found in the stony horizon while SF77 and SF164 were found in the brushwood layer. Both SF5 and SF77 are made from a schist and have fractured laterally and across the perforation (figure 54d and e). Although roughly half of each survives, they are not conjoining. They are approximately 35 and 26mm in diameter respectively. The original thickness of each would have been roughly double that which remains (they would have been about 4mm thick) as indicated by the chamfering of the perforation in SF5. The perforation for SF5 is slightly eccentric and that for SF77 more centrally placed.

These whorls can be classed as disc whorls, comprising two flat faces and probably cylindrical perforations drilled from both sides (see discussion Walton Rogers 1997, 1736, fig 807 Form B). The form is simple and known from Iron Age contexts at The Howe (Ballin-Smith 1994, 192) to Viking and beyond (for example, Walton Rogers 1997). A larger diameter example was noted from Dunadd (Lane & Campbell 2000, 191 no 890)

with slightly chamfered perforation on the upper side. These obviously suggest domestic thread production. A number of pin-shaped objects without head or tip were found in the wood assemblage which could have been spindles. SF150/151a (figure 25a) in particular is a good candidate and both SF5 and SF77 would have sat comfortably over the bulge on its shaft.

BAKING STONES/CONTAINER LIDS?

Three items described as baking stones were recorded in the site find book, SF33, SF36 and SF91. The latter has been discounted as an artefact and SF36 is missing. SF33 was found in the brushwood layer and is one half of a flat stone which has been deliberately shaped into a round, 310mm in diameter (figure 56). Fragments of cloth adhere to one surface.

A number of flattish stones have been identified as bakestones from other sites, such as The Howe (Ballin-Smith 1994, 204) and most particularly from The Biggings, Papa Stour (Crawford & Ballin-Smith 1999, 134–9) where scored schist baking plates were imported to the site in the Late Norse period. All baking plates have common features and that is the flatness of the upper surface and the thinness of the stone used (schist is particularly good because it laminates and is a good heat conductor when scored). SF33 is rather thicker than is common for a baking stone and neither surface is particularly flat. This may represent opportunistic use of a local resource but SF33 would never have functioned particularly well as a baking stone. Furthermore, it does not appear to

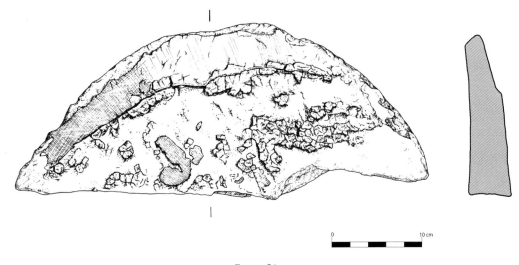

FIGURE 56
Potlid, SF33. Note the textile impressions

107

have been affected by heat – there is no discoloration or crazing.

It could also be a lid or cover for a container. Stone 'potlids' are a common find, particularly on sites in the Northern and Western Isles dating from the Neolithic to the Viking period. Its use as a lid may explain the presence of the cloth because a cloth wrapped around the stone lid would have created a better seal between lid and container. If the container had been used for storing fatty- or sugar-based foodstuffs the absorption and subsequent concretion of the foodstuffs into the cloth might explain its adhesion to the stone.

MISCELLANEOUS

Two items fall within this category, a stone ball, SF75 and a split pebble, SF113, both found within the brushwood layer. SF75 is a perfectly smooth and rounded stone ball, with a maximum diameter of 62mm but it has not been worked in any way (Alastair Gunning *pers comm*). It resembles the category of finds labelled 'slingstones' from other sites such as The Howe (Ballin-Smith 1994, 191) and Clickhimin (Hamilton 1968, 80).

SF113 is a small split pebble, domical in shape and with a flat lower surface (figure 54f). It was originally described as a possible slickstone, used for polishing wood or preparing leather, but at only 20mm in height it is not an easy size to grasp in the hand and the 'base' is irregular. Much larger river pebbles were used for this purpose at Dunadd where they displayed traces of polish presumed to be tallow and animal fat from the processing of hides (Lane & Campbell 2000, 179). Another possibility is that this is a gaming counter, although it is somewhat larger than the wooden equivalents found on the crannog (Chapter 4.1).

# CATALOGUE OF ILLUSTRATED ARTEFACTS

Numbers in brackets are Kelvingrove accession numbers.

**SF1 (A6046ce)**
Slightly tapering stone, possible traces of charring. Length c 80mm, max width 35mm

**SF2 (A6046bz)**
Possible sling stone, max diameter 20mm

**SF3 (A6046ca)**
Possible sling stone of banded stone and some discoloration. Max diameter 30mm

**SF4 (A6046cb)**
Possible sling stone of dark brown stone with flecks of schist and small indentation at the top. Max diameter 30mm

**SF5 (A6046ci)**
Schist spindle whorl, fragmentary, approx ½ remaining. Max diameter 35mm

**SF21 (A6046cf)**
Slightly tapering stone with deep notch on one side, narrower end discoloured. Length c 215mm × max width 64mm

**SF33 (A6046bx)**
Almost semi-circular baking stone with remains of cloth attached. 292mm × 125mm × 34mm

**SF75 (A6046en)**
Stone ball with superficial pitting and cracking (containing iron panning), signs of burning. Max diameter 62mm

**SF77 (A6046cj)**
Part of stone spindle whorl, with worn broken edge. Approx diameter 26mm

**SF93 (A6046cc)**
Possible sling stone, pale brown and egg shaped. Max diameter 20mm

**SF113 (A6046cl)**
?Slickstone, smooth on one side, dome shaped and smooth on other. 47mm × 39mm × 20mm

**SF129 (A6046cd)**
Possible sling stone of very rough stone of irregular shape. Max diameter 30mm

**SF131 (A6046ek)**
Smooth, worn stone pounder. Length c 145mm × 60mm wide

**SF132 (A6046el)**
Smooth, worn stone pounder, slightly roughened in centre of underside. Length c 110mm × 60mm wide

**SF135 (A6046cg)**
Badly worn stone with one side notched and broken and split at one end. Length max 100mm × width c 45mm

**SF219 (A6046em)**
Possible quartzite hammerstone, very smooth and spherical and slightly flattened on one side. Overall diameter c 60mm

# Chapter 5

# The Date of the Crannog

## 5.1 THE ARTEFACTUAL EVIDENCE

The artefactual evidence for the chronology of the crannog is summarized in figure 57. Only a handful of objects can be ascribed any chronological significance.

Stratigraphic evidence from a host of sites in Western Britain points to the importation of E ware in the late 6th/7th centuries AD (Chapter 4.2). Residues on the Loch Glashan E ware provided an opportunity to investigate the chronology of their use in Britain; the results are summarized below (Chapter 5.2). The crucibles also support evidence for activity on the crannog at about this time. The type of crucible found at Loch Glashan, sub-triangular with a rectangular lug on the lid, has been found in 7th-century AD metalworking deposits at Dunadd and in mid-7th-century AD deposits at Buiston crannog (Crone 2000, 150–1). Although the general type, with a handle on the lid (Tylecote's Type E1), is found in a wider date-range of sites in Britain and Ireland, from the 6th to 10th centuries, those with rectangular-sectioned handles are so far known only from these two 7th-century Scottish contexts.

Typological parallels for the penannular brooch place it in the 8th/early 9th century AD but there is little concrete evidence for the actual date of manufacture of this style of brooch (Chapter 4.4). However, the 8th/9th century date gains credence from the presence of the glass bead. The fact that the bead is silver-in-glass rather than gold-in-glass makes an 8th/9th century date for its manufacture more likely although, as Campbell points out (Chapter 4.7), an earlier 5th to 7th century date cannot be entirely ruled out. Both items are objects of personal adornment and may have been part of a cache deposited at the same time. However, the fact that the bead is broken suggests it was a casual loss. Brooches are fairly common finds on Irish crannogs and, although most may be casual losses in a watery environment, Newman (2002, 114–16) has recently re-interpreted those at Balinderry No 2 as the result of ritual hunting/bathing pre-crannog activity. However interpreted, in trying to date the deposition of the bead and brooch it should be remembered that, as valuable items, they may well have assumed heirloom status by the time of their deposition in the loch. A 9th century

date for these artefacts thus seems credible. The iron axe appears to be a Norse type dateable to the 9–11th centuries, reinforcing a possible 9th century date for this group of artefacts.

The only items amongst the wooden artefacts which may have some chronological significance are the turned container, SF149 and the gaming counters, SF151b and SF123 (Chapter 4.1). If the container is accepted as a skeuomorph of E ware pottery then it must have been manufactured sometime during the period that E ware was being imported and used, ie the late 6th/7th century AD. This interpretation is however thought to be unlikely (Chapter 4.2). The gaming counters, if they are accepted as copies of Norse counters, must have been manufactured sometime in the 9th to 11th centuries.

The leather assemblage provides little in the way of chronologically significant artefacts apart from the satchel. Its chronological significance resides in its interpretation as a book satchel rather than as a bag *per se*. Its overall shape and design, square with a flap and strap, accords well with contemporary written descriptions and visual depictions of book satchels (Chapter 4.10). Perhaps more significantly, the carefully tapered shape of the side panels and the construction of a flat base mimic the outline of a bound codex, the thicker spine uppermost in the satchel. It is difficult to see why such care would have been taken in the design of these details if the satchel were simply a general holdall. Books and their associated paraphernalia were part of the cultural package that accompanied the introduction of Christianity into Dál Riata, through the ministry of Columba on Iona. The scriptorium in the monastery there was probably producing books from its inception in the second half of the 6th century and the monastic community there and elsewhere would henceforth have required book satchels.

The coarse stone objects and the querns are not particularly chronologically sensitive (Chapters 4.11 and 4.12). However, the large size of many of the querns and some of their features suggest that they are typologically late, possibly medieval or more likely post-medieval in date.

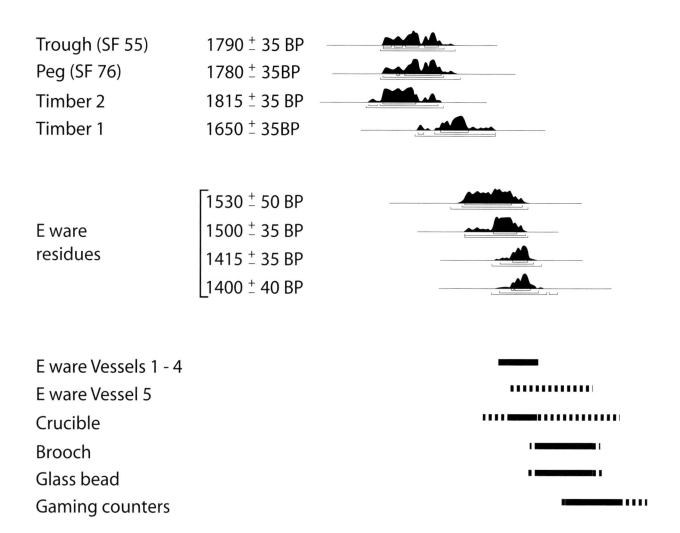

Trough (SF 55)    1790 ± 35 BP

Peg (SF 76)    1780 ± 35BP

Timber 2    1815 ± 35 BP

Timber 1    1650 ± 35BP

E ware
residues    ⎡1530 ± 50 BP

1500 ± 35 BP

1415 ± 35 BP

⎣1400 ± 40 BP

E ware Vessels 1 - 4

E ware Vessel 5

Crucible

Brooch

Glass bead

Gaming counters

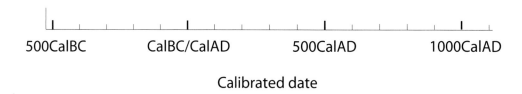

500CalBC        CalBC/CalAD        500CalAD        1000CalAD

Calibrated date

FIGURE 57
Graph showing the calibrated ranges of the radiocarbon dates and the date ranges of the chronologically diagnostic artefacts

In summary, there is evidence in the artefact assemblage for at least two episodes of deposition, one in the late 6th/7th century AD represented by the E ware and the crucibles, and one in the 9th century AD represented by the brooch, the bead, the axe, and possibly the gaming counters. The satchel could belong to either of these episodes. The unusual E ware Vessel 5 could fall between these two groups of dates. The querns probably represent a later episode of deposition.

## 5.2 RADIOCARBON-DATING OF THE E WARE RESIDUES

The dating of E ware has been controversial in the past, but is a key element in dating many Early Historic sites in western Britain and Ireland. Initially, before the ware was recognized as a Continental import, some E ware vessels were identified as Roman (for example, Henken 1950, 124), while others were thought to be local wares of the 8th century (for example, Craw 1930, 126). Thomas' original age range of 5th to 8th centuries, in the seminal paper where the ware was first defined (Thomas 1959, 104), was reiterated in a series of publications (Peacock & Thomas 1967; Thomas 1976; 1981). During this period Richard Warner published stratigraphic information from the royal site of Clogher, Tyrone, which suggested that E ware was not reaching the site before the late 6th century (Warner 1979). Following a detailed study of all the stratified occurrences of the pottery, a *floruit* in the first half of the 7th century was proposed on the basis of a wide variety of types of evidence, with a date-range of 575–700 (Campbell 1991, 39; 1996b, 92). Later, the large-scale excavations at Whithorn provided the best stratified sequence of deposits containing E ware, suggesting that while this dating was generally valid, a

few vessels could have been imported as early as the mid-6th century (Hill 1997, 324).

The Loch Glashan material offered the opportunity to obtain direct dates from E ware vessels using techniques already used on Iron Age pottery (Campbell 2003; Campbell *et al* 2004). The advantage of this direct method of dating is that it is not affected by problems of taphonomy in pottery assemblages. For example, it is possible that the E ware sherds stratified in early and late contexts at Whithorn were the result of contamination and residuality respectively.

Samples were chosen from the interior and exterior of the vessels, where there was sufficient carbonized material to provide samples. The carbonized exteriors were due to sooting during the heating of the vessels over fires, while the interior deposits were from the overheating of foodstuffs. Sufficient material was found on the exteriors of Vessels 1, 2 and 4, and on the interior of Vessel 4. Unfortunately, there was no dating material on Vessel 5, which is thought to be typologically later than most other E ware (Chapter 4.2), and thus to represent the final phase of importation. Exterior deposits were not taken in the Iron Age studies previously mentioned, as there was a strong possibility of peat being used as a fuel, thereby producing spuriously early dates. In a wooded environment such as Argyll, this was thought to be unlikely, though there is still the possibility that old wood or charcoal was used on fires. Dates from exterior deposits may therefore be slightly older than those from the interior, which should date to the period of use of the pottery. Fortunately, samples were available from both the interior and exterior of Vessel 4, enabling a check to be carried out.

The results of the determinations are fairly clear (Table 3) and support the dating of E ware put forward by Warner and Campbell. Two of the calibrated dates,

Table 3   Radiocarbon dates. The calibrated age ranges are determined using OxCal v.3

| Lab No. | Context | Material | Species | Date (BP) | δ¹³C (‰) | 1σ cal AD | 2σ cal AD |
|---------|---------|----------|---------|-----------|----------|-----------|-----------|
| GU-11525 | Timber 2 | Wood (conserved) | *Quercus* sp | 1815 ± 35 | −25.4 | 130–250 | 120–330 |
| GU-11522 | SF55 | Wood (conserved) | *Alnus glutinosa* | 1790 ± 35 | −28.0 | 130–330 | 130–350 |
| GU-11523 | SF76 | Wood (conserved) | Unknown | 1780 ± 35 | −28.6 | 180–340 | 130–350 |
| GU-11524 | Timber 1 | Wood (unconserved) | *Quercus* sp | 1650 ± 35 | −25.1 | 340–440 | 260–540 |
| GU-11860 | SF15 | Wood (conserved) | *Fraxinus excelsior* | 1650 ± 40 | −27.2 | 260–440 | 260–540 |
| GU-11394 | Vessel 2 ext | sooting | | 1530 ± 50 | −30.8 | 430–600 | 420–640 |
| GU-11395 | Vessel 4 ext | sooting | | 1500 ± 35 | −29.9 | 535–620 | 430–650 |
| GU-11396 | Vessel 4 int | food residue | | 1415 ± 35 | −29.5 | 605–660 | 560–680 |
| GU-11397 | Vessel 1 ext | sooting | | 1400 ± 40 | −27.0 | 605–670 | 560–700 |

on Vessel 4 interior and Vessel 1 exterior (GU-11396; GU-11397) lie solidly within the 7th century, indeed within the earlier part of that century. This restricted age range is due to the steepness of the calibration curve for this period. The date from the sooting on the exterior of Vessel 4 (GU-11395) falls mainly in the later 6th and early 7th centuries. This might suggest the possibility that old wood was used in fires. Large oak branches, for example, might have provided a certain proportion of carbon from tree-rings up to 50–100 years old. However, the interior and exterior dates are not statistically distinguishable, so this may be pushing the evidence too far, and the difference may be due to chance. The final date, from the exterior of Vessel 2 (GU-11394), has a much wider range, through most of the 5th, 6th and early 7th centuries. This 'smearing' of the early part of the range is mainly due to the flattening of the calibration curve in the period before the 7th century, though the larger error range also contributes. The same smearing effect applies, though to a much lesser extent, to the date from the exterior of Vessel 4. This interpretation of the dates is supported by the evidence from Buiston, where dates from timbers gave calibrated dates ranging over 475 calendar years, while dendrochronological results showed they represented an event which took place over only 26 years between AD 583 and AD 609 (Crone *et al* 2000, 58; and see Chapter 5.3). The four dates form a consistent group, though it would not be permissible to combine them statistically as they do not necessarily represent one episode of deposition.

One further aspect of the dates to be discussed is the carbon-13 determinations, whose values range from −27.0 to −30.8. These are slightly more negative than might be expected. The Hebridean examples of charred food residues varied from −24.6 to −26.0 (Campbell *et al* 2004), while wood is typically −24 to −28. This might indicate some contamination from old peat that would presumably have occurred through the use of peat in fires. However, there was no mention in the excavation accounts of any peat ash, which is distinctive, being found on the site. It seems unlikely that an experienced excavator such as JGS would have missed this, though it is possible that any such ash could have been concentrated on an unexcavated portion of the site. The effect, if it exists, can be shown to be small and would make little overall difference to the calibrated dates, making them slightly older than their true age. If this is the case, then only GU-11397 with its value of −27 is most likely to be unaffected and would provide the most reliable date. However, if there had

been the use of peat as fuel, the dates would not have formed such a coherent group, and some would have prehistoric dates related to the age of formation of the peat. As the dates form a statistically indistinguishable group, the possibility of peat soot contamination can be ruled out.

Taken all together, the dates support a date range for E ware in the later 6th and 7th centuries. These dates however, only give a *terminus post quem* for the later Vessel 5, whose dating still relies on typological arguments. Whatever the stratigraphic position of the sherds, and the interpretation of the structural history of the crannog, there is no doubt that the crannog was occupied during the 6th/7th centuries AD.

## 5.3 RADIOCARBON-DATING OF THE STRUCTURAL TIMBERS AND WOODEN ARTEFACTS

The artefacts cannot directly date episodes of construction on the crannog. Furthermore, the nature of the deposits in which most of the artefacts were found is uncertain, as is the relationship between those deposits and the crannog structure (Chapter 3.5 and see below). Consequently other means of dating the crannog structure were sought.

The records of the 1960 excavations indicated that much of the structural timber used on the crannog consisted of large oaks (figure 5 and plate 11). This type of material is ideal for dendrochronological analysis which could provide precise dates for construction and occupation on the crannog. However, only two structural oak timbers had been sampled during the 1960 excavations. These were examined as part of an earlier project to develop an Early Historic tree-ring chronology for Scotland but could not be dated, probably because of the small size of the dataset combined with the absence of any dated master chronologies for western Scotland (Crone 1998). Sampling of a larger assemblage of timbers was therefore one of the objectives of the underwater investigation but the depth of silt which had built up over the crannog made it impossible (Chapter 3.4). Samples from the two structural oaks were therefore submitted for radiocarbon dating.

As few of the organic artefacts were typologically dateable (Chapter 4.1) samples from two of the wooden artefacts were also submitted for radiocarbon dating. A sample from the wooden container, SF15 was also submitted because it would provide a *terminus post quem* for the insertion of the stakes which destroyed it,

### THE STRUCTURAL TIMBERS

Timber 1 is a large horizontal timber lying within the halo of piling surrounding the crannog (figure 5). Some of the piles appear to cluster around it, suggesting that it may have been deliberately pinned in position there, possibly as part of a causeway to the shore. JGS had the timber lifted in its entirety, on the advice of Professor Harry Godwin who recommended that it be curated for 'future tree-ring analysis' (letter 24 Aug 1960; see Kelvingrove archive). Presumably as a consequence of its destined use, it was not conserved, unlike the rest of the wood assemblage. The surface of the timber was decayed and all the sapwood rings and at least some of the outermost heartwood rings were missing but analysis of its tree-ring pattern still recorded a very long sequence of 321 years (Crone 1998, 489). Circa 10 of its outermost heartwood rings were submitted for radiocarbon-dating, yielding a date of $1650 \pm 35$ BP (GU-11524).

Timber 2 is a pile of undressed roundwood with a forked top (figure 5 and plate 9). It had been conserved using carbowax. Tree-ring analysis indicated that it was a young oak, with only 62 growth-rings, its sub-bark surface still intact (Crone 1998, 489). Circa 10 of its outermost sapwood rings were submitted for radiocarbon-dating, yielding a date of $1815 \pm 35$ BP (GU-11525).

### THE WOODEN ARTEFACTS

The following criteria were used in selecting two artefacts for radiocarbon-dating; firstly, artefacts made from short-lived, diffuse-porous species were preferred and secondly, the artefact had to be suitable for display/presentation purposes in the new Kelvingrove Museum, ie its function had to be immediately obvious. It should be reiterated here that all of the wooden artefacts had been conserved with carbowax.

SF55 is one of the large wooden troughs (figure 12). It was provisionally identified as alder (*Alnus glutinosa*), and had been converted from the original tree trunk in such a way that the outermost growth-rings lie at the basal corners of the trough. This meant that the outermost rings could be readily sampled by paring a splinter of wood from one corner of the trough, with minimal damage to the artefact. Radiocarbon-dating of the splinter yielded a date of $1790 \pm 35$ BP (GU-11522).

SF76 is a peg with a shaped head and broken shaft (figure 23c). Although its exact species could not be ascertained it is clear that it had been fashioned from a length of short-lived, diffuse-porous roundwood. A small piece sawn off the broken end of the shaft of the peg yielded a date of $1780 \pm 35$ BP (GU-11523).

SF15 is a tub-like container (figure 11) which had been carved out a log of ash (*Fraxinus excelsior*) in such a way that the walls of the container consisted of the outermost rings of the log. A small fragment yielded a date of $1650 \pm 40$ BP (GU-11860).

### DISCUSSION

The calibrated ranges of the dates are presented in Table 3. The radiocarbon dates from Timber 2, SF55 and SF76 are statistically indistinguishable from each other and are subsequently referred to as Date Group 1. They imply that construction or refurbishment of the pile palisade, as represented by Timber 2, and occupation on the crannog, as represented by at least some of the wooden artefacts, are contemporaneous and occurred sometime in the 2nd to 4th centuries AD. Timber 2 is unlikely to have been re-used timber: it was young roundwood, with bark intact and was probably felled immediately prior to its insertion in the crannog.

This group of dates is significantly earlier than the chronology indicated by the artefactual evidence. One possible hypothesis which was explored to explain the Date Group 1 determinations is that the conservation medium, carbowax, was not fully removed during the pre-treatment process and had contaminated the dates. However, the three age measurements form a very coherent set with a spread of only 35 $^{14}$C years between them and with a 35 year one-sigma error on each. Since they were all pre-treated separately, it would seem improbable that the same amount of conservation medium could be retained in each sample. More importantly, the pre-treatment scheme employed (Hoper *et al* 1998) was designed specifically to remove waxes and resins for the preparation of $\alpha$-cellulose from wood samples and employed sequential soxhlet extractions with ethanol/chloroform, ethanol and then water. The subsequent bleaching step was not used because of the potentially large sample losses in many old samples of wood. However, an extensive extraction using acid, alkali, alkali and acid was used to complete the sample pre-treatment (Gordon Cook *pers comm*). These same procedures were applied to SF15 which produced a statistically distinct date. It is therefore difficult to imagine any contamination process which would produce the coherent set of dates found in Date Group 1.

The radiocarbon dates from Timber 1 and the wooden container, SF15, are virtually identical and are referred to here as Date Group 2. These dates can be statistically distinguished from those in Date Group 1 indicating that they represent a separate event. This is further emphasized by the fact that the trunk of Timber 1 had probably lost at least 50 growth rings (see above) so its real felling date was probably later rather than earlier in the calibrated date range. It is possible that the true age of Date Group 2 lies outside the calibrated age range altogether. Support for this proposition comes from Buiston crannog, where an extensive dating programme was complemented by dendrochronological analysis of structural timbers. Buiston Date Group 3 consisted of 15 dates which could not be divided on statistical grounds into smaller sub-groups (Crone *et al* 2000, 57–8). They spanned 190 radiocarbon years from $1530 \pm 50$ BP to $1720 \pm 50$ BP which, when calibrated spanned 475 calendar years from AD 150 to AD 625 (at the 2-sigma range). However, the dendochronological results from timbers from the same stratigraphic units showed that all the activity represented by those

deposits took place over a very short period from AD 583 to AD 609. While this date range was encompassed within that of the calibrated radiocarbon dates it fell at the very recent end of the range. It was argued at the time that the conflict between the long duration of activity implied by the calibrated radiocarbon dates and the short duration of activity indicated by the dendro dates was an artefact of the calibration curve (*ibid*, 58). As the radiocarbon dates from Date Group 2 fall within the same date range, it must be conceivable, on the evidence from Buiston, that their real date is also somewhat later than their calibrated calendrical range, ie in the late 6th/early 7th century AD and therefore contemporary with the occupation which produced the E ware and crucible.

The combined evidence of the radiocarbon dates and the artefact typologies suggests that there were up to four episodes of activity of the crannog: in the middle Iron Age, the 6/7th centuries, the 8/9th centuries, and the medieval period. The nature of these episodes, their duration and significance is discussed in the following chapter, together with the implications of this chronology for the interpretation of the remains on the crannog.

# Chapter 6

# Discussion and Interpretation

## 6.1 CHRONOLOGY

It is clear that there are inconsistencies and conflicts in the available evidence that will never be fully resolved. Consequently several alternative chronologies are presented below. Chronology 1 embraces *all* the available dating evidence, both radiocarbon and artefactual, while Chronologies 2 and 3 present variant hypotheses.

CHRONOLOGY 1

| Episode 1 | 2nd–4th centuries AD |
| | —————————————— abandonment |
| Episode 2 | late 6th/7th centuries AD |
| | —————————————— abandonment |
| Episode 3 | 8th/9th centuries AD |
| | —————————————— abandonment |
| Episode 4 | medieval |

*Episode 1*
Timber 2 is inserted in the crannog some time during the 2nd to 4th centuries AD. JGS records that Timber 2 was 'immovably fixed in mud … like the other solid earthfast oak timbers' (see plate 8) and postulated that these timbers might derive from an earlier building. There is no evidence for activity prior to this date so these timbers may well represent the initial construction of the crannog. Some of the wooden artefacts are associated with this episode.

*Episode 2*
The crannog is refurbished and re-occupied in the late 6th/7th century AD. Timber 1 is laid down as part of the refurbishment and the E ware, crucibles and some of the wooden artefacts are used on the crannog. The book satchel, and by implication, the bulk of the leather assemblage, could be associated with this episode.

*Episode 3*
The insertion of the stakes which split the abandoned wooden container, SF15, may represent building activity which took place during this episode. The brooch, the bead, the gaming counters and possibly Vessel 5 and the axe are used on the crannog. The book

satchel and the leather assemblage could also belong to this episode.

*Episode 4*
The crannog may still have been visible to the occupants of the 14th-century settlement on the nearby island and it may have been they who were responsible for the dumping of the stones on the north-western quadrant of the crannog, perhaps to create a fishing stance or possibly to form a cairn of stones, with a projecting post, to signal the location of the hazard that the decaying crannog presented. The concentration of typologically late querns found on the surface of the crannog may have been part of the same dump. Alternatively, the querns may have been brought out to the crannog from the mainland as part of a move to take them out of circulation following the outlawing of hand mills in 1284 AD (Chapter 4.11).

CHRONOLOGY 2

| Episode 1 | late 6th/7th century AD |
| | —————————————— abandonment |
| Episode 2 | 9th centuries AD |
| | —————————————— abandonment |
| Episode 3 | medieval |

Some doubt will always remain about the radiocarbon dates taken from samples of conserved wood (Chapter 5.3) and, as these provide the only evidence for the 2nd–4th century AD episode, they are excluded from consideration in Chronology 2.

*Episode 1*
The crannog is constructed during this episode and refurbished at least twice, Timber 1 representing the first refurbishment and the stakes which pierced SF15 representing the second. Most of the artefacts found on and around the crannog, with the possible exception of the querns, and those items which define Episode 2, are associated with this episode.

*Episode 2*
This episode is defined by only the brooch, the bead, the axe and the gaming counters, all personal items.

There is no clear evidence for construction on the crannog during this episode so it is possible that these objects represent no more than a visit to the island sometime in the 9th century AD.

*Episode 3*
As per Episode 4 in Chronology 1.

CHRONOLOGY 3

| Episode 1 | late 6th/7th–9th centuries AD |
| | ————————— abandonment |
| Episode 4 | medieval |

*Episode 1*
The entire artefact assemblage, with the possible exception of the querns, is considered to represent activity which spanned at least two centuries. The typologically late E ware vessel 5 is crucial to this chronology, suggesting as it does, activity into the 8th century.

*Episode 2*
As per Episode 4 in Chronology 1.

DISCUSSION

Two of the three chronologies assume activity on the crannog over long periods of time, five to seven centuries in the case of [1] and two centuries in the case of [3]. It is unlikely that this activity was continuous over these periods; first and foremost the structural evidence does not support such an interpretation. A crannog which was occupied even for short durations would have needed constant refurbishment to deal with settlement and the destabilizing effects of wave action. At Buiston the crannog was occupied at most for 80–90 years and lay within a small, shallow loch where wave fetch would have been relatively limited. Yet the palisades were refurbished six times (Crone 2000, fig 58) leaving a virtual forest of vertical timbers of varying type encircling the crannog (*ibid*, fig 132). The same history of frequent repair is also apparent in the multiplicity of piling seen at Lochlee (Munro 1882, figs 34–5). There is no such evidence at Loch Glashan; the piling is sparse in comparison and appears relatively homogenous, the only distinction apparent being that between the short line of squared oak piles and the undressed roundwood piles (figure 5). Without tree-ring analysis or radiocarbon dating the chronological relationships of the piling will never be known but we argue that there is little structural evidence at Loch Glashan to support continuous activity over a long period. At most the structural evidence indicates three episodes of activity, one of initial construction and two of refurbishment. These episodes may have been separated by a period of abandonment, the duration of which may have been prolonged, but the episodes themselves were probably not of any duration, maybe a generation at most.

Assessment of dendrochronological and radiocarbon evidence from both wetland and dryland sites suggests that episodic settlement of short duration was probably more commonplace than is normally accepted for later prehistoric and Early Historic sites (Halliday 1999; Barber & Crone 2001; Cowley 2003). Certainly, the duration of each episode is crucial to the issue of the nature of the occupation on the crannog. Even within the micro-scale of the episode we must also consider whether the occupation was permanent, intermittent or more regularly seasonal. Crannogs, by their very location on the edge of sometimes large waterbodies, would have been uncomfortable places to inhabit during the winter months. Despite the unequivocal evidence that Buiston was a domestic settlement there are fragments of evidence which suggest that the occupation there was, if not seasonal, at least intermittent (Crone 2000, 110). Morrison (1985, 66) suggests that some crannogs may have been '… specialized out-stations located at some distance from the home base …', ie sites which were only ever occupied for short periods and for specific functions. We know, from more recent descriptions of crannogs, that they were often put to fitful, occasional use as prison-islands, boltholes, feasting islands, etc (*ibid*, 66–7).

How does the chronological evidence from Loch Glashan fit with that from other crannogs? Firstly, if the radiocarbon determinations in Date Group 1 are accepted as valid, then Loch Glashan is the first crannog in Scotland to have been used during this period. The 3rd to 5th centuries AD present a noticeable gap in the radiocarbon chronology for crannogs (Crone 1993b, 248). Crannogs were being built and occupied throughout the latter half of the 1st millennium BC and up until the 2nd century AD, after which the next spate of crannog-building begins in the late 6th century AD (*ibid*). This apparent gap is corroborated by the artefactual evidence; virtually all Roman material found on crannogs has been 1st–2nd century AD in date while no 3rd–4th century AD artefacts have been found (Robertson 1970; Oakley 1973, 106–8). Similarly, in

Ireland there are no crannogs with dates in this period. A possible crannog at Lisnamunchin, Co Antrim has produced a date of 243–341 AD (UB-3383 – quoted in Stout 1997, 28). Very little is known about this site but the date does not conform to the general pattern of dated crannogs in Ireland which indicate a major crannog-building phase beginning in the late 6th century AD (O'Sullivan 1998, 131–3; Fredengren 2002, 94, 102–3). This widespread gap in dates in the Late Roman period could be seen to support doubts about the validity of the radiocarbon dates from the conserved wood at Loch Glashan.

The overwhelming majority of radiocarbon-dated crannogs in Scotland are later prehistoric in date (Henderson 1998; Crone & Henderson forthcoming). Apart from Loch Glashan only five other crannogs have produced Early Historic radiocarbon dates; these are Buiston, Barean and Milton Loch 3, all in south-west Scotland (Crone 1993b), Eilean nam Breaban in Loch Tay in the central Highlands (Dixon 2004, 94), and Loch Seil, Argyll (Cavers forthcoming). Artefacts retrieved during antiquarian investigations in the 19th century demonstrate that a number of other crannogs were also in use during the Early Historic period (Oakley 1973; MacSween 2000, 151). These include Dowalton (from which a leather shoe was recently dated to the period – see Chapter 4.8), Lochlee (E ware), possibly Lochspouts (E ware), and Loch Inch-Cryndil (double-sided composite bone comb), again all in south-west Scotland. The E ware recently found at Ederline crannog, in Loch Awe, Argyll (Chapter 2.3) adds another site to this list.

Many of the crannogs which have been scientifically dated have produced evidence for at least two episodes of use separated by long intervals of non-use. Buiston was built in the 1st-2nd centuries AD, abandoned and then re-used from the mid-6th century AD (Crone 2000, 64). There was building activity on the crannog in Barean Loch in the latter half of the 1st millennium BC and again sometime in the 7th–9th centuries AD (Crone 1993b, 246). Radiocarbon dates from other crannogs also hint at re-use but over less clearly distinguished periods of time (*ibid*). Loch Glashan is therefore not unusual in the evidence it presents for multi-period use, if Chronology 1 is accepted.

In summary, it is impossible to decide between the alternative chronologies presented above, and this should be borne in mind in the discussions which follow. Leaving aside the question of the 2nd–4th century dates, one of the authors (AC) inclines towards Chronology 2, and the other (EC) to Chronology 3.

## 6.2  TAPHONOMY

The dating evidence presented in the previous section indicates that there were multiple episodes of activity on the crannog, rather than the single phase of occupation envisaged by the excavator. The consequences of this chronology are considerable for the interpretation of the artefact assemblage because it can no longer be regarded as a coherent whole and forces us to address the exact nature of the deposits in which the bulk of the artefacts were found. The artefacts were invariably described as being found in 'the brushwood layer' and there is no evidence from the recorded stratigraphy to indicate that this deposit represents anything other than a single depositional event. Yet it contained artefacts that had been manufactured possibly as much as five to seven centuries apart.

JGS interpreted these deposits as the midden (Chapter 3.3) but there are a number of problems with this interpretation. Firstly, it seems inconceivable that the occupants would have thrown their rubbish in exactly the same spot over a period that would have amounted to some five to seven centuries. Secondly, the location is problematic; the deposits lie on the landward side of the crannog (figure 7) where the water would have been at its shallowest and more sheltered, and through which the occupants would have had to make their way to the shore. Does it not seem more likely that the occupants would have thrown their debris off the loch side of the crannog, where it would have sunk into deeper water or been dispersed by wave action? Thirdly, many of the artefacts do not look like broken, discarded objects. One might expect the occasional, accidental loss of a tool such as the axe or a small personal object such as the brooch but it is more difficult to imagine that the substantial wooden troughs and bowls, most of which were still functional, were discarded by accident. It would surely have been more efficient to burn discarded wooden artefacts than to turf them over the side of the crannog.

Rather, elements of the assemblage look as though they have been abandoned. The range of artefacts found at Buiston survived because they were abandoned, the sudden collapse of the crannog causing the house and its contents to sink below the water, thus preventing their retrieval (Crone 2000, 111). There is no evidence of a similar catastrophic collapse at Loch Glashan (although it is feasible given that the crannog was not built on a solid foundation – see Chapter 3.3) but if the settlement was abandoned for whatever reason, settlement debris might have been eventually swept or washed over to the landward side of the crannog. Some objects might have ended up in the water at that time, while others might have become buried within the mound as it was refurbished at each re-occupation, only eroding out on that side of the crannog as the organic mound deflated after final abandonment (see Chapter 3.5). A similar set of circumstances must have prevailed at Llangorse crannog in Wales. Here, virtually the entire artefact assemblage, which contained a rich variety of metalwork and metalworking waste (Redknap 1995), was found on the lake bed in a spread lying to the south and west of the crannog; none came from the crannog itself (Redknap & Lane 1994). There had been considerable build-up of silt on the sheltered, shore-facing side of the crannog, where many of the artefacts were found. It is thought that the final distribution of the artefacts was due to erosion and the scouring of the crannog deposits, possibly middens on the periphery of the site, by water and wave action (*ibid*, 200).

At Loch Glashan this depositional model would more readily explain the location of the artefacts and the mixing of material from multiple phases, with the prevailing wind concentrating the material washed off the mound into the lee side of the crannog. The condition of the organic artefacts could have had a bearing on their pre-depositional history but unfortunately conservation has masked much of the surface detail. There is some slight evidence that some lay abandoned on the surface of the crannog for some time before submersion in the loch. On one face of the tool, SF119 (figure 20a), there are woodworm tracks which suggest that the object was discarded and lay somewhere dry for some time before final burial (see Catalogue). Similarly, the trough, SF121 appears to have decayed before it came to settle in the loch silts (figure 13 and plate 15).

The condition of the E ware pottery, particularly the large sherd size, suggests that it had not been moved about much after deposition. It may have been refuse that had been swept to the edge of the crannog prior to dumping over the palisade, an act which was not completed. As at Llangorse we could perhaps envisage a rubbish heap at the periphery of the crannog. The pottery may not have been washed over the edge because it was low in the rubbish heap.

In whatever scenario is envisaged, the lack of structural debris in the deposits off the crannog is puzzling. The only material recovered, which might have had a structural function, was the group of squared timbers characterized by a pierced, projecting ridge (Chapter 4.1 and figure 29). If the crannog was

abandoned the superstructure would surely have decayed and the timberwork would have fallen or been swept off the crannog. The superstructure could have been dismantled and the timbers taken away for re-use but then why leave perfectly functional tools and equipment behind? The absence of any structural debris in deposits which have preserved so much has implications for the nature of the superstructure of the crannog; this issue is pursued further below.

## 6.3   THE NATURE OF OCCUPATION ON THE CRANNOG

Why was the crannog built and who built it? Early Historic crannogs in Scotland tend to be seen as the settlements of high status individuals (Alcock 1988; Nieke & Duncan 1988) and Loch Glashan was certainly seen by its excavator in terms of a domestic settlement site (Scott 1960). In the most recent commentary on crannogs Fredengren (2002) exhorts us to move away from such functional, economistic interpretations and hierarchical high status/low status narratives and view the crannog more as a phenomenon which articulated contemporary communal and personal perceptions. It is certainly important to bear in mind that crannogs may have had other 'significances' to their builders over and above somewhere to live and work but the most basic questions must be addressed before we can move on to broader issues. The reliability of the evidence is vital and at Loch Glashan there are so many queries hanging over the stratigraphy and depositional history of the site as to make even questions of function and status difficult to address. In this section the evidence for the nature of the occupation on the crannog is discussed and takes into consideration the artefact assemblage, and the size, structure and location of the crannog in determining variables such as status and function.

### THE FINDS ASSEMBLAGE

#### Site status

The first point to make in any discussion of the finds from Loch Glashan is the overall number of finds compared to other Argyll sites of 1st millennium AD date (table 4). The figures in the table should be taken as a general indication only, as some sites are multi-phase within the 1st millennium, and others have restricted periods of occupation. Some have later medieval occupation which may have increased the number of iron objects from unstratified contexts. Some sites have

Table 4   Summary of finds by type of material from mainland Argyll sites with 1st millennium AD occupation (totals for all phases). 'Imported pottery' includes samian ware and is expressed as Minimum Number of Vessels

| Site | Imported pottery | Copper alloy | Iron | Metal-working | Glass | Stone | Bone | Wood | Leather |
|---|---|---|---|---|---|---|---|---|---|
| Dunadd | 31 | 29 | 346 | 1386 | 40 | 345 | 28 | | |
| Loch Glashan | 5 | 1 | 1 | 1 | 1 | 1 | | 106+ | 74+ |
| Dunollie | 4 | 4 | 68★ | 17 | 4 | 3 | 10 | | |
| Kildonan | 1 | 2 | 21★ | 30 | 3 | 12 | | | |
| Kildalloig | 1 | 2 | 1 | | | 1 | 3+ | | |
| Ardifuir | 2 | 1 | | 1 | | 7 | | | |
| Dun an Fheurain | 1 | 6 | 7 | | | 9 | 30 | | |
| Dun Eilean Righ 1 | | 1 | 1 | | 1 | 1 | | | |
| Bruach an Druimein | 1? | 1 | 56★ | 1 | 3 | 1+ | | | |
| Dun Fhinn | 1 | 2 | | | | | | | |
| Ugadale | | 1 | | 2 | 3 | 5 | | | |
| Leccanmore | | 2 | | | | 1 | 2 | | |
| Balloch | | | | | 10 | | | | |

KEY ★ possible medieval contamination

only antiquarian collection of 'relics', others modern scientific excavation.

However, despite these caveats, table 4 shows that Dunadd is in an entirely different category from all other sites in most categories of finds. It could be argued that this site has had the most excavation (three campaigns), and the greatest area excavated, but the vast majority of the finds are from the recent, very restricted areas of excavation (Lane & Campbell 2000, 30). Dunadd is clearly much more productive than any other site in Argyll. The total number of objects, particularly those requiring extra expense in manufacture or trade, gives some indication of the status of the inhabitants of the sites. Loch Glashan falls into a second rank of sites in terms of total numbers of objects, along with sites such as Dunollie and Kildonan. However, almost all of the Loch Glashan objects are organic, and if these had not been preserved the site would be classified alongside sites such as Eilean Righ 1 which have produced only a handful of artefacts. This situation illustrates both what has been lost on sites with no organic preservation, and the difficulties of making comparisons between sites with differing preservation.

There are some indications from the inorganic finds that Loch Glashan had a rather higher status than other small sites of the period. The first is the imported pottery, as expressed by the minimum number of vessels (MNV) represented by the sherds. This measure has been shown to be a good indicator of status (Campbell

1991; 1995), with three ranks of site being identified. Loch Glashan falls into the middle rank of sites, while Dunadd falls into the first category, as an import and redistribution centre. These second rank sites received their imports from the primary centres, probably as gifts to clients of the kings, who controlled the trade in these items. Loch Glashan compares in number of imported vessels to sites such as the royal crannog of Lagore, Co Meath (Henken 1950), or the royal site of Clogher, Co Tyrone (Warner 1988), perhaps suggesting that it could itself be of royal, or at least aristocratic, status. The close links with Dunadd are further attested by the purple dyestuff identified on Vessel 3, which is also found at Dunadd (Chapter 4.2). The dyestuff itself is an indication of high status, if the Irish Laws which specify the restriction of red colours to nobility (Kelly 2000, 263) can be taken to apply to Gaelic Scotland.

The second indication of status is the brooch and the evidence of fine metalworking. It has been shown that brooches were used as a sign of individual status in the early medieval period, with silver and gold being reserved for aristocracy and royalty (Nieke 1993; Campbell 1996a). The production of brooches has also been associated particularly with royal sites (Campbell 1996a, table 4.1). While there is no direct evidence of brooch *production* at Loch Glashan, the presence of the brooch is significant. Apart from Dunadd, where at least 45 examples are represented by mould fragments (Lane & Campbell 2000, 106), the only other site in

Argyll to have produced early medieval brooches is Kildonan, though both Kildalloig and Dun Fhinn have produced Roman period brooches. Although the Loch Glashan brooch is of copper alloy, the identification of silver in the crucible analysis (Appendix 7.2) shows that precious metals were being worked on the site, probably to produce brooches or pins. The brooch is also particularly carefully made, and it may be that the use of a brass-coloured quaternary copper alloy was intended to imitate gilding.

Comparative work on sites in other areas of the Gaelic west has shown that the presence of precious metals on a metalworking site is one element of a set of characteristics associated with royal sites (Campbell 1996a, table 4.1). Loch Glashan has several of these characteristics, namely the presence of imported pottery, a defended situation requiring mobilization of considerable resources in its construction, and the presence of precious metals and metalworking. This might be seen as supporting such a royal status for Loch Glashan, but the picture is not so clear. Firstly, recent work has shown that some Scottish sites of low status have silver working. This applies to the contemporary site of Eilean Olabhat, North Uist (Armit et al forthcoming) and other Hebridean sites. This may be due to a different social organization in this area, with less centralization of power (Campbell & Heald forthcoming), but it does suggest caution. Secondly, several important characteristics of the 'high status package' are missing from Loch Glashan, for example evidence of brooch production, glass-working and weapons.

Loch Glashan therefore has a number of characteristics which mark it out as being unusual, and possibly associated with royalty (cf Campbell 1996a, table 4.1). However, there is very little in the assemblage apart from the imported pottery and the silver-working which gives any hint of it being a special site. The wooden and leather objects, although abundant, are undecorated and utilitarian. Only the bead is exotic, like the pottery indicating long-distance contacts, presumably articulated through Dunadd. It is possible that this reflects one of the alternative chronologies of the site, with this utilitarian material dating to the 2nd to 4th centuries, and the other material to the 6th to 8/9th century occupation. However, the relatively small size of the crannog (see below) militates against its interpretation as a royal habitation site, so it may have served some other specialist function, such as a craftworking site.

This explanation would account for the fact that undeniably high status material (imported pottery and dyestuff; silver; possible gaming pieces) was present on the site, without other indications of occupation by high status individuals. In this scenario, the high status material was provided to craftworkers to produce items for high status individuals who lived elsewhere, presumably at Dunadd.

*Cultural contacts: production and consumption*

The finds assemblage is mainly of local origin, and can be firmly located in a generally Gaelic and specifically Dál Riata context. All the stone, leather, wood and iron artefacts have parallels in these areas. However, a small number of items show contacts further afield.

The bead is ultimately of Mediterranean origin, though as discussed above, the route by which it reached Loch Glashan is debatable. It may have been part of the trading network which brought Mediterranean, and later Continental, pottery to Atlantic Britain from the south, but it is more likely to have arrived from the north through contacts with early Norse or *Gall-Gaedhil*, mixed Norse/Gaelic, settlers. Supporting this interpretation, the axe, though of a form which may continue into the medieval period, also appears to be of a Norse type.

The other exotic material consists of the imported E ware pottery, and its contents. This originated in western France, but was almost certainly brought to the site from Dunadd, which was the major import and redistribution centre for this material (Campbell 1996a). Although the only content which has been certainly identified is the red/purple dyestuff from the plant Dyers' madder (*Rubia tinctorum*), other luxuries such as nuts, spices, olives, sweetmeats and honey have been suggested as possible goods on the basis of documentary and archaeological evidence (Campbell 1995, 92). The immediate implication is that the inhabitants of Loch Glashan were allowed access to these exotica because they were of sufficient status in society to receive them from the king, if they were not royalty themselves. The second implication is that dyeing took place on the site, in particular dyeing of red/purple material. This is significant because purple clothing was associated with royalty, and red with nobility in early Gaelic laws (Kelly 2000, 263). This association holds even if, as Kelly claims, madder was being grown in Ireland as early as the 8th century, rather than being imported as a ready-made dyestuff (*ibid*, 267).

The final evidence for long-distance contacts comes from the brooch. This has traditionally been seen as of Pictish provenance, but as was argued above (Chapter 4.4), it is perhaps better to ascribe it to a southern

Highlands regional milieu rather than a specifically Pictish context. It does seem to show some exposure to eastern Scottish influences, though whether this was merely through some form of exchange, or through hybridity of art styles on the site depends on whether or not the brooch was made at Loch Glashan. This remains no more than a possibility in the absence of mould fragments.

These exotic items show a pattern of consumption very similar to sites such as Dunadd, though on a very much smaller scale. It is perhaps significant that such material has not turned up so far on other contemporary small settlements in Argyll. However, if Chronology 2 is accepted, the bead and the brooch may not relate to occupation of the crannog, but a casual visit at a later period.

*Production*

The local material raises other questions about the function of the site, particularly in terms of production. The querns are excluded from this discussion, as they probably post-date the occupation of the site. The wooden material is unusual in that no turning waste was present in the recorded finds, whereas other waterlogged sites of the period, for example Iona and Buiston, have all produced such material. These wasters are unlikely to have been missed by the excavators, so it seems likely that wood-turning was not carried out on the site. The single turned vessel (SF149) was probably obtained from elsewhere, whether by gift, tribute or other form of exchange. The other wooden objects may have been made on site, though no wood shavings were collected or recorded, but these would have been much less obvious than lathe core debris. The lengths of prepared hazel hoops indicate that stave-built vessels were being repaired, if not manufactured, on the crannog.

It is only with the leather material that we have definite evidence of substantial production on the site, in the form of numerous offcuts. It is most likely that these relate to the making of shoes, and possibly other items. Apart from the metalworking, this is the only evidence of any surplus material being used to produce goods on the site. However, even here there is some doubt, as Thomas suggests (Chapter 4.8) that most of the scraps were from recycled pieces of old leather. It seems inherently unlikely that a leather-worker would specialize only in recycled material, so it seems safe to assume that leather working was indeed a significant function of the site. The surrounding area would have been suitable for cattle ranching using the small black cattle of the period attested at Dunadd (Lane

& Campbell 2000, 227), producing enough hides to service such a craft activity. It should be pointed out that leather products of the Gaelic areas were apparently sought after and exported. An 8th-century *vita* of St Filibert tells of 'a Gaelic ship (*Scothorum navis*) … with an abundance of shoes and clothing' appearing at Noirmoutier at the mouth of the Loire (Krush 1880, 603; Wooding 1996, 71). The lack of decoration on most of the fragments perhaps militates against the production of high quality leather goods such as the contemporary shoe from Dundurn (Alcock *et al* 1989, illus 16, 50), though if the decoration was added after the cutting out of the pieces one might not expect decoration on the scraps and offcuts. One item was recorded as decorated (SF171), but does not survive. A more tantalizing possibility is that hides were being used for vellum production. The original finds catalogue has one small find consisting of pieces of 'thin leather', all other finds being described as 'leather' or 'thick leather'. It is possible that these could be fragments of calf-skin vellum, although this hypothesis cannot be substantiated as the 'thin leather' finds do not survive. Furthermore, some of the other wooden implements, such as the large troughs (ie SF55), the pierced timber 'frame' (ie SF155) and the spatulate knives (SF138 and SF205) which are paralleled at Iona, would have been suitable for use in the production of vellum. The presence of the book satchel on the site is very significant, even though it was worn and may have been in the process of being recycled. It raises the possibility that such satchels were in secular hands, with the implication of literacy among the secular elite. There is little point in having a book satchel without a book, though it would be possible to argue re-use for another function. Another pointer to secular use is that all the other existing satchels are decorated with crosses, and were almost certainly used in ecclesiastic contexts. If the satchel was solely used in a monastic context, it is difficult to see why it should have been brought to Loch Glashan.

The total range of activities represented by the finds is restricted. There is little sign of agricultural or hunting activities (if the querns post-date the occupation), apart from a dubious ard (SF45). Certain activities included small-scale production of leatherware and fine jewellery. Other probable activities include dyeing (E ware stains and large trough SF55), weaving (?loom pegs SF112 and SF187) and linen production (?flax beater SF119). These activities are more than the mundane level of activity suggested by most of the finds, and suggest specialist craftworkers in residence. The gaming counters (SF151b and SF123) and possible pegs from musical instruments (SF107 and SF152a), suggest leisure activities associated with the *topos* of the feasting hall, or the making of such items. Taken together these lines of evidence suggest a specialized function for the site, with craftworkers sponsored by an elite aristocracy.

SIZE, STRUCTURE AND LOCATION

Loch Glashan crannog probably measured approximately 18m in diameter; the recorded piling appears to describe an oval but we cannot be certain whether this was due to slumping or whether it was deliberate. During Phase III at Buiston the crannog was an oval shape measuring 19m by 15.5m (Crone 2000, fig 4), which expanded to a final size of 24m × 20m by the mid-7th century AD. In its final phase Lochlee was also about 24m in diameter (Munro 1882, fig 35). Loch Glashan is thus somewhat smaller than its Early Historic counterparts. What also distinguishes Loch Glashan is that it lacks any evidence for the sophisticated carpentry seen on these other Early Historic crannogs. It appears to have had a simple palisade with none of the radial and tangential elements used on those sites to brace and strengthen the structure.

The question of the kind of structure that might have stood on top of the crannog has already been posed. The fact that no structural debris was retrieved from the deposits around the crannog raises the possibility that there was no structure at all. Alternatively, the structure may have been a very simple construction of undressed roundwood, brushwood and withies. Despite the massive nature of the palisades at Buiston the walls of the roundhouse they encircled were constructed almost entirely of wickerwork with no evidence of large timbers or complex carpentry (Crone 2000, 23–5). Very similar roundhouses with double walls of wickerwork have been found on Irish sites of Early Historic date, notably the crannog in Moynagh Lough, Co Meath (Bradley 1993) and the raised rath at Deerpark Farms, Co Antrim (Lynn 1987; 1994). Debris from such structures, when decayed and broken up, may not have been that distinguishable from the natural debris in the loch itself. The only possible evidence for the superstructure at Loch Glashan consists of the forked piles, of which Timber 2 was one. The use of undressed roundwood which utilizes the natural features of the tree bespeaks an unsophisticated construction. This may be because the function of the crannog did not merit undue amounts of labour in its construction or it may be because the builders did not have access to the type of timber needed for more complex joinery, ie that it

was a question of status. Oak was certainly at a premium in Ireland by the Early Historic period (Kelly 1976) and supply may have been restricted but plenty of oak, albeit mostly of small scantling, was used in the Loch Glashan crannog. Overall, the crannog can be characterized as a simple construction in which no great investment of effort and resources has been made.

Let us now consider the location of the crannog in Loch Glashan and what that might tell us in terms of function. The most striking aspect of its location is that it lies some 50m from the natural island on which a settlement was built in the medieval period (Chapter 2.3). The immediate reaction is to question why the builders ignored the island and chose instead to spend time and energy building from scratch. This situation, where natural islands have been ignored in favour of fully artificial construction, is paralleled in many lochs. At the north-east end of Loch Awe, for instance, several crannogs were built just offshore in an area where there are plentiful small natural islands (Morrison 1985, 72). Similarly, Fredengren (2002, 89) noted that the natural islands in Lough Gara, both large and small, were ignored in favour of very specific locations. In the case of Loch Awe, Morrison was able to demonstrate that 17 of the 20 crannogs found in the loch had been built adjacent to patches of land with arable potential on the shore, a correlation made more significant by the very limited nature of such land around the loch (Morrison 1985, 74).

No such correlation can be made for Loch Glashan because it is surrounded by moorland, none of which ever had much agricultural potential. Roy's map of mid-18th century farming settlements in the area (reproduced in Lane & Campbell 2000, 258, illus 7.18) shows the landscape at a time when all available arable land was probably fully exploited. Even at that time the nearest cultivated land lay to the east around the shores of Loch Gair and up the valley of the *Abhainn Mhor*, and much further west along the River Add. It is therefore probably safe to say that the location of the crannog in Loch Glashan was not chosen for access to cultivable land. The surrounding moorland would have provided grazing land for cattle and this may have played some part in the location of the crannog.

Morrison also noted that the location of crannogs and duns around Loch Awe was mutually exclusive and postulated that their distribution represented a response to the need for security which was determined by the nature of the shore and loch topography (Morrison 1985, 75). Again, this is not the case at Loch Glashan where the dun overlooks the very same stretch of shoreline in which the crannog sits. In fact the crannog and dun are part of a nexus of monuments which cluster around the outlet from the loch (figure 3 and Chapter 2.3) suggesting that this particular location was important for the better part of a millennium or longer. Is this about control of a routeway, possibly connected to cattle droving? In discussing the location of the medieval island settlement Fairhurst (1969, 47) pointed out that it lay close to a natural routeway from Loch Gair to Loch Crinan which wended its way along the eastern and northern shore of Loch Glashan. Might it not have been easier to cross the waters of the loch by boat from the mouth of the outlet to the northern shore and then proceed by foot to the valley of the River Add? Could we speculate that the crannog, and possibly the dun before it, were so placed to control movement along this routeway? It has been suggested that this is the reason for the cluster of marine crannogs at Erskine, Langbank and Dumbuck, straddling as they do, the last major fording point across the Clyde before it opens up to the sea (Sands & Hale 2002, 50).

While this discussion has thrown up some useful insights into the possible function of the crannog it still has not addressed the question posed earlier – why invest labour in constructing the crannog when the island was available? Security is the most obvious explanation; the natural island is only 10m from the shore, its larger perimeter would have made it more difficult to defend and would have required more manpower. In comparison the small, compact crannog, situated some 50m from the shoreline, would have been relatively easy to defend. An alternative, less functional, explanation might be that the *process* of building the crannog served an important social function, binding a community together by their communal effort, much as has been suggested for major prehistoric ritual monuments. On the same note, Fredengren sees the boundaries of the crannog, created by the palisade and by its position out in the water, not as defensive boundaries but as serving to strengthen the identity of the people who used or inhabited them (2002, 242).

IRISH COMPARISONS

Recent excavations in Ireland are challenging the notion that all Early Historic crannogs were high status settlements of long duration and provide some interesting parallels for Loch Glashan.

Bofeenaun crannog in Lough More, Co Mayo is a small, low-lying mound encircled by an irregular palisade of roundwood posts, one of which was dendro-dated to AD 804±9 (Keane 1995). There was no

evidence for a structure on the crannog and the artefact assemblage consisted primarily of large quantities of metal slag. It has been interpreted as a single-phase structure of short duration which was used exclusively for iron-working and may not have been occupied at all (O'Sullivan 1998, 122).

Craigywarren crannog, Co Antrim, a site excavated at the beginning of the 20th century (Coffey 1906) also seems to have been used for only a short period of time possibly in the 6th/7th century AD (O'Sullivan 1998, 111). Again, it was a small, low-lying mound encircled by a simple palisade. The evidence for a domestic structure is slight although the artefact assemblage was much richer and more varied than that from Bofeenaun, including a great deal of metalwork, pottery, crucibles and some leatherwork. O'Sullivan has postulated that Craigywarren may not have been a domestic residence at all but a locus where craft activities took place (*ibid*).

Fredengren's work at Lough Gara, Co Sligo has demonstrated that these types of crannogs were probably commonplace in some parts of Ireland (Fredengren 2002). She has identified numerous 'low cairn' crannogs in the lough, one of which has been excavated. Sroove crannog consisted of a low mound of material, no more than 1.2m in height above the level of the water meadow within which it was built (*ibid*, 221). The crannog was contained within a palisade consisting of a single, occasionally double, line of roundwood posts within which there was a rectangular structure which shows no evidence of ever having been refurbished. Although the excavator claims great chronological depth for the site, identifying five phases of activity (*ibid*, 223–40), the excavated evidence could as readily be interpreted as the remains of a single-phase structure of short duration. The site has produced a tight cluster of radiocarbon dates indicating activity sometime during the late 7th–10th centuries AD (*ibid*, 94) and an artefact assemblage which included items of bone, iron nails, bronze studs, slag and a possible bowl-furnace – nothing that would indicate high status occupancy.

Sroove is of interest to a discussion on the function of crannogs for a number of reasons. First, its height implies that there were times during the year when it would have been easily accessible from the shore, thus negating the idea of its defensiveness. In summer it lay within the water meadow along the shores of the loch and only in winter was it an island. Second, it lay within a water body which contains at least one high status crannog, Rathtinaun, which was occupied during the 7th to 8th centuries AD. This crannog produced a rich artefact assemblage which included a bronze brooch, pins, rings and armlet, bone combs and pins, beads, Merovingian glass, crucibles and clay mould fragments, iron weapons and tools, as well as wooden vessels (O'Sullivan 1998, 118–21). A frequently refurbished perimeter and evidence for a round house denotes its status as a defended settlement. The juxtaposition of these two dissimilar but possibly contemporary crannogs suggests that during the Early Historic period crannogs were being built by the same communities but for very different functions.

## 6.4   CONCLUSIONS

It will be clear from the previous sections that analysis of the records from the excavations at Loch Glashan crannog has raised serious problems of interpretation. This is hardly surprising, given that the site was excavated over half a century ago, before modern standards of conservation of organic remains, before modern standards of excavation recording, before systematic collection of environmental samples, before proper funding of post-excavation work, and most importantly, before the modern understanding of taphonomic processes in waterlogged environments. The alternative chronologies presented in Chapter 6.1 are therefore not merely a post-modernist nod to the concept of multivocality, but reflect the authors' difficulties in understanding and agreeing on the processes at work on the site, given the limitations of the evidence. Despite these problems, the site has made significant contributions to our understanding of 1st millennium Dál Riata. These can be discussed under the headings of artefacts and settlement studies.

ARTEFACTS

The finds assemblage as a whole, though limited in range, fills a large gap in our knowledge by showing the variety of organic artefacts utilized in this period on a secular Gaelic site, and allows comparison with other recently excavated sites such as the contemporary monastic site of Iona and the British site of Buiston crannog. This helps to counterbalance the impression that an impoverished material culture is found on non-waterlogged sites in the region (table 4). This holds true whether these objects date to the 2nd/4th centuries AD, as the radiocarbon assays suggest, or to the main period of occupation of the crannog. However, if the radiocarbon dates are accepted, then these objects are of further importance as the first wooden artefacts to be securely ascribed to this period in Scotland and Ireland. The leatherworking artefacts seem to provide evidence for one of the major activities on the site, as far as can

be ascertained from the finds. Individual finds are also of significance beyond the site itself. The re-identification of the leather 'jacket' as an early medieval book satchel is of international significance, being only the second found in an archaeological context, and the earliest so far known. Its presence on the crannog, even if being re-cycled as scrap, raises questions about the possibility of literacy in a secular context in Dál Riata, something which has been suggested recently in relation to Dunadd (Lane & Campbell 2000, 253–4). Of the other finds, the 8/9th century silver-in-glass bead is a surprising find, indicating contact with Norse or, perhaps more likely, Gall-Gaedhil, early in the Norse period. The axehead is also of Norse type, supporting this interpretation. The recent recognition of a motif piece bearing Norse style ring-plait ornament at the contemporary settlement at Bruach an Druimein, Poltalloch (Campbell in Abernethy forthcoming) perhaps strengthens this argument. Previously there has been little physical evidence for Norse influence in this area of mainland Argyll. Finally, the first direct scientific dates obtained from the imported E ware on the site confirm a welcome fixed point in the chronology of artefacts of the period, which are otherwise bedevilled by art historical debates and problems with taphonomic interpretation. E ware is crucial in identifying and dating occupation of the 6/7th centuries in Scotland, Ireland, Wales and south-west England. The identification of red dyestuffs on the E ware adds the site to a growing list of such occurrences and shows the site had some connection with the Continental trading network which was articulated through Dunadd.

SETTLEMENT STUDIES

The site contributes to our understanding of the settlement pattern in 1st millennium Argyll. We now have detailed knowledge of four contemporary early medieval sites in the Kilmartin valley: the royal fort of Dunadd (Lane & Campbell 2000); the open settlement at Bruach an Druimein (Abernethy forthcoming); the older excavations at the unusual low-lying dun at Ardifuir (RCAHMS 1988, 171–2); and Loch Glashan crannog itself. Recently, a further crannog of the period has been identified at the west end of Loch Awe at Ederline boathouse and will provide important comparative material to Loch Glashan (Chapter 2.3). In addition, stray finds, sculptured stones and placenames fill in this framework (Lane & Campbell 2000, illus 1.35). It is clear that this was a densely settled landscape with a wide variety of settlement types in use. Surprisingly, what has emerged is that some similar types of activity were present on all four sites even though they are all of different form and location. Evidence of metalworking, both ferrous and non-ferrous, including precious metals was found on all the sites. This shows that these activities were not under the direct control of the elite at the royal site of Dunadd, and that costly materials, such as imported pottery, beads, dyestuffs and silver, could find their way to sites of much lower status. The locations of these sites are all very different, and each seems to have served a specific function. It has been suggested that Dunadd is located not just for its defensive possibilities, but for its place in a symbolic landscape (Campbell 2003, 52–5). Bruach an Druimein lies on the fertile gravel terraces of the Kilmartin valley, one the largest areas of good quality arable land in Argyll. Ardifuir has a coastal situation, perhaps sited for the extensive outlook down the Sound of Jura where it could control access to the estuary of the River Add. Loch Glashan is in an upland setting, far from agricultural land, but perhaps located to be close to resources such as cattle and fishing. Ederline crannog is sited on the major trans-Highland route from Argyll which runs along Loch Awe, through Glen Dochart, to eastern Scotland. It may be significant that this site, Ardifuir, and Loch Glashan itself are all sited at points where they could control access routes to Dunadd. Until further sites are excavated we cannot know what the 'typical' site of the period looked like, but this is clearly a well-developed settlement pattern adapted to exploitation of a variety of environments.

The site also contributes to our understanding of the development of settlement patterns over time. The variety of sites in the immediate vicinity of the crannog indicates some form of occupation for at least two millennia. The recent excavations at the dun on the hill above the loch have produced a small yellow bead which shows that it was certainly occupied around the 2nd century AD and this is supported by radiocarbon dates (Gilmour & Henderson *pers comm*). The crannog itself was occupied perhaps in the 2/4th centuries, and certainly at some times in the late 6th/9th centuries. The enclosed island settlement seems to have been occupied during the 13th and 14th centuries. The unenclosed post-medieval settlement is undated at present, but a settlement is marked here on Timothy Pont's map of the early 17th century (named *Derren Loch*) (Stone 1989, map 15a), and stray 17th century and later craggan pottery was also found on the island settlement and in silts near the crannog (Fairhurst 1969, 59–60). It is not possible to say whether these were successive monuments, or whether there was overlap in the occupation of the sites. Whatever the case, the location near the outlet of Loch Glashan has clearly been important over an extended period of time, despite the apparently poor upland location far from agricultural land. Whether the settlements were located to take advantage of upland resources, such as cattle, or fish from the loch, or were sited to control routeways, or for some other more opaque symbolic reasons, is a matter for debate. However, the succession of sites seems in microcosm to reflect a widespread regional pattern of settlement change which can be discerned taking place in the 1st millennium. The excavations at Loch Glashan have thus contributed a great deal to throwing some light on the process which led to the evolution of the present day landscape of dispersed farming settlements.

## BIBLIOGRAPHY

Abernethy, D forthcoming 'Bruach an Druimein: Excavations by the late Eric Cregeen 1960–2', *Scottish Archaeology Internet Reports*.

Alcock, L 1963 *Dinas Powys, an Iron Age, Dark Age and early medieval settlement in Glamorgan*. Cardiff: Univ of Wales.

Alcock, L 1988 'The activities of potentates in Celtic Britain, AD 500–800: a positivist approach', *in* Driscoll, S T & Nieke, M R (eds) *Power and politics in early medieval Britain and Ireland*, 22–46. Edinburgh: EUP.

Alcock, L 2003 *Kings and warriors, craftsmen and priests*. Edinburgh: Soc Antiq Scot Monog Ser.

Alcock, L & Alcock, E A 1987 'Reconnaissance excavations on Early Historic fortifications and other royal sites in Scotland, 1974–84: 2, Excavations at Dunollie Castle, Oban, Argyll, 1978', *Proc Soc Antiq Scot* 117, 73–101.

Alcock, L, Alcock, E & Driscoll, T 1989 'Reconnaissance excavations on Early Historic fortifications and other royal sites in Scotland, 1974–84:3 Excavations at Dundurn, Strathearn, Perthshire, 1976–7', *Proc Soc Antiq Scot*, 119, 189–226.

Alexander, J J G 1978 'Insular Manuscripts, 6th to the 9th century, a survey of manuscripts illuminated in the British Isles 1', *in* Lowe, E A (ed) 1978.

Allen, J R 1903 *Early Christian Monuments of Scotland III*. Edinburgh: Soc Antiqs Scot.

Armit, I 1991 'The Atlantic Scottish Iron Age: five levels of chronology', *Proc Soc Antiq Scot*, 121, 181–214.

Armit, I (ed) 1990 *Beyond the Brochs. Changing perspectives on the Late Iron Age in Atlantic Scotland*. Edinburgh.

Armit, I, Campbell, E, & Dunwell, S forthcoming 'Excavations at Eilean Olabhat, North Uist', *Proc Soc Antiq Scot*.

Atkinson, J A, & Photos-Jones, E 1999 'Brave at heart: clanship and the work of the Highland smith', *in* Young, S M M, Pollard, A M, Budd, P & Ixer, R A (eds), *Metals in Antiquity*, BAR Int Ser 792, 271–9.

127

Ballin-Smith, B (ed) 1994 *Howe: four millennia of Orkney prehistory.* Edinburgh: Soc Antiq Scot Monog Ser 9.

Barber, J 1981 'Excavations at Iona, 1979', *Proc Soc Antiq Scot*, 111, 282–380.

Barber, J W & Crone, B A 2001 'The duration of structures, settlements and sites: some evidence from Scotland', *in* Raftery, B & Hickey, J (eds) *Recent Developments in Wetland Research*, 69–86. Seandálaíocht: Mon 2, Dept Archaeol, UCD & WARP Occ Paper 14. Dublin: Dept Archaeol, Univ College Dublin.

Batey, C & Graham-Campbell, J 1998 *Vikings in Scotland.* Edinburgh.

Bersu, G 1948 'Preliminary report on the excavations at Lissue, 1947', *Ulster J Archaeol*, 11, 131–3.

Boon, G C 1977 'Gold-in-glass beads from the ancient world', *Brittannia*, 8, 193–207.

Bourke, C 2001 'Antiquities from the River Blackwater III: iron axeheads', *Ulster J Archaeol* 3rd series 60, 63–93.

Bradley, J 1993 'Moynagh Lough: an insular workshop of the 2nd quarter of the 8th century', *in* Spearman, M & Higgitt, J (eds) 1993, 74–81.

Bradley, R & Fulford, M 1980 'Sherd size in the analysis of occupation debris', *Bulletin of the Institute of Archaeology*, 17, 85–95.

Braunfels, W 1968 *Die Welt der Karolinger und ihre Kunst.* Munich.

Breslin, L 1999 *A landscape survey of the Iron Age settlements of Mid Argyll and Lorn.* Unpubl undergraduate dissertation, Dept Archaeol, Univ Glasgow.

Brisbane, M A (ed) 1992 *The Archaeology of Novgorod, Russia: recent results from the town and its hinterland.* Lincoln: Soc Med Archaeol Monog No 13.

Brown, M P 2003 *The Lindisfarne Gospels. Society, spirituality and the scribe.* London: British Library.

Bruce-Mitford, R 1983 *The Sutton Hoo Ship Burial*, vol. 3, ii. London: British Museum.

Brugmann, B 2004 *Glass beads from Anglo-Saxon graves.* Oxford: Oxbow Books.

Butter, R 1999 *Kilmartin: an introduction and guide.* Kilmartin.

Callmer, J 1977 *Trade beads and bead trade in Scandinavia, 800–1000 AD.* Lund: Acta Archaeol Lund 11.

Campbell, E 1987 'A cross-marked quern from Dunadd and other evidence for relations between Dunadd and Iona', *Proc Soc Antiq Scot,* 117, 105–118

Campbell, E 1991 *Imported goods in the Early Medieval Celtic West with special reference to Dinas Powys.* Unpubl PhD thesis, Univ Wales, College of Cardiff.

Campbell, E 1995 'New evidence for glass vessels in western Britain and Ireland in the 6th/7th centuries AD', *in* Foy, D (ed) *Le Verre de l'Antiquité tardive et du Haut Moyen Age*, 35–40. Association Française pour l'Archéologie du Verre/Musée Archéologique du Val D'Oise.

Campbell E 1996a 'Trade in the Dark Age West: a peripheral activity?', *in* Crawford, B (ed), *Scotland in Dark-Age Britain*, 79–91. St Andrews: St John's House Papers No 6.

Campbell E 1996b 'The archaeological evidence for contacts: imports, trade and economy in Celtic Britain had 400–800', *in* Dark, K R (ed), *External contacts and the economy of Late Roman and Post-Roman Britain*, 83–96. Woodbridge: Boydell & Brewer.

Campbell, E 1997 'The early medieval imports', *in* Hill, P 1997, 297–322.

Campbell, E 2000 'A review of glass vessels in western Britain and Ireland AD 400–800', *in* Price, J (ed) *Glass in Britain, AD 350–800*, 33–46. London: British Museum Press.

Campbell, E & Lane, A 1993 'Celtic and Germanic interaction in Scottish Dalriada: the seventh-century metalworking site at Dunadd', *in* Higgitt, J & Spearman, R M (eds) 1993, 52–63.

Campbell, E 2001 'Were the Scots Irish?', *Antiquity* 75, 285–92.

Campbell, E 2003 'Royal Inauguration in Dál Riata and the Stone of Destiny', *in* Wellander, R, Breeze, D, & Clancy, T (eds) *The Stone of Destiny: artefact and icon*, 43–59. Edinburgh: Soc Antiq Scot Monog 24.

Campbell, E, Housley, R & Taylor, M 2004 'Charred food residues from Hebridean Iron Age pottery: analysis and dating', *in* Housley, R & Coles, G (eds) *Atlantic Connections and Adaptations: economies, environments and subsistence in lands bordering the North Atlantic*, 64–85. Oxford: Oxbow Monograph (= AEA/NABO symposium 21).

Campbell, E & Heald, A forthcoming 'A Pictish brooch mould from North Uist: Implications for the organization of metalworking in the later 1st millennium AD'.

Carlson, J, Pretzel, B & Price, B (eds) 2000 *Infrared & Raman Users Group (IRUG) spectral database,* edition 2000. Philadelphia: IRUG.

Carver, M 1979 'Three Saxo-Norman tenements in Durham City', *Med Archaeol*, 23, 26–35.

Cavers, G forthcoming 'An underwater survey of crannogs in Argyll'.

Chinnery, V 1986 *Oak furniture; the British tradition.* Woodbridge: Woodbridge Antique Collectors Club.

Clarke, A 1997 'The coarse stone artefacts', *in* Driscoll, S T & Yeoman, P A *Excavations within Edinburgh Castle in 1988–91*, 122–6. Edinburgh: Soc Antiq Scot Monog Ser 12.

Clarke, A 1998a 'Small rounded pebbles', *in* Sharples, N 1998, 178–80.

Clarke, A 1998b 'Cobble tools', *in* Sharples, N 1998, 140–4.

Clarke, A forthcoming a 'The coarse stone tools from Pool, Sanday'.

Clarke, A forthcoming b 'The coarse stone tools from Bayanne, Shetland'.

Coffey, G 1906 'Craigywarren crannog', *Proc Roy Irish Academy* 26C, 109–18.

Cowgill, J, de Neergard, M & Griffiths, N 1987 *Knives and Scabbards: Medieval Finds from Excavations in London: 1.* London: HMSO.

Cowley, D C 'Changing places – building life-spans and settlement continuity in northern Scotland', *in* Downes, J & Ritchie, A (eds) *Sea change. Orkney and northern Europe in the Later Iron Age AD 300–800*, 75–81. Balgavies: Pinkfoot Press.

Craw, J H 1930 'Excavations at Dunadd and at other sites on the Poltalloch Estates, Argyll', *Pro. Soc Antiq Scot* 64, 111–27.

Crawford, B E & Ballin-Smith, B 1999 *The Biggings. Papa Stour, Shetland. The history and archaeology of a royal Norwegian farm.* Edinburgh: Soc Antiq Scot Monog Ser 15.

Cregeen, E 1960 'Poltalloch', *Discovery Excav Scot 1960*, 10.

Crone, B A 1988 *Tree-ring analysis and the study of crannogs.* Unpubl PhD thesis, Univ Sheffield.

Crone, B A 1993a 'A wooden bowl from Loch à Ghlinne Bhig, Bracadale, Skye', *Proc Soc Antiq Scot,* 123, 269–75.

Crone, B A 1993b 'Crannogs and chronologies', *Proc Soc Antiq Scot* 123, 245–54.

Crone, B A 1998 'The development of an Early Historic tree-ring chronology for Scotland', *Proc Soc Antiq Scot,* 128, 485–93.

Crone, B A 2000 *The history of a Scottish lowland crannog: excavations at Buiston, Ayrshire 1989–90.* Edinburgh: STAR Monog Ser 4.

Crone, B A unpubl *The waterlogged wood assemblage from Tuquoy, Westray.* Unpubl report for Historic Scotland.

Crone, B A & Barber, J 1981 'Analytical techniques for the investigation of non-artefactual wood from prehistoric and medieval sites', *Proc Soc Antiq Scot,* 111, 510–15.

Crone, B A, Henderson, J C & Sands, R 2001 'Scottish crannogs: construction, collapse and conflation. Problems of interpretation', *in* Raftery, B & Hickey, J (eds) *Recent Developments in Wetland Research,* 55–68. Seandálaíocht: Mon 2, Dept Archaeol, UCD & WARP Occ Paper 14. Dublin: Dept Archaeol, Univ College Dublin.

Crone, B A & Henderson, J forthcoming 'Later prehistoric crannogs in south-west Scotland'.

Curwen, E C 1937 'Querns', *Antiquity* 11, 133–51.

Curwen, E C 1941 'More about Querns', *Antiquity,* 15, 15–32.

Curzon, Robert 1849 *Visits to Monasteries in the Levant.* London.

Davies, O 1942 'Contributions to the study of crannogs in South Ulster', *Ulster J Archaeol,* 5, 14–30.

Dhondt, J 1962 'Les problemes de Quentovic', *Studi in Onore di Aminote Fanfani,* 217–18. Milan.

Dixon, T N 1984 *Scottish crannogs: Underwater excavation of artificial islands with special reference to Oakbank Crannog, Loch Tay.* Unpubl PhD thesis. Univ Edinburgh.

Dixon, N 2004 *The crannogs of Scotland.* Stroud: Tempus.

Dobbin, S 1977 *The disc querns from Loch Glashan.* Dept Archaeol, Univ Glasgow, Undergraduate dissertation.

Duck, R W & McManus, J 1987 'Side-scan sonar applications in limnoarchaeology', *Geoarchaeology* 2, 223–30.

Earwood, C 1988 'Wooden containers and other wooden artefacts from the Glastonbury Lake Village', *Somerset Levels Papers* 14, 83–90.

Earwood, C 1990 'The wooden artefacts from Loch Glashan crannog, mid-Argyll', *Proc Soc Antiq Scot,* 120, 79–94.

Earwood, C 1992 'Turned wooden vessels of the Early Historic period from Ireland and western Scotland', *Ulster J Archaeol* 54–5, 154–9.

Earwood, C 1993a *Domestic Wooden Artefacts in Britain and Ireland from Neolithic to Viking Times.* Exeter: EUP.

Earwood, C 1993b 'The dating of wooden troughs and dishes', *Proc Soc Antiq Scot,* 123, 355–62.

Earwood, C 1998 'Typology of Bronze Age wooden containers: new dating evidence from Islay', *Proc Soc Antiq Scot,* 128, 161–6.

Earwood, C unpubl *Deer Park Farms, Co. Antrim: Catalogue of Wooden Artefacts,* Unpubl DoE NI report.

East, K 1983 'The shoes', *in* Bruce-Mitford 1983, 792–5.

Fairhurst, H 1969 'A mediaeval island-settlement in Loch Glashan, Argyll', *Glasgow Archaeol J,* 1, 47–67.

Feachem, R W 1966 'The hill-forts of Northern Britain', *in* Rivet, A L F 1966 (ed) *The Iron Age in Northern Britain,* 59–87. Edinburgh.

Flemming, B W 1976 'Side Scan Sonar: A Practical Guide', *Int Hydrographic Review,* 53, 65–91.

Foster, S 1996 *Picts, Gaels and Scots.* London: Batsford.

Forbes, R J 1987 *Studies in Ancient Technology.* Vol IV. Leiden: Brill.

Fredengren, C 2002 *Crannogs. A study of people's interaction with lakes, with particular reference to Lough Gara in the north-west of Ireland.* Dublin: Wordwell.

Gilmour, S 2000 'First millennia settlement development in the Atlantic West', *in* Henderson, J (ed) 2000, 155–70.

Gladwin, P F 1987 'Loch Glashan (Lochgair parish): iron bloomery site', *Discovery & Excavation Scotland,* 40–1.

Goodman, W L 1964 *The history of woodworking tools.* London: Bell & Hyman.

Graham-Campbell J 2001 'National and regional identities: the "Glittering Prizes"', *in* Redknap, M, Edwards, N & Youngs, S (eds) *Pattern and purpose in Insular art,* 27–38. Oxford.

Groenman-van Waateringe, W 1975 'Society ... rests on leather', *in* Renaud, J G N (ed), 1975, *Rotterdam Papers II,* 23–34. Rotterdam.

Groenman-van Waateringe, W 1981 'The leather from ditch I', *in* Barber, J 1981, 318–28.

Groenman-van Waateringe, W 2000 'The leatherwork', *in* Crone, B A 2000, 128–33.

Guido, M 1978 *The glass beads of the prehistoric and Roman periods in Britain and Ireland.* London: Soc Antiqs Lond.

Guido, M 1999 *The glass beads of Anglo-Saxon England* c AD 400–700. Woodbridge: Boydell Press.

Hald, M 1972 *Primitive shoes.* Copenhagen: National Museum Publications ser 1, XIII.

Hall, A J & Photos-Jones, E 1998 'The bloomery mounds of the Scottish Highlands: Part II – a review of iron mineralization in relation', *J Historical Metallurgy Society,* 32 (2), 54–66.

Halliday, S 1999 'Hut-circle settlements in the Scottish landscape', *in* Frodsham, P, Topping, P & Cowley, D (eds) *'We were always chasing time' – papers presented to Keith Blood,* 49–65. Northern Archaeology 17/18.

Hamilton, J R C 1968 *Excavations at Clickhimin, Shetland.* Edinburgh: HMSO.

129

Harbison, P 1992 *The High Crosses of Ireland. An Iconographical and Photographic Survey*. Bonn.

Harding, D 1997 'Forts, duns, brochs and crannogs: Iron Age settlements in Argyll', *in* Ritchie, G (ed) 1997, 118–40.

Hayden, B & Cannon, A 1983 'Where the garbage goes: refuse disposal in the Maya highlands', *J Anthrop Archaeol*, 2, 117–63.

Hencken, H O'N 1936 'Ballinderry Crannog No 1', *Proc Roy Ir Acad*, 43c, 103–239.

Hencken, H O'N 1942 'Ballinderry Crannog No 2', *Proc Roy Ir Acad*, 47c, 1–76.

Hencken, H O'N 1950 'Lagore Crannog: An Irish Royal residence of the 7th to 10th centuries AD', *Proc Roy Ir Acad*, 53c, 1–248.

Henderson, J 1998 'Islets through time: the definition, dating and distribution of Scottish crannogs', *Oxford J Archaeol* 17.2, 227–44.

Henderson, J 2000 'Shared traditions? The drystone settlement records of Atlantic Scotland and Ireland 700 BC–AD 200', *in* Henderson, J (ed), 117–54.

Henderson, J (ed) 2000 *The prehistory and Early history of Atlantic Europe*. Oxford (= British Archaeological Report International Series 861).

Henry, F 1956–7 'Early monasteries, beehive huts, and dry-stone houses in the neighbourhood of Caherciveen and Waterville, Co Kerry', *PRIA*, 58C, 45–166.

Herren, M W (ed) 1974 *The Hisperica famina: I. The A-Text. A new critical edition with english translation and philological commentary*. Toronto: Pontifical Institute of Medieval Studies.

Higgitt, J & Spearman, R M (eds) 1993 *The Age of Migrating Ideas. Early medieval art in Northern Britain and Ireland*. Edinburgh: National Museums Scot.

Hill, P *Whithorn and St Ninian: The excavations of a monastic town 1984–91*. Gloucester: Sutton.

Hingley, R, Moore, H L, Triscott, J E & Wilson, G 1997 'The excavation of two later Iron Age fortified homesteads at Aldclune, Blair Atholl, Perth and Kinross', *Proc Soc Antiq Scot*, 127, 407–66.

Hodges, R 1981 *The Hamwih pottery: the local and imported wares from 30 year's excavation at Middle Saxon Southampton and their European context*. London: Council Brit Archaeol Research Rep 37.

Holdsworth, P 1976 'Saxon Southampton: a new review', *Med Archaeol*, 20, 26–61.

Hoper, S T, McCormac, F G, Hogg, A G, Higham, T F G & Head, M J 1998 'Evaluation of wood pretreatments on oak and cedar', *Radiocarbon* 40, 45–50.

Hourihane, C 2003 *Gothic Art in Ireland*. London: Yale Univ Press.

Hunt, J 1974 *Irish Medieval Figure Sculpture, 1200–1600: a study of Irish tombs with notes on costume and armour*. Dublin: Irish Univ Press.

James, H 2003 *Medieval and Later landscape and settlement in Mid-Argyll and Knapdale, 2003*. Glasgow: GUARD report.

Jones, E W 1945 'Biological flora of the British Isles: *Acer pseudoplatanus* L', *J Ecol*, 32, 220–37.

Keane, M 1995 'Lough More, Co Mayo. The crannog', *Irish Archaeol Wetland Unit Trans* 4, 16–82.

Kelly, F 1976 'The old Irish tree-list', *Celtica*, 2, 107–24.

Kelly, F 1988 *A guide to Early Irish Law*. Dublin: Dublin Institute for Advanced Studies.

Kelly, F 2000 *Early Irish farming*. Dublin.

Kelly, E P 1994 'The Lough Kinale book shrine: the implications for the manuscripts', *in* O'Mahony, F (ed) *The Book of Kells, Proceedings of a Conference at Trinity College Dublin, 6–9 September 1992*, 280–9. Aldershot.

Khoroshev, A S K & Sorrokin, A N 1992 'Buildings and Properties from the Lyudin End of Novgorod', *in* Brisbane, M A (ed) 1992, 107–59.

Krusch, B 1880 *Studien zür Christlich-mittlealterlichen Chronologie*. Leipzig.

Laing, L 1974 'Cooking pots and the origins of the Scottish medieval pottery industry', *Archaeol J*, 130, 183–216.

Lamm, K 1977 'Early medieval metalworking on Helgo in Central Sweden', *in* Oddy, W A (ed) *Aspects of early metallurgy*, 97–115. London: British Museum Occ Pap 17.

Lane, A 1984 'Some Pictish problems at Dunadd', *in* Friell, J & Watson, W G (eds) *Pictish Studies*, 43–62. Oxford (= British Archaeol. Rep. 125).

Lane, A 1990 'Hebridean pottery: problems of definition, chronology, presence and absence', *in* Armit, I (ed) 1990, 108–30.

Lane, A & Campbell, E 2000 *Dunadd: An early Dalriadic capital*. Cardiff Studies in Archaeology. Oxford: Oxbow.

Lewis, R 2003 *Loch Glashan: conservation report on a leather 'jerkin' (satchel) and two iron artefacts*. Unpubl report for Historic Scotland.

Lynn, C 1978 'A rath in Seacash townland', *Ulster J Archaeol* 41, 55–74.

Lynn, C J 1987 'Deer Park Farm, Glenarm, Co Antrim', *Archaeology Ireland* 1, 11–15.

Lynn, C J 1994 'Early Medieval houses', *in* Ryan, M, *Irish Archaeology Illustrated*, 126–31. Dublin.

Loyn, H R & Percival, J 1975 *The reign of Charlemagne*. London: Edward Arnold.

Lucas, A T 1956 'Footwear in Ireland', *County Louth Archaeol J* 13, 309–88.

Lucas, A T 1972 'National Museum Acquisitions', *J Royal Soc Antiq Ireland*, 102, 204–5.

Lucas, A T 1973 *Viking and Medieval Dublin. National Museum Excavations 1962–78*. Dublin: National Museum.

McCarthy, M R & Brooks, C M 1988 *Medieval Pottery in Britain AD 900–1600*. Leicester: Leicester Univ Press.

McGrail, S 1987 *Ancient boats in NW Europe*. London: Longmans.

Mackie, E W 1974 *Dun Mor Vaul, an Iron Age Broch on Tiree*. Glasgow.

MacKie, E 1987 'Leckie Broch. The impact on the Scottish Iron Age', *Glasg Archaeol J*, 14, 1–18.

MacKie, E 1997 'Dun Mor Vaul revisited: fact and theory in the reappraisal of the Scottish Atlantic iron Age', *in* Ritchie, G (ed) 1997, 141–80.

MacKie, E W 2002 'Two querns from Appin', *Scot Archaeol J*, 24.1, 85–92.

MacKintosh, J 1988 *The woods of Argyll and Bute. Research and Survey in Nature Conservancy 10*. Peterborough: Nature Conservancy Council.

MacSween, A 2000 'Integrating the artefact assemblages from the 19th and 20th century excavations', *in* Crone 2000, 143–51.

MacSween, A 2003 'The pottery from Minehowe, Orkney: aspects of contextual interpretation', *in* Gibson, A (ed) *Prehistoric pottery: people, pattern and purpose*, 127–34. Oxford: BAR 1156.

Mack, A 1997 *Field guide to the Pictish symbol stones*. Balgavie: Pinkfoot Press.

Madsen, H B 1984 'Metal-casting', *in* Bencard, M *Ribe Excavations 1970–76*, Vol 2, 15–189.

Marner, D 2002 'The Sword of the Spirit, the Word of God and the Book of Deer', *Med Archaeol*, XLVI, 1–28.

Matson, M 1998 *The historical uses of leather in Britain: with reference to the leatherwork from Loch Glashan*. Unpubl undergraduate dissertation, Dept Archaeol, Univ Glasgow.

Meehan, B 1994a 'Elements of manuscript production in the Middle Ages', *in* Ryan, M (ed) *Irish Archaeology Illustrated*, 139–43. Dublin: Country House.

Meehan, B 1994b *The Book of Kells. An illustrated introduction to the manuscript in Trinity College Dublin*. London: Thames & Hudson.

Moar, P & Stewart, J 1944 'Newly discovered sculptured stones from Papil, Shetland', *Proc Soc Antiq Scot* 78, 91–9.

Moorhouse, S 1986 'Non-dating uses of medieval pottery', *Medieval Ceramics* 10, 85–124.

Morris, C 1984 *Anglo-Saxon and Medieval woodworking crafts: the manufacture and use of domestic and utilitarian artefacts in the British Isles 400–1500 AD*. Cambridge: unpubl PhD thesis.

Morrison, I 1981 'The extension of the chronology of the crannogs of Scotland', *Int J Nautical Archaeol*, 10.4, 344–6.

Morrison, I 1985 *Landscape with lake dwellings*. Edinburgh: EUP.

Mould, Q, Carlisle, I & Cameron, E 2003 *Leather and Leatherworking in Anglo-Scandinavian and Medieval York. The Archaeology of York, The Small Finds 17/16 Craft, Industry and Everyday Life*. York.

Mowat, R J C 1996 *The logboats of Scotland*. Oxford. Oxbow Monog 68.

Mullarkey, P A 2000 *Irish book shrines: a reassessment*. Unpubl PhD thesis, vol 1A. Trinity College Dublin.

Munro, R 1882 *Ancient Scottish lake-dwellings or crannogs*. Edinburgh: David Douglas.

Munro, R 1893 'Notes of crannogs or lake-dwellings recently discovered in Argyllshire', *Proc Soc Antiq Scot*, 27, 205–22.

Newman, C 2002 'Balinderry crannog no 2, Co Offaly: Pre-crannog early medieval horizon', *J Irish Archaeol*, 11, 99–124.

Nieke, M R 1990 'Fortifications in Argyll: retrospect and future prospect', *in* Armit, I (ed) 1990, 131–42.

Nieke, M 1993 'Penannular and brooches: secular ornament or symbol in action?', *in* Higgitt, J & Spearman, R M (eds) 1993, 128–34.

Nieke M R & Duncan, H B 1988 'Dalriada: the establishment and maintenance of an Early Historic kingdom in northern Britain, *in* Driscoll, S T & Nieke, M R (eds) *Power and politics in early medieval Britain and Ireland*, 6–21. Edinburgh: EUP.

Oakley, G E M 1973 *Scottish crannogs*. unpubl MPhil thesis. Univ Newcastle-upon-Tyne.

Ohlgren, T H 1986 *Insular and Anglo-Saxon illuminated manuscripts. An iconographic catalogue* c AD *625–1100*. New York: Garland Pub.

O'Neill, T 1997 'Columba the scribe', *in* Bourke, C (ed) *Studies in the Cult of Saint Columba*, 69–79. Dublin.

O'Sullivan, A 1998 *The archaeology of lake settlement in Ireland*. Dublin: Discovery Programme Monog 4.

OS *Dunoon and Loch Fyne*. Ordnance Survey 1 inch Map. Sheet 65.

Ottaway, P 1992 *Anglo-Scandinavian ironwork from Coppergate. The archaeology of York. The small finds 17/6*. London: CBA.

Owen, O 1999 'The gaming pieces', *in* Owen, O & Dalland, M, *Scar. A Viking boat burial on Sanday, Orkney*, 127–32. Edinburgh: Historic Scotland.

de Paor, L 1955 'A Survey of Sceilg Mhichíl', *J Roy Soc Antiq Ir*, 174–87.

Peacock, D P S & Thomas, A C 1967 'Class E imported post-Roman pottery: a suggested origin', *Cornish Archaeol*, 6, 35–46.

Pertz, G W (ed) 1874 *Monumenta Germaniae Historica*, Diplomata spuria 1. Berlin.

Photos-Jones, E, Atkinson, J A, Hall, A J & Banks, I 1998 'The Bloomery Mounds of the Scottish Highlands. Part I: The archaeological background', *J Historical Metallurgy Society*, 32 (1), 15–32.

Raftery, J (ed) 1941 *Christian Art in Ancient Ireland* Vol II. Dublin: Stationary Office.

Raine, J (ed) 1835 *Reginaldi monachi Dunelmensis libellus de admirandis beati Cuthberti virtutibus quae novellis patratae sunt temporibus*. Surtees Society.

RCAHMS 1988 *Argyll. An inventory of the ancient monuments. Vol 6. Mid-Argyll and Cowal. Prehistoric and early historic monuments*. Edinburgh: HMSO.

RCAHMS 1992 *Argyll. An inventory of the ancient monuments Vol 7. Mid Argyll and Cowal, Medieval and later monuments*. Edinburgh: HMSO.

Redknap, M 1995 'Insular non-ferrous metalwork from Wales of the 8th to 10th centuries', *in* Bourke, C (ed) *From the Isles of the North*, 59–74. Belfast: HMSO.

Redknap, M & Lane, A 1994 'The early medieval crannog at Llangorse, Powys: an interim statement on the 1989–1993 seasons' *Int J Nautical Archaeol* 23.3, 189–205.

Rees, S E 1979 *Agricultural implements in Prehistoric and Roman Britain*. Oxford: BAR Brit Ser 69.

Reeves, W 1857 *The Life of St Columba, Founder of Hy / written by Adamnan*. Dublin & Edinburgh.

Ritchie, J 1942 'The lake dwelling or crannog in Eaderloch, Loch Treig; its traditions and its construction', *Proc Soc Antiq Scot*, 76, 8–78.

Ritchie, A 1977 'Excavation of Pictish and Viking-age farmsteads at Buckquoy, Orkney', *Proc Soc Antiq Scot*, 108, 174–227.

Ritchie, G (ed) 1997 *The archaeology of Argyll*. Edinburgh: EUP.

Robertson, A 1970 'Roman finds from non-Roman sites in Scotland', *Britannia* 1, 198–226.

Rodziewicz, M 1984 *Alexandrie III. Les Habitati romaines Tadives d'Alexandrie*. Warsaw.

Rogerson, A & Dallas, C 1984 *Excavations in Thetford 1948–59 and 1973–80. East Anglian Archaeology Report* 22. Gressenhall (Norfolk): EAA.

Ryan, M (ed) 1983 *Treasures of Ireland. Irish Art 3000 BC – AD 1500*. Dublin: Royal Irish Academy.

Sands, R & Hale, A 2002 'Evidence from marine crannogs of later prehistoric use of the Firth of Clyde', *J Wetland Archaeol* 1, 41–54.

Schiffer, M B 1972 'Archaeological context and systemic context', *American Antiquity*, 37, 156–65.

Schiffer, M B 1976 *Behavioural archaeology*. New York: Academic Press.

Schiffer, M B 1996 *Formation processes of the archaeological record*. Salt Lake City: Univ Utah Press.

Scott, J 1960 'Loch Glashan', *Discovery & Excavation Scotland*, 8–9.

Scott, J 1961a 'Loch Glashan crannog', *Med Archaeol*, 5, 310–11.

Scott, J 1961b 'Loch Glashan crannog' *Archaeol Newsletter*, 7.1, 20–1.

Scott, B G 1990 *Early Irish Ironworking*. Ulster Museum Pub 266. Ulster: Ulster Museum.

Sharpe, R 1985 'Latin and Irish Words for "Book-Satchel"', *Peritia*, 4, 152–6.

Sharpe, R (ed) 1995 *Adomnán of Iona, Life of St Columba*. London: Penguin.

Sharples, N 1998 *Scalloway: A broch, Late Iron Age settlement and medieval cemetery in Shetland*. Oxford: Oxbow Monograph 82.

Simpson, I A 1997 'The physical nature of the burial environment in archaeological sites and landscapes', *in* Corfield, M, Hinton, P, Nixon, T & Pollard, M (eds) 1997 *Preserving archaeological remains in situ*, 55–9. London: MOLAS.

Small, A, Thomas, C & Wilson, D M 1973 *St Ninians Isle and its Treasure*. London: Oxford Univ Press.

Sode, T & Feveile, C 2002 'Segmented metal foil glass beads and hollow, blown glass beads with a coat of metal from the marketplace at Ribe', *By, marsk og geest* 14, 5–14.

Sommer, U 1990 'Dirt theory, or archaeological sites seen as rubbish heaps', *J Theoretical Archaeol*, 1, 47–60.

Stevenson, R B K 1952 'Celtic carved box from Orkney', *Proc Soc Antiq Scot*, 86, 187–90.

Stout, M 1997 *The Irish ringfort*. Dublin: Four Courts Press.

Stokes, M 1892 *Six months in the Apennines*. London.

Stokes, W 1877 *Three Middle-Irish homilies on the Lives of Saints Patrick, Brigit and Columba*. Calcutta.

Stokes, W (ed) 1905 *The Martyrology of Oengus the Culdee*. Dublin: Dublin Institute for Advanced Studies.

Stone, J C 1989 *The Pont Manuscript Maps of Scotland*. Tring.

Stuart, J 1867 *The Sculptured Stones of Scotland II*. Edinburgh.

Szabo, M, Grenander-Nyberg, G & Myrdal, J 1985 *Elisenhof in Eiderstadt: Die Holzfunde*. Frankfurt am Main: Peter Lang.

Taylor, M 1981 *Wood in Archaeology*. Aylesbury: Shire Publications.

Taylor, G W 1991 'Dyepots – method of analysis', *in* Vince, A 1991, 169–70.

Thomas, C 1959 'Imported pottery in dark-age western Britain', *Med Archaeol*, 3, 89–111.

Thomas, C 1963 'The interpretation of the Pictish symbols', *Archaeol J*, 120, 1–97.

Thomas, C 1976 'Imported Late-Roman Mediterranean pottery in Ireland and western Britain: chronologies and implications', *Proc Royal Irish Acad* 76C, 245–55.

Thomas, C 1981 *A provisional list of imported pottery in post-Roman western Britain and Ireland*. Redruth (= Inst Cornish Studies Special Rep 7).

Thomas, M C forthcoming 'The leather', *in* Bogdan, N Q & Thomas, M C forthcoming *Excavations in High Street, Perth 1975–77*.

Thornton, J H 1990 'Shoes, boots, and shoe repairs', *in* Biddle, M 1990 *Artefacts from Medieval Winchester: object and economy in Medieval Winchester*, 591–617. Oxford: OUP.

Vince, A 1991 *Aspects of Saxon and Medieval London I. Finds and environmental evidence*. London.

Wallace, P F & Ó Floinn, R 1988 *Dublin 1000. Discovery & excavation in Dublin, 1842–1981*. Dublin.

Walton, P 1988 'Dyes of the Viking Age: a summary of recent work', *Dyes in History and Archaeol*, 7, 14–20.

Walton, P 1989 *Textiles, cordage and raw fibre from 16–22 Coppergate. The Archaeology of York* 17/5. London: CBA.

Walton Rogers, P 1997 *Textile Production at 16–22 Coppergate. The Archaeology of York* 17/11. York: CBA.

Walton Rogers, P, 1999 'Identification of dye on Middle Saxon pottery from Christ Church College', *Canterbury's Archaeology 1996–1997. 21st Annual Report of Canterbury Archaeological Trust*, 36. Canterbury.

Walton Rogers, P, 2001a 'The textiles', *in* Haughton, C & Powlesland, D *West Heslerton, The Anglian Cemetery vol I. The excavation and discussion of the evidence*, 143–71. West Heslerton: The Landscape Research Centre.

Walton Rogers, P, 2002b 'Tests for dye in textile samples', *in* Filmer-Sankey, W & Pestell, T *Snape Anglo-Saxon Cemetery: Excavations and Surveys 1824–1992*, 212–14. *East Anglian Archaeology 95*.

Walton Rogers, P, 2001c 'The re-appearance of an old Roman loom in medieval England', *in* Walton Rogers, P, Bender Jorgensen, L & Rast-Eicher, A *The Roman textile industry and its influence: a birthday tribute to John Peter Wild*, 158–71. Oxford: Oxbow.

Walton Rogers, P and Taylor, G W 1991 'The characterization of dyes in textiles from archaeological excavations', *Chromatography and Analysis*, 17, 5–7.

Walton Rogers, P unpubl a *Dye on 7th–8th century potsherd from Teeshan, nr Ballymena, Co Antrim*. TRA Report to R Warner. Ulster Museum, 7 May 1985.

Walton Rogers, P unpubl b *Dye analysis of sherds of E ware from Dunadd and Buiston*. TRA Report to National Museums of Scotland, 29 July 1986.

Walton Rogers, P unpubl c *Tests for dye on potsherds from The Brooks, Winchester*. TRA Report 15 February 1996.

Walton Rogers, P unpubl d *Dye on potsherds from Norwich*. TRA Report to P Murphy, UEA, 22 April 1985.

Walton Rogers, P unpubl e *Tests for dye on textile samples from Dublin Castle Yard, Waterford City, Deerpark Farm and Loch Tay*. TRA Report to E Heckett, 20 January 1989.

Warner, R B 1988 'The archaeology of Early Historic Irish kingship', *in* Driscoll, S T & Nieke, M R (eds) *Power and politics in early Medieval Britain and Ireland*, 47–68. Edinburgh: EUP.

Warner, R B 1979 'The Clogher yellow layer', *Medieval Ceramics* 3, 37–40.

Waterer, J W 1986 'Irish book-satchels or budgets', *Med Archaeol*, XII, 70–82.

Wellander, R, Batey, C & Cowie, T 1987 'A Viking burial from Kneep, Uig, Isle of Lewis', *Proc Soc Antiq Scot*, 117, 149–74.

Werner, A E 1963 *Scientific examination of the penannular brooch from Loch Glashan crannog*. Unpubl report, British Museum.

Whiting, M C 1983 'Appendix 2: Dye analysis', *in* Crowfoot, E 'The textiles', *in* Bruce-Mitford, R 1983, 465.

Wild, J P 1970 *Textile Manufacture in the Northern Roman Provinces*. Cambridge: CUP.

Wilson, D M 1973 'The treasure', *in* Small, A *et al* (eds) 1973, 45–148.

Wilson, D M (ed) 1976 *The Archaeology of Anglo-Saxon England*. London: Methuen.

Wilson, D M 1981 *The Anglo-Saxons*. Harmondsworth: Penguin.

Wooding, J 1996 *Communication and commerce along the western seaways AD 400–800*. Oxford: BAR 654.

Youngs, S (ed) 1989 *'The Work of Angels': Masterpieces of Celtic metalwork, 6th–9th centuries AD*. London: British Museum Publications.

# Chapter 7

# Appendices

## APPENDIX 7.1   FTIR MICROANALYSIS OF RESIDUE ON VESSEL 4

*Anita Quye*

### INTRODUCTION

Residual matter was found on the internal surface of Vessel 4, a base sherd from an E ware pot. To determine the source of the residue and test the hypothesis that the vessel may have been used as a lamp, the residue was sampled for analysis by Fourier transform infrared (FTIR) microspectrometry.

### SAMPLE DESCRIPTION

The inner surface of the sherd was coated with a visible pale brown residual layer present as three-dimensional concentric circles. Examination with a low-powered light microscope at ×80 magnification showed a dark brown crystalline-like material between the friable and crazed pale brown layer. Four samples were transferred with a scalpel from the areas shown in plate 33 to individual glass microscope slides with a central well (sample 3 was taken from the layer below sample 2). The samples were covered with a plain glass slide secured to the well slide with sticking tape prior to analysis by FTIR microspectrometry.

### FTIR MICROSPECTROMETRY

The four residue samples were analysed by FTIR microspectrometry. Samples from each were prepared individually for analysis using a diamond-window compression cell (μSample Plan, Spectratech). Instrumental parameters were:

| | |
|---|---|
| microscope: | Nic Plan (Nicolet); MCT-A detector; ×15 Cassegrain objective & condenser |
| mode: | transmission (single diamond window) |
| scans: | 64 |
| resolution: | 8cm$^{-1}$ |
| velocity: | fast |
| apodization: | Happ-Genzel |
| software: | OMNIC 3.1 (Nicolet) |

### RESULT AND DISCUSSION

Comparative infrared absorption spectra for the four samples of residue on the sherd are shown in figure 58a. Samples 1, 3 and 4 were similar in their spectral characteristics, displaying features relating to organic

PLATE 33
E ware Vessel 4 showing the areas sampled for infrared microspectrometric analysis

Table 5   Infrared spectral peak positions

| Sample No | Peak Position (cm$^{-1}$) | Bond vibration |
|---|---|---|
| 1, 3, 4 | 3300 | O-H stretch |
| 1, 3, 4 | 2950–2850 | C-H stretches |
| 1, 4 | 1641 | C=O, Amide I band |
| 4 | 1515 | N-H, Amide II band |

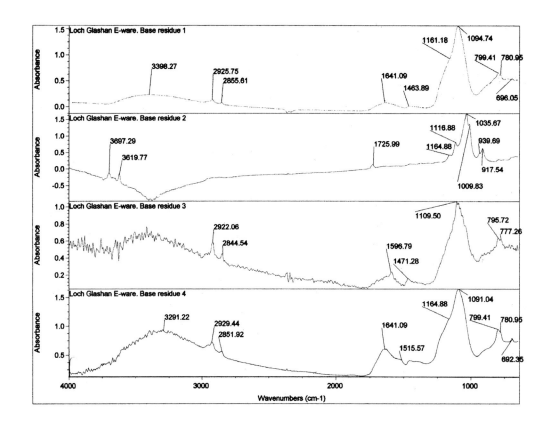

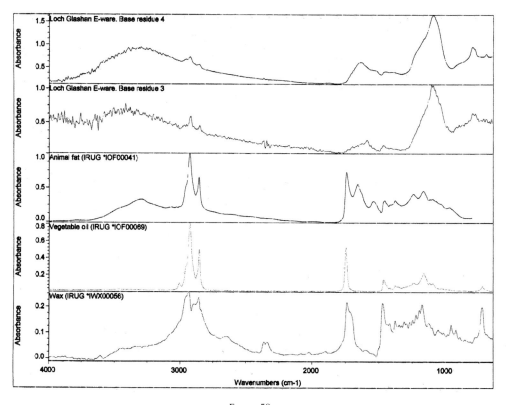

FIGURE 58

a) Comparative absorption infrared spectra of four residue samples from E ware sherd from Loch Glashan; b) Comparative infrared absorption spectra of Loch Glashan residues 3 and 4 with references of representative lipidic sources

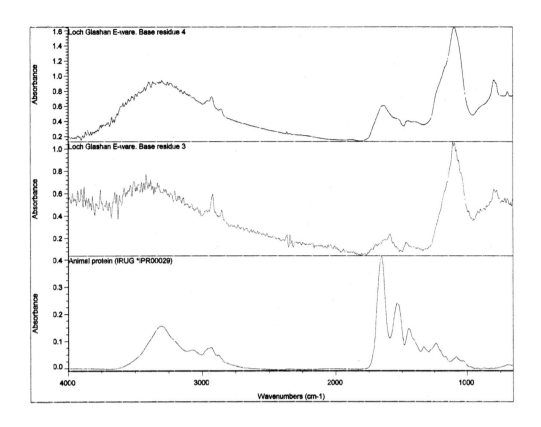

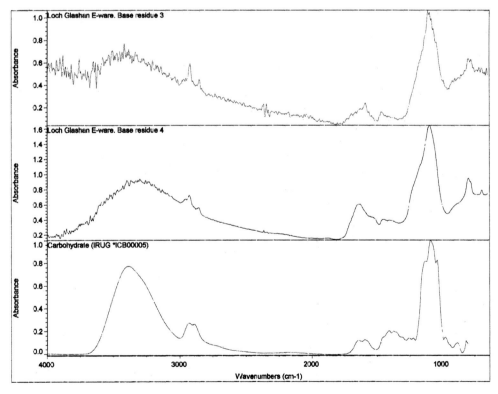

FIGURE 59

a) Comparative infrared absorption spectra for residues 3 and 4 and an animal protein reference; b) Comparative absorption infrared spectra of samples 3 and 4 and a representative carbohydrate reference (Carlson et al 2000)

137

compounds (table 5). The spectrum for sample 2 indicated it was predominantly inorganic, most probably accumulated dirt. If any organic material was present in sample 2, it was below detections limits.

No lipidic compounds, which are the principle chemical components of waxes, fats and oils, were detectable in the spectra for samples 1, 3 and 4 (figure 58b). Instead, the spectrum for sample 4 showed two spectral characteristics associated with proteinacous compounds (figure 59a), and samples 1, 3 and 4 showed spectral characteristics associated with carbohydrates (figure 59b). Carbohydrates include natural gums, sugars and starches which are the principle chemical constituents of many organic materials, examples being binding media, adhesives, foods and paper. Categorization of the carbohydrate source, even at a basic level, is unfortunately not possible by FTIR analysis.

CONCLUSIONS

The residue on the inner surface of Vessel 4 is carbohydrate-based, with protein residues possible in some areas. The residue could originate from a range of natural carbohydrate sources. No detectable traces of lipids, the principle components of oils, fats and waxes, were found, but these may be absorbed into the pottery fabric which was not sampled.

## APPENDIX 7.2   ANALYSIS OF THE CRUCIBLE LID AND CRUCIBLE CONTENTS

*Effie Photos-Jones*

THE CRUCIBLE CONTENTS (SF11) (figure 34a)

The interior of the crucible was partly slagged suggesting that it has been used in metal melting. A small sample was scraped off from the interior, a small fraction of which was then mounted on a stub and subsequently carbon-coated for SEM-EDAX analysis. The other fraction was subjected to X-ray diffraction analysis. SEM-EDAX analysis showed the presence of silver and sulphur together with other metallic impurities like copper, lead, tin and iron (table 6a). Plate 34a shows an SEM-SE image of acicular acanthite $Ag_2S$ amidst plates of kaolin. Other natural materials include feldspar and quartz. Plate 34b shows an XRD pattern of the contents of the crucible, which includes acanthite as well as iron arsenopyrite and proustite, the latter two arsenical sulphides of iron and silver respectively.

THE CRUCIBLE LID (SF12) (figure 34b)

SF12 is a crucible lid with handle, of light grey colouration with black patches due to localized reduction, the fabric resembling that of the crucible, SF11. The fabric consists of a silica rich material displaying the beginning stages of vitrification. A small section was removed for semi-quantitative SEM-EDAX examination and analysis.

Three area analyses at × 100 showed the presence of potassium iron alumino-silicates with minor amounts of calcium and magnesium (table 6b). Sulphur must have been absorbed into the fabric from the burial environment. Phosphorus appears to be an integral part of the fabric of the vessel and may have been introduced, in the form of bone ash as a strengthener.

CONCLUSIONS

SEM-EDAX analyses suggest that the crucible was used in silver melting. Spot analyses show that the silver was relatively free of impurities. The crucible was probably used for the melting of other alloys like arsenical and tin bronzes. Silver sulphide and indeed the other sulphides must have formed as a result of the crucible having been buried in an environment where conditions were anaerobic.

## APPENDIX 7.3   ANALYSIS OF THE BROOCH

*Effie Photos-Jones*

The analytical investigation of the brooch was designed to provide information on;

a) the alloy composition of both hoop and pin
b) the possibility of gilding as suggested by an earlier investigation by the National Museum of Scotland (NMS Lab Report No 7092)
c) the possible use of inlaying with niello, a copper/ lead/silver sulphide.

METHODOLOGY

The Loch Glashan brooch was examined non-destructively with the scanning electron microscope (a Leo stereoscan-S360) attached to an ISIS analyser with ZAF correction package. All elements shown in table 7 were sought; the composition is given in weight per cent. Internal calibration was carried out using a Co standard. Operating voltage was 20Kev and working distance was 25mm. Typical limits of detection for SEM-EDAX are of 0.1%wt–0.5%wt on

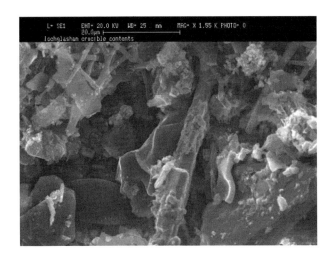
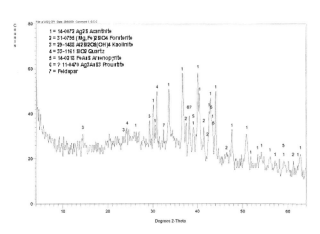

PLATE 34
a) SEM-SE image of acicular acanthite with plates of kaolin and a spore (oval shaped) (Bar = 20 microns);
b) XRD pattern of the contents of the Loch Glashan crucible, to include primarily silver sulphide (acanthite); natural materials include quartz, feldspar, kaolin and various silicates

a polished surface. Given that no sample was removed, the results presented in table 7 should be considered as semi-quantitative. It was not necessary to carbon coat the brooch.

ANALYSIS

SEM-EDAX area and spot analyses were undertaken on the hoop, the pin, the pin head, the right and left terminals and the hoop panel (table 7). SEM-SE images (plate 35a-d) show the areas analysed and should be read in association with table 7.

CONCLUSIONS

The hoop and pin appear to have been cast. Some level of decoration must have been present in the as-cast state but additional engraving must have been carried out subsequent to casting.

All sections of the brooch are made of a copper-based alloy with small amounts of zinc, tin, iron, arsenic and lead. Compositional variations are minimal and in accordance with expected levels of surface depletion in elements like tin and arsenic, resulting from surface weathering and cleaning/conservation.

Table 6 a) SEM-EDAX semi-quantitative analysis of crucible contents (SF11): composition in weight percent;
b) SEM-EDAX semi-quantitative analysis of crucible lid (SF12): composition in weight percent

| a) | Mg | Al | Si | P | S | Cl | K | Ca | Ti | V | Cr | Mn | Fe | Cu | Zn | As | Ag | Sn | Sb | Pb | Total |
|---|---|---|---|---|---|---|---|---|---|---|---|---|---|---|---|---|---|---|---|---|---|
| Spot analysis 1 | n/d | 3.82 | 1.06 | n/d | 11.6 | n/d | n/d | n/d | n/d | n/d | n/d | n/d | 4.59 | 2.58 | n/d | n/d | 62.14 | 13.58 | n/d | 2.08 | 101.45 |
| Spot analysis 2 | n/d | 0.45 | n/d | n/d | 18.94 | n/d | n/d | n/d | n/d | n/d | n/d | n/d | 1.86 | 2.09 | 0.85 | n/d | 72.55 | n/d | n/d | 2.28 | 99.02 |

| b) | $Na_2O$ | $K_2O$ | $Al_2O_3$ | $SiO_2$ | MgO | CaO | $TiO_2$ | MnO | FeO | $P_2O_5$ | $SO_3$ | BaO | Total |
|---|---|---|---|---|---|---|---|---|---|---|---|---|---|
| Area analysis 1 | 1.44 | 4.81 | 27.31 | 47.69 | 1.56 | 1.17 | 1.28 | 0.3 | 7.5 | 4.99 | 1.87 | 0.02 | 99.94 |
| Area analysis 2 | 0.33 | 0.79 | 14.76 | 72.69 | 0.16 | 1.45 | 0.28 | 0 | 2.18 | 6.55 | 0.79 | 0 | 99.98 |
| Area analysis 3 | 0.62 | 5.8 | 26.47 | 50.9 | 1.88 | 0.7 | 1.32 | 0.18 | 6.97 | 4.25 | 0.57 | 0.28 | 99.94 |
| *mean* | 0.8 | 3.8 | 22.85 | 57.09 | 1.2 | 1.11 | 0.96 | 0.16 | 5.55 | 5.26 | 1.08 | 0.1 | 99.96 |

Table 7  SEM–EDAX semi-quantitative analyses of the brooch: composition in weight percent

| | Mg | Al | Si | P | S | Cl | K | Ca | Ti | V | Cr | Mn | Fe | Cu | Zn | As | Ag | Sn | Sb | Pb | Total |
|---|---|---|---|---|---|---|---|---|---|---|---|---|---|---|---|---|---|---|---|---|---|
| **Hoop** | | | | | | | | | | | | | | | | | | | | | |
| Area Analysis 1 | n/d | 1.02 | 1.47 | nd | 10.43 | 2.87 | 1.43 | 0.95 | n/d | n/d | n/d | n/d | 2.82 | 66.69 | 9.53 | n/d | n/d | 3.51 | n/d | n/d | 100.72 |
| Area Analysis 2 | n/d | 7.27 | 1.57 | nd | 8.01 | 2.3 | 1.23 | 0.6 | n/d | n/d | n/d | n/d | 2.93 | 61.51 | 7.52 | n/d | n/d | 2.34 | n/d | 3.66 | 98.94 |
| Area Analysis 3 | n/d | 4.42 | 1.9 | nd | 11.65 | 2.38 | 1.33 | 0.6 | n/d | n/d | n/d | n/d | 5.86 | 59.83 | 4.45 | n/d | n/d | 2.55 | n/d | 3.23 | 98.2 |
| *Mean* | n/d | 4.24 | 1.65 | nd | 10.03 | 2.52 | 1.33 | 0.72 | n/d | n/d | n/d | n/d | 3.87 | 62.68 | 7.17 | n/d | n/d | 2.8 | n/d | 2.3 | 99.31 |
| **Pin** | | | | | | | | | | | | | | | | | | | | | |
| Area Analysis | n/d | 8.64 | 2.22 | nd | 7.44 | 2.81 | 1.23 | 0.62 | n/d | n/d | n/d | n/d | 6.92 | 54.84 | 6.16 | n/d | n/d | 2.54 | n/d | 5.49 | 98.91 |
| **Hoop panel: setting for amber** | | | | | | | | | | | | | | | | | | | | | |
| Area Analysis | 0.76 | 0.4 | 1.05 | nd | 4.87 | 1.14 | n/d | n/d | n/d | n/d | n/d | n/d | 1.22 | 83.01 | 5.44 | n/d | n/d | 2.11 | n/d | n/d | 100 |
| **Left terminal** | | | | | | | | | | | | | | | | | | | | | |
| Area Analysis | n/d | 2.97 | 1.45 | nd | 2.15 | 1.09 | n/d | n/d | n/d | n/d | n/d | n/d | 5.16 | 65.83 | 7.11 | n/d | n/d | 6.58 | n/d | 7.65 | 99.99 |
| **Right terminal** | | | | | | | | | | | | | | | | | | | | | |
| Area Analysis 1 | n/d | n/d | 0.94 | nd | 4.63 | 0.85 | n/d | n/d | n/d | n/d | n/d | n/d | 1.53 | 78.56 | 7.47 | n/d | n/d | 2.78 | n/d | 1.93 | 98.69 |
| Area Analysis 2 | n/d | 4.58 | 1.13 | nd | 5.45 | 0.96 | 0.57 | n/d | n/d | n/d | n/d | n/d | 0.46 | 77.63 | 3.76 | n/d | n/d | 2.54 | n/d | 1.82 | 98.9 |
| *Mean* | n/d | 2.29 | 1.03 | nd | 5.04 | 0.9 | 0.28 | n/d | n/d | n/d | n/d | n/d | 0.99 | 78.09 | 5.61 | n/d | n/d | 2.66 | n/d | 1.87 | 98.76 |
| **Pin head** | | | | | | | | | | | | | | | | | | | | | |
| Area Analysis | n/d | 0.82 | 2.00 | nd | 3.87 | 2.17 | 0.85 | 0.64 | n/d | n/d | n/d | n/d | 10.15 | 56.7 | 9.48 | n/d | n/d | 5.1 | n/d | 8.21 | 99.99 |

SEM-EDAX imaging and analysis with the back-scattered detector on various locations within the sample show quite clearly that there is no mercury gilding.

Significant levels of sulphur are recorded throughout the artefact reflecting the presence of sulphides. There are no suggestions that there have been *specific* areas decorated with niello.

## APPENDIX 7.4   ANALYSIS OF THE GLASS BEAD

*Effie Photos-Jones*

SAMPLING AND ANALYSIS

The bead consisted of four glass spherules attached to each other in a straight line. Only half the bead is preserved, the section of the spherules being that of a semicircle, with a long thin core in the middle. Sampling strategy involved the removal of one of the four spherules, thus preserving the overall shape of the bead. The spherule was mounted in metallographic resin, ground with a series of silicon carbide papers and polished with 6 and 3-micron diamond paste. The polished block was subsequently carbon-coated in preparation for SEM-EDAX analysis. Three spot

analyses were carried out per glass layer and a mean is calculated for each layer. Furthermore, three particles of silver were also analysed. However no mean was calculated for the latter. In the process of removal of the spherule, fragments of glass broke off and these were subsequently mounted on separate block, ground and polished in the same way. Their analyses are reported separately and confirm the results above.

The glass bead was examined with the scanning electron microscope (a Leo stereoscan-S360) attached to an ISIS analyser with ZAF correction package. All elements shown in table 8 were sought, composition given in weight per cent. Internal calibration was carried out using a Co standard. Operating voltage was 20Kev and working distance was 25mm. Typical limits of detection for SEM-EDAX are of 0.1%wt-0.5%wt. Higher amounts for elements like sodium are expected. Elements with values below the limit of detection are denoted as nd. The sample was examined with the backscatter detector which made readily apparent the compositionally different areas of the sample.

DISCUSSION

The glass spherule consists of two layers of glass, a clear exterior overlaying an opaque interior of similar

Table 8   SEM-EDAX analyses of the glass bead; all results are normalized (to 100%) unless otherwise specified

| | $Na_2O$ | MgO | $Al_2O_3$ | $SiO_2$ | $SO_3$ | Cl | $K_2O$ | CaO | FeO | CuO | $AS_2O_3$ | $SnO_2$ | PbO | $Ag_2O$ | Total |
|---|---|---|---|---|---|---|---|---|---|---|---|---|---|---|---|
| surface layer, spot 1 | 14.72 | 4.91 | 1.43 | 68.6 | n/d | 0 | 2.85 | 6.47 | 0.76 | n/d | n/d | n/d | n/d | n/d | 99.74 |
| surface layer, spot 2 | 14.51 | 4.77 | 1.7 | 68.19 | n/d | 0 | 2.82 | 6.62 | 0.43 | n/d | n/d | n/d | n/d | n/d | 99.04 |
| surface layer, spot 3 | 15.42 | 5.62 | 1.4 | 68.5 | 0.68 | 0 | 2.6 | 6.25 | 0.52 | n/d | n/d | n/d | n/d | n/d | 100.99 |
| *mean* | *14.88* | *6.74* | *1.97* | *68.43* | *n/d* | *0* | *2.76* | *6.45* | *0.57* | *n/d* | *n/d* | *n/d* | *n/d* | *n/d* | *101.8* |
| space between two glasses, | | | | | | | | | | | | | | | |
| Ag grain 1 | n/d | n/d | 22.96 | n/d | n/d | n/d | n/d | n/d | n/d | n/d | 2.97 | n/d | n/d | 74.5 | 100.43 |
| Ag grain 2 (unnormalized) | 2.7 | n/d | 23.01 | 7.65 | 2.94 | 0 | n/d | n/d | n/d | n/d | n/d | n/d | n/d | 58.1 | 94.4 |
| Ag grain 3 | 3.89 | n/d | 24.98 | 9.4 | 2.66 | n/d | n/d | n/d | n/d | n/d | 4.17 | n/d | n/d | 54.85 | 99.95 |
| interior layer, spot 1 | 15.71 | 4.67 | 1.89 | 66.9 | n/d | n/d | 2.47 | 6.79 | 0.69 | n/d | n/d | n/d | n/d | n/d | 99.12 |
| interior layer, spot 2 | 15.4 | 5.83 | 2.12 | 67.31 | n/d | n/d | 2.57 | 6.48 | n/d | n/d | n/d | n/d | n/d | n/d | 99.71 |
| interior layer, spot 3 | 15.66 | 4.63 | 1.88 | 66.45 | 0.64 | n/d | 2.88 | 6.42 | n/d | n/d | n/d | n/d | n/d | n/d | 98.56 |
| *mean* | *15.59* | *5.03* | *1.93* | *66.89* | *n/d* | *n/d* | *2.64* | *6.56* | *0.69* | *n/d* | *n/d* | *n/d* | *n/d* | *n/d* | *98.64* |
| separate fragment of clear glass (surface layer) | 15.96 | 4.98 | 0.8 | 71.14 | n/d | n/d | 2.78 | 6.24 | n/d | n/d | n/d | n/d | n/d | n/d | 101.9 |
| separate fragment of opaque glass (interior layer) | 15.6 | 5.12 | 1.39 | 67.92 | n/d | n/d | 2.99 | 6.17 | 0.94 | n/d | n/d | n/d | n/d | n/d | 100.13 |

KEY n/d: not-detected or below the limit of detection

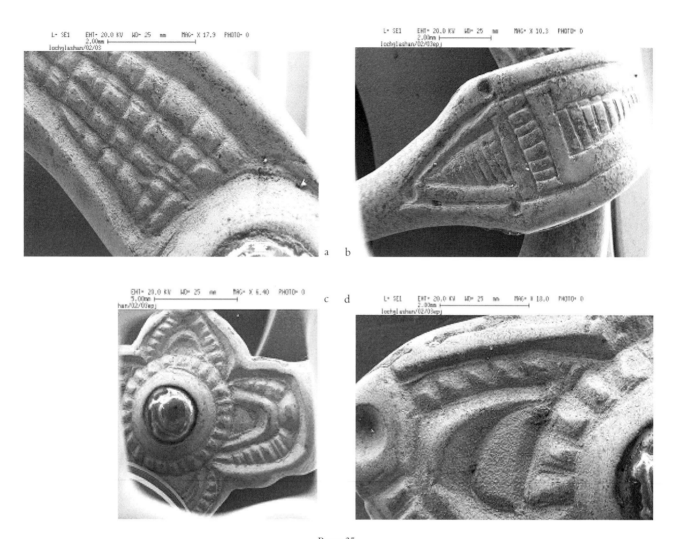

a    b

c    d

PLATE 35
SEM-SE images of details of the brooch: a) hoop panel; b) section of pin head; c) section of right terminal with amber bead; d) engraved area within
right terminal

composition (see plate 36a and table 8). Both layers have a greenish hue. The thickness of the exterior layer is c 0.7mm, that of the interior c 2.5mm at its core and c 1.5mm at the periphery. There is a thin gap of <20 microns between the two layers (plate 36b). Gas bubbles are trapped within the body of the interior layer and elongated along the line of rotation of the bead as it was formed. The composition of both layers is that of sodium, magnesium, calcium silicate glass with small amounts of potassium and traces of iron; the latter is responsible for the greenish hue.

The thin gap between the two layers is at places filled with a thin 'layer' of silver (maximum particle size c 10 microns) hardly visible to the naked eye (plate 36c). The metal is impure, an 'alloy' of arsenic and silver. The rest of the elements shown in Table 8 originate from both the resin and earthy material (dirt) which collected on the surface prior to the application of silver and should not be taken into account as part of the composition of the metal. It is most likely that the bead would have been dipped into the metal 'alloy' and allowed to solidify, prior to the application of the external layer.

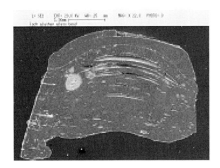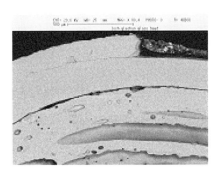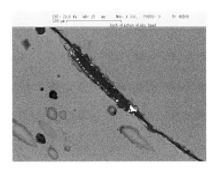

PLATE 36

The silver-in-glass bead

a) SEM-SE image of a transverse section of one of the four spherules of the bead. It consists of two glass layers overlaying one another. (Bar = 1 microns; × 22.3); b) SEM-BS image of the spherule at higher magnification showing elongated gas bubbles within the interior layer, the fine gap (< 20 microns) separating the two and the exterior layer, its upper section cracked (thin hairline crack). Earthy material deposited on the surface is seen at the upper right hand corner. (Bar = 500 microns; × 80.4); c) SEM-BS image of the space between the two glass layers showing fine particles (bright specks) of metallic silver 'alloyed' with arsenic. (Bar = 100 microns; × 333)

# Index

wooden artefacts (*cont*)
  containers 29–35
  radiocarbon dating 115
  tools 35–8
  *see also* lathe-turned; timber
Wooding, J 123

Wroxeter 71
wustite 69, *69–70*

York 37, 62, 68, 77
Youngs, S 67